# THE SCIENCE OF SATYUG

SUNY series in Hindu Studies

Wendy Doniger, editor

# THE SCIENCE OF SATYUG

## Class, Charisma, and Vedic Revivalism in the All World Gayatri Pariwar

**Daniel Heifetz**

SUNY
PRESS

Cover image of the Havan or Homa, igniting sacrificial or ceremonial fire in copper square kunda; from www.123rf.com

Published by State University of New York Press, Albany



Printed in the United States of America



For information, contact State University of New York Press, Albany, NY
www.sunypress.edu

**Library of Congress Cataloging-in-Publication Data**

Name: Heifetz, Daniel, author.
Title: The science of satyug : class, charisma, and Vedic revivalism in the All World Gayatri Pariwar / Daniel Heifetz.
Description: Albany : State University of New York Press, [2021] | Series: SUNY series in Hindu Studies, Wendy Doniger, editor. | Includes bibliographical references and index.
Identifiers: 9781438481715 (hardcover : alk. paper) | ISBN 9781438481708 (pbk. : alk. paper) | ISBN 9781438481722 (ebook)
Further information is available at the Library of Congress.

10 9 8 7 6 5 4 3 2 1

# Contents

# Illustrations

# Preface

Like many academic books, *The Science of Satyug* is rooted in confusion and frustration—confusion as to why things are the way they are and frustration with the available explanations. This book resolves confusion that I felt late in my doctoral coursework, when my primary interest was global guru movements. I'd been noticing how ubiquitous appeals to scientific authority were in such movements, but I could not square these appeals with my presumption that guru movements attracted followers by offering an escape from disenchantment. This confusion was compounded by a frustration with the frequently dismissive scholarly treatment these appeals to scientific authority often received. It seemed that such a widespread cultural pattern deserved to be taken seriously. As I continued to work through these issues, I found that the field of postcolonial science and technology studies had laid substantial groundwork for understanding these issues, but I still could not see what it was about the contemporary situation that had caused such a proliferation of scientific discourse in global guru movements.

These interests were what led me to pursue research on the All World Gayatri Pariwar. I had not heard of the movement before I began searching for a suitable case to explore my interests. It quickly became clear that it was an ideal case: not only was their discourse rooted in laboratory research conducted on site, but also the movement had never seen sustained scholarly attention despite its wide popularity in North India. My suspicions were confirmed during a short preliminary visit in August 2010. This visit culminated in me seeking permission to conduct my research in the community. Commenting on a research proposal I had shared, one community leader suggested that I ought to read Thomas Kuhn's *The Structure of Scientific Revolutions*. As this book is a foundational work in the field of science and technology studies, I was already familiar with it, but the mere fact that my contact made this suggestion confirmed my sense that there was a great deal I could learn from the Gayatri Pariwar.

# Acknowledgments

I am very fortunate to have studied a community that was so enthusiastic about my project. Not only were my hosts at Shantikunj very hospitable in providing me with a home in their community during my fieldwork, but they were also kind and patient in educating me about their movement by putting me in touch with so many thoughtful community members who could answer my many questions. Chinmay, Somnath, Piyush, and Gagan played particularly crucial roles in situating me in their community and facilitating my research. I am also grateful for the time and energy that was invested in my project by my interview contacts, and the countless other community members I interacted with during my stay. My greatest hope for this book is that it does their community justice, and that they will feel as if their efforts were worthwhile.

Transforming the inchoate tangle of information I gathered from the field into a coherent piece of writing would not have been possible without significant support. As I worked toward this project's initial form as a dissertation, the fantastic community of scholars at Syracuse University played a major role. As my dissertation advisor, Joanne Waghorne provided excellent advice on my project especially in her encouragement to think about spatial theory and the nature of the Gayatri Pariwar's middle class. Ann Gold provided a number of helpful comments as well, sharpening my ethnographic research and writing skills and compelling me to think with greater nuance about the Gayatri Pariwar's gendered leadership. Gareth Fisher similarly supported my project's ethnographic components while supporting my thought with helpful points of comparison from his work on contemporary Chinese Buddhism. Gail Hamner made immense contributions to my theoretical framework through her knowledge of science and technology studies and affect theory. Many of my other colleagues at Syracuse played a major role in this project, including James Watts, Susan Wadley, Anand Dwivedi, Lawrence McCrea, Carol Babiracki, Donovan Schaefer, Wendy DeBoer, Jenny Caplan, John Borchert, Emera Bridger Wilson, Ian Wilson, Nidhi Vij, Jocelyn Kilmer, Drew Thomases, Yoshina Hurgobin, Sravani Biswas, Alisa Weinstein, Jonathan Jackson, and the rest of the religious studies, South Asian studies, and anthropology communities at Syracuse University.

A little something was missing from the dissertation, and the evolution of this project into its current form rested on the support of some of the fantastic scholars I have known since. Of particular importance was the process of adapting my work to two thematic journal issues. The first of these was *Where Class Meets Religion: Examining Middle-Class Religiosity in India* in the *International Journal of Hindu Studies*, organized by Jenn Ortegren. This piece helped solidify parts of my analysis of middle-class identity that are foundational to my argument in this book. Parts of chapter 2 are based on this article (reprinted by permission from Springer Nature: "Religion, Science, and the Middle Class in the All World Gayatri Pariwar," *International Journal of Hindu Studies* 23, no. 1 (2019): 27–42). Contributing to the volume *The Moralizing of Dharma in Everyday Hinduisms* in *Nidān: International Journal for Indian Studies* organized by Antoinette DeNapoli and Tulasi Srinivas was also important for allowing me to develop my thoughts on the role of morality in relation to the larger themes of my research. Parts of chapter 4 are based on this article (reprinted with permission: "Yajña without Dharma? Ritual and Morality in the All World Gayatri Pariwar," *Nidān: International Journal for Indian Studies* 1, no. 2 (2016): 14–31). Finally, parts of chapter 3 also appeared in an earlier article (republished with permission of Brill Academic Publishers: "From Gurudev to Doctor-sahib: Religion, Science, and Charisma in the All World Gayatri Pariwar," *Method & Theory in the Study of Religion* 30, no. 3 (2018): 252–78; permission conveyed through Copyright Clearance Center, Inc).

In addition to these projects with colleagues at other institutions, I have been grateful for the support of my religious studies colleagues at Mercyhurst University and Bucknell University. I felt fortunate to have worked with these departments, as they engaged with me as a researcher in ways that contingent faculty so rarely experience.

My family has played an important role in this work as well. My parents, Pamela, David, and Kimberly Cheifer, have encouraged me to chase my dreams, supporting me from the very beginning of my academic career. My wife, Maria Carson, has been a presence in my life since the earliest stages of my writing process at Syracuse University. Her contributions to this project are innumerable. She has been an important intellectual interlocutor, offering me feedback and constructive criticism on the basis of her excellent grasp of theory. She has been an important emotional support, offering both sympathy and encouragement when I struggled. Finally, she has been willing to make sacrifices as we have negotiated the two-body problem. For these things and more, I am grateful.

My field research was only possible with financial support by a FLAS fellowship through the Syracuse University South Asia Center. Additional support at the writing stage came from a Syracuse University Humanities Center Dissertation Fellowship. The American Institute for Indian Studies and the Centre for Studies in Science Policy at Jawaharlal Nehru University were instrumental in allowing me to gain access to India as a researcher.

# Note on Translation and Transliteration

Many Gayatri Pariwar publications were originally written in Hindi, and I conducted interviews in Hindi, English, or a mix of both languages, depending on the preferences of my contacts. My aim is to make this book accessible to non-Hindi speakers while representing the importance of Hindi for the movement I studied. Accordingly, I have tried to limit Sanskrit and Hindi terms in the body of the text to words and phrases I consider crucial, and have included a glossary of important and recurring names, terms, and acronyms that non-specialist readers may find difficult. Aside from proper nouns and words that have entered the English lexicon, Hindi and Sanskrit terms are italicized and written with appropriate diacritics. With respect to literature, I have used the movement's own translations where possible and placed the original Hindi version in a footnote, along with citations to both texts. When I present material from a text that is only available in Hindi, I note that this is the case and provide my own translation. With respect to bilingual interviews, I italicize all portions of the interview that I have translated from Hindi in the body of the text and present the original Hindi in an endnote.

# Introduction

When I arrived at the All World Gayatri Pariwar's ashram Shantikunj one afternoon in January 2012, it was taken as one indicator among many that the fulfillment of the movement's eschatological hopes for the revival of *satyug* was at hand. As far as I knew, I had selected the Gayatri Pariwar for my research on Hindu traditions and science because their mixture of Vedic revivalism, populism, and science seemed like an intriguing case. But upon arriving at Shantikunj, the movement's main ashram in Haridwar, community members were quick to offer a different perspective. I had been brought to Shantikunj by their guru, Shriram Sharma, who has guided the movement in incorporeal form since he voluntarily shed his body in 1991. Gurudev had brought me to Shantikunj, I learned, to utilize my scholarly authority to help the Gayatri Pariwar spread beyond India and its diaspora, ultimately bringing about a new *satyug*, a Hindi term (from the Sanskrit Satya Yuga) that the Gayatri Pariwar translates as "golden era."[1]

There were a number of synchronicities that strengthened this sense of divine purpose among some Gayatri parijans.[2] For example, the timing of my arrival at Shantikunj seemed particularly auspicious: Republic Day, Basant Panchami, and the anniversary of Gurudev's first meeting with his incorporeal master all took place within my first three days in the ashram.[3] The year leading up to my arrival had been a momentous one, full of signs that *satyug* was imminent. First and foremost, it has been the year of Gurudev's birth centenary. It had also been the year when Shantikunj hosted its first extended visit by a Westerner—a man named Simon. Simon had left Shantikunj by the time of my arrival, but I came to know him somewhat through a book he had published under the name "Brahmavarchas" called *Thought Revolution: A Western Introduction to the Work of Acharya Shriram Sharma*, which was released during the holiday festivities that took place during my first few days in the ashram. In this book, Simon framed Gurudev's teachings as solutions to the emerging global ecological crisis. His writing took place against the background of the Arab Spring, the *Indignados*, and Occupy Wall Street, and the book reflects the revolutionary optimism that filled the air and the sense that humanity seemed to be on the brink of some eschatological change:

> In recent months, social uprisings that began in Egypt, Syria, Libya, and India have migrated into Western countries as well. All over the world change seems to be spreading like wild fire. . . . According to Acharya Sharma, the changes that the human race will witness during the course of the 21st century will dwarf anything the world has witnessed in recent centuries.[4]

Gayatri parijans' confidence that their movement would go global, bringing about the return of *satyug* in the process, was based not solely in this series of auspiciously timed events. Rather, their eschatology is data-driven. The movement ties its hopes for the revival of *satyug* at least in part to scientific data about their practices generated through laboratory experiments. For example, picture a Brahmin male clad in a saffron *dhotī* sitting in front of a shallow pit in the floor near the banks of the Ganges. Chanting Sanskrit mantras, he kindles the firewood inside. He purifies himself and worships a number of ritual implements nearby. Upon completing all of the needed preliminary steps, he takes a pinch of herbs between his fingers, holding it ready, and begins to chant the Gayatri mantra:

> *Oṃ bhūr bhuvaḥ svaḥ tat saviturvareṇyaṃ*
> *bhargo devasya dhīmahi dhiyo yo naḥ pracodayāt*

Completing the mantra, he tosses the herbs into the fire and begins to repeat the process. The fire crackles with each offering, its smoke rising upwards. Whither does it ascend? Not to Savitṛ or even Gayatri Mata; rather, it is collected by an exhaust hood and pumped into a small glass chamber labeled "Dhūmr Kakṣ," or "Smoke Chamber." Cultures of various pathogens sit in this chamber, awaiting exposure to the ritual's smoke. The officiant-scientist wants to see if the smoke from his ritual-experiment has had any medical benefits. If only he could produce scientific proof, rational people the world over would be persuaded as to the benefits of this practice and take it up themselves.

Figure I.1. The *Yajña* Laboratory, Brahmavarchas Shodh Sansthan.

I gathered many fascinating images and anecdotes during my study of the All World Gayatri Pariwar,[5] but this vignette remains the most provocative. Perhaps this is because Vedic-style fire rituals have meant so many things throughout their long history. To name a few of the most obvious ones: a means to solicit boons from the gods, proof of a king's sovereignty, a metaphor for yogic practice, and a way of tying public spaces to Hindu identities of a particular kind. What, then, does it mean when such a ritual is performed in a laboratory, under an exhaust hood? How does it fit into the broader institutional framework in which it occurred? And what might it tell us about the broader cultural and historical context that has made such an image possible?

Such laboratory rituals attempt to marshal scientific authority to solve certain modern problems for the Gayatri Pariwar. These problems often date back to the colonial period, but many are particularly urgent in the age of globalization. The Gayatri Pariwar wants their practices to seem legitimate not only in rural India and among the growing numbers of STEM-educated[6] middle-class Hindus, but also globally, to those who do not share their cultural or religious sensibilities. A laboratory ritual like the one I have described above generates a rhetoric about universal human health and well-being, rather than a rhetoric that is specific to religious, cultural, class, caste, or gender identities. Put in slightly broader terms, the apparently universal authority of science allows for the unsettling of context-specific ideologies and facilitates the circulation of those ideologies first through India, a postcolonial nation in search of an identity, and eventually, with the help of contemporary communication technology, through the entire world.

In this book, I am particularly interested in the post–IT boom STEM-educated middle-class Hindus who are prominent members of the Shantikunj community. Over the course of my conversations with these Shantikunj residents, it became clear that they have experienced a kind of moral crisis, in which they perceive the lifestyles of contemporary urban professionals in India as lacking in meaning and values. Shantikunj residents who are affected by this crisis are able to find a kind of resolution through involvement in the ritual life of the Gayatri Pariwar, which reconciles their commitments to scientific and technological pursuits with their desire to pursue a lifestyle they perceive as moral and meaningful.

## Introducing the Gayatri Pariwar

In order to ground and provide context for this argument, I want to start by providing a brief overview of the Gayatri Pariwar's most fascinating features. While it may seem to share numerous characteristics with the plethora of other guru-centered "reform" or "neo-Hindu" movements on the scene today, the convergence of these particular features make the Gayatri Pariwar rather noteworthy, and so it offers a distinctive lens on Hindu modernity. Despite the analytical opportunities the movement presents and its apparent popularity in north India, it has received limited scholarly attention, most notably in highly polemical works by Lise McKean and Meera Nanda. McKean's brief account of the Gayatri Pariwar in *Divine Enterprise* treats the Gayatri Pariwar as a shill for capitalist and Hindu nationalist interests,[7] while Nanda characterizes the movement's use of scientific rhetoric to appeal to middle-class Hindus as a kind of cynical "crafty genius."[8]

Nanda emphasizes the Gayatri Pariwar's middle-class associations, but once I took an interest in the organization it quickly became apparent to me that it was quite socioeconomically diverse. Hindu-based reform movements are often most closely connected to educated, urban, middle-class networks, and the Gayatri Pariwar does enjoy some popularity with this segment of the population in India and among the Indian diaspora. But the movement has been particularly successful in rural India not only with upwardly mobile segments of the population but also among those with less formal education. A number of factors may be responsible for this popularity: a large network of centers in small towns and villages, a pragmatic, populist orientation, and an overwhelming tendency to favor Hindi over English in official materials.

Like many modern movements rooted in Hindu traditions, the Gayatri Pariwar was founded by a charismatic guru—in this case, Shriram Sharma (1911–1991). The gurus who found reform Hindu-based movements often advocate for delving into India's past to revive traditions they associate with a better time. In the case of Sharma, or as his followers call him, Gurudev,[9] these practices are *yajña* and recitation of the Gayatri mantra.[10] It is often the case that this revival comes with a twist: these old practices must be presented as fitting modern rationalist and universalist sensibilities in accordance with intellectual norms imposed by British colonialism. Accordingly, Gurudev presented Gayatri recitation and *yajña* as having a scientific basis and being open to all, not just Brahmin males. Like his counterparts in other reform movements, Gurudev opposed social ills like dowry, caste discrimination, and "superstitions."

The roots of the Gayatri Pariwar lie in the late colonial period. During this period, Gurudev was quite involved with the Arya Samaj and also participated in Gandhi-inspired grassroots organizing in the independence movement. This aspect of Gurudev's history provides fascinating connections to major historical currents within India. Gurudev's Arya Samaj association does not just provide a clear link to earlier reform currents within Hindu traditions; it also has political ramifications, given the Arya Samaj's character as a proto–Hindu-nationalist organization.[11] Gurudev's Gandhian connections are perhaps even more fascinating because it provides a window on how the legacy of Gandhian nation-building plays out in the Gayatri Pariwar's own efforts to revitalize India as a healthy, moral, coherent nation.

Shantikunj, the ashram and global headquarters of the Gayatri Pariwar, illustrates what such a utopian nation might look like in microcosm. Located near the Ganges in Haridwar, Shantikunj is a massive ashram that accommodates thousands of visitors, especially when pilgrimage season is in full swing. Permanent residents, generally clad in saffron saris or *kurtā*-pajamas, contribute a variety of skills to the community, making it surprisingly self-sufficient. They have even marshaled the resources needed to found their own school and more recently a university called Dev Sanskriti Vishwavidyalaya (Divine Culture University; DSVV hereafter) near Shantikunj to see to the education of the ashram's young people and any others who choose to avail themselves of these facilities. Children do in fact grow up in Shantikunj—some families come to live at Shantikunj already formed, while others marry and have children while living at the ashram (although Gayatri parijans are expected to abstain from non-procreative sex and keep their families small). Gurudev also practiced this form of partial celibacy, and was married to a woman named Bhagwati Devi, whom Gayatri parijans call "Mataji."

Their daughter and son-in-law, Shailbala and Pranav Pandya, known to the Gayatri Pariwar as "Jiji" and "Doctor-sahib," respectively, took up leadership of the movement in 1995, after both Sharmas had passed and while India's new liberal economy was opening the doors to the forces of globalization. While many guru-based movements have struggled after the death of their charismatic founders, the Gayatri Pariwar remains quite robust. Doctor-sahib may owe his success in these regards partly to his status as a medical doctor. Prior to becoming head of the movement, he had applied his medical knowledge to conducting experiments at the Gayatri Pariwar's research institute, Brahmavarchas Shodh Sansthan (Light of Brahma Research Institute). At this facility, Doctor-sahib worked intensively to prove that there are medical benefits to reciting the Gayatri mantra and performing *yajña*. Such experience clearly serves him well in appealing to the multitude of STEM-educated professionals flooding India's new economy. His background has also helped him to open up DSVV in 2002. It is not coincidental that the Pandyas' tenure as leaders has also seen expanded efforts toward expanding the Gayatri Pariwar's appeal among the Hindu diaspora and beyond. The movement sees its scientific activities as essential in bringing about these global aspirations, but it is not yet clear just how this will play out.

## Methods and Scope

This project is based on seven months of field research at Shantikunj and critical readings of an archive of key Gayatri Pariwar texts in Hindi and

English that I curated with assistance from contacts in the Gayatri Pariwar. During this time, I lived in a private room on the premises of the ashram. The exact nature of my involvement in the community changed over the course of my stay there, but it involved participation in the daily ritual life of the community, working as a volunteer to help with cleaning, studying quietly with a group of students at DSVV, and eating at least one of my daily meals in public ashram spaces. I was able to conduct about fifty interviews during the period of my research. In general, these interviews were arranged by one of two men. At Shantikunj itself, Somnath assisted me with great patience and diligence as I met with a number of prominent members of the community. Somnath worked in Abroad Cell, an office that coordinated a number of aspects of the Gayatri Pariwar's international efforts, especially arranging visas. Generally speaking, Somnath was my main liaison to the community and helped a great deal with the Kafkaesque process of acquiring a residency permit. Somnath was what many ethnographers call a community gatekeeper. He worked tirelessly to help me get settled at Shantikunj and to arrange numerous meetings for me. I have no doubt that his assistance in this regard enriched my project greatly. At DSVV, an endlessly enthusiastic student in the Department of Scientific Spirituality named Gagan introduced me to a number of faculty and students in various departments. Earlier in my research, one of his senior colleagues, Piyush, provided me with similar assistance before becoming overburdened with teaching responsibilities.

In terms of the scope of this project, my focus is generally on the residents of Shantikunj and DSVV rather than on the Gayatri Pariwar writ large. I consider this to be an important distinction because the Gayatri Pariwar as a whole is much larger than the ashram community, and seems to have a different demographic profile. As I have already hinted, one of the noteworthy aspects of the Gayatri Pariwar is its popularity as a reform Hindu movement among less formally educated segments of the rural Indian population. This sense is imparted by the literature I have examined and was easily confirmed by my observations at Shantikunj. For most of the year, there are so many of these visitors at Shantikunj that they outnumber the residents significantly. This is especially true during pilgrimage season, when Shantikunj sees a substantial flow of visitors who are passing through Haridwar on their way to the Choṭā Cār Dhām in the Himalayas.[12]

This holds true of the movement as a whole and of visitors to Shantikunj, but not of the community's permanent and semi-permanent residents. When considering the demographic makeup of ashram residents specifically, the community seems to be much more in line with other reform Hindu movements: mostly middle and especially upper middle class. According to Somnath, roughly 80 percent of ashram residents have a bachelor's or often a master's degree. While I hope that my future research will allow me to learn more about Shantikunj residents with less formal education as well as non-resident Gayatri parijans, I have found it analytically useful and logistically necessary to limit the scope of this study to middle-class permanent and long-term ashram and university residents and a handful of non-resident Gayatri parijans who are full-time volunteers for the movement. This has allowed me to think specifically about how the Gayatri Pariwar's scientific rhetoric relates to contemporary India's middle class.

## Key Terms

### Religion-*Dharm* and Spirituality-*Adhyātmavād*

In choosing to characterize the Gayatri Pariwar as a *religious* movement, I am somewhat at odds with Gayatri parijans, who tend to think of what they do as a kind of spirituality or *adhyātmavād*. In conversation, Gayatri parijans acknowledge there is some overlap between the two concepts. They sometimes take spirituality as the "essence" of religion, or what is left when religion is stripped of superficial cultural accretions. But according to them, spirituality is not simply inherited like religion; rather, it is chosen for personal reasons. Perhaps more importantly, they understand spirituality as something that is homogenous, universal, and shared by all of humanity because it deals with invariant aspects of the human experience. Religions have such spiritual elements embedded within them, but also have extra elements that are not universal. Some of these non-universal elements may have context-specific relevance: they are valuable for some people but not all. Other such elements are corruptions and empty superstitions that may do more harm than good. Either way, religions, unlike spirituality, are tied to specific identities.

In some cases, when Gayatri parijans talk about religion, it is clear that they are using the term in a different sense than Westerners might in either academic or everyday contexts because they are relying on indigenous concepts. A conversation I had with a Shantikunj resident named Dina illustrates this well. A woman of about fifty, Dina grew up in Ahmedabad but had been a resident of Shantikunj for at least ten years. She had inquired with Somnath about my presence in the ashram, and arranged to meet with me out of curiosity. Dina had opted to speak with me in English, and when I asked her to talk about what *religion* and *spirituality* meant, it became clear that she understood *religion* through the concept of *dharm*, following a common translational practice between Indian languages and English:

> Religion is one type of virtue. It is a duty, religion is. . . . Suppose you are coming from outside. What is my religion? What is my duty? That I should give all the comforts and whatever you want, what is your need, we should fulfill all those things. That is original ritual, means, we say, "*dharma*." Means what is my duty? What is our duty? That is *dharma*. And spirituality is different. Spirituality means we have to improve our inner things. That we have, what to say, *karuṇā* [compassion], *dayā* [mercy], *prem* [love], *udārtā* [generosity], *ātmiyatā* [closeness, intimacy], and all the real qualities of insight, that is spirituality. . . . That is spirituality, and spirituality develops all these things.

As Dina illustrates, when Gayatri parijans distinguish between religion and spirituality there is an implicit sense that religion-*dharm* has to do with behaviors that are obligatory for persons with particular identities. The claim of being "spiritual but not religious," so common in the American context that it has become almost laughably trite, does not seem to hold here. Embedded in the Gayatri Pariwar's use of these terms is the notion, common in South Asia, that one's religious identity and community is fixed at birth. Whether or not one upholds the religion of one's parents in practice does not generally change the sense that one identifies as, say, a Muslim. Spirituality could be found within Islam for such a person, but, since spirituality is ultimately disconnected from religious identities for Gayatri parijans, Muslims could also look for spirituality elsewhere without changing their religious identity at all. This is crucial for understanding how the Gayatri Pariwar sees itself: since it is a spiritual movement, its practices may be taken up by everyone, alongside extant religious obligations, without any need to change their religious identity.

Moving from the emic to the etic, I rarely use *spirituality* as an analytical term. While it is an important component of my project to interrogate what Gayatri parijans mean when they talk about spirituality, I tend to utilize the term *religion* in my analysis. When I talk about religion, I am doing so in a different, much broader sense than most Gayatri parijans. Like many contemporary religious studies scholars, when I talk about religion, I do so in the tradition of Jonathan Z. Smith, who characterized religion as a "second-order, generic concept" that we may deploy for particular scholarly ends.[13] Accordingly, when I deploy it, I am pointing to a vast array of social phenomena that occasionally bear certain resemblances to one another and to a vast array of scholarly theories that have attempted to offer insight into these phenomena. Given the breadth of this category, what the Gayatri Pariwar calls *spirituality* falls well within the scope of what Smith and many others in the field would call *religion*.

## Science-*Vijñān*

*Science* is a central concern of this project, and developing a rigorous understanding of the term has been essential to the development of my argument from an early stage. Like religion, science does not have a stable meaning between historical and cultural contexts—it is clear enough that when Gayatri parijans talk about spiritual science, Evangelical Christians talk about creation science, and New Atheists talk about science, they are not talking about quite the same thing. My goal is not to take a side in any such debate, but rather to understand how the concept of science affects the lives to the people I am studying, and so I find myself wanting a way to understand the concept that is rigorous but non-essentialist. If this were the only issue, I might easily take a similar approach to the one Smith takes with *religion* as I have described above, treating it as an intellectual category, but I have found that this still falls somewhat short.[14]

It has fascinated and at times frustrated me to note the wide variety of meanings scholars intend when they talk about science. Some of this is clearly disciplinary. Many in the scientific community seem to think of science as a method. Meera Nanda, in her effort to differentiate "real science" from "Vedic science," quotes at length from a brief that she boasts was prepared by "72 Nobel Laureates and scientific organizations":

> Science is devoted to formulating and testing naturalistic explanations for natural phenomena. It is a process for systematically collecting and recording data about the physical world, then categorizing and studying the collected data in an effort to infer the principles of nature that best explain the observed phenomena.[15]

The influential philosopher of science Karl Popper similarly focused on method when he argued that the essence of science was in its never-ending refinement of propositions by means of critique and refutation.[16]

A different approach, quite common in the field of science studies, is to treat science as a social institution. In *Sciences from Below*, Sandra Harding illustrates this view of science when she says, "The new sociologies, histories, and ethnographies of science have revealed how scientific inquiry has been a social institution with many features of other social institutions."[17] We can trace this approach, as Harding does, all the way back to Thomas Kuhn, who illustrated how scientific institutions undergo paradigm shifts as old theories crumble under the weight of new evidence. While Kuhn's focus tended toward the institutional side, he understood this institution to be very much tied to a particular and changing canon of scientific knowledge.[18] At other times, science studies scholars see science as functioning primarily as a form of authority. Such a conception often takes center stage in Gyan Prakash's *Another Reason*, which exposes the role of scientific authority in consolidating British control over India by signifying its supposed civilizational superiority.[19]

I have found no particular need to side with any of these ways of understanding science: as method, institution, body of knowledge, or form of authority. This arises in part from my frustration with a certain tendency—most commonly in popular conversations and a handful of conference papers I have sat through—to drag the term "science" through two or more of these significations over the course of a single argument, without clarification. In my work, I too need to refer to these multiple facets of science, but I wish to be clearer. I thus tend to prefer to speak of *scientific methods* utilized by *scientific institutions* to generate forms of *scientific knowledge* projected to the populace by *scientific authority*. These four facets are not necessarily intended as exhaustive, but they are among those that I use most commonly, and are enough to provide a sense of how I use the terms.[20]

I have found that this multifaceted way of thinking about science has mitigated some of the essentialisms that troubled my earlier efforts to think about science across multiple cultural and historical contexts. Rather than having to say that the British brought science to India, for example, I can speak of how Western scientific institutions wielded more scientific authority in a colonial context, forcing Indian scientific institutions to adopt a hybrid approach, integrating Western scientific knowledge with their own and adapting Western scientific methods to indigenous purposes. This is not to say that I only ever use the adjectival form, *scientific*. Sometimes I do use the nominal *science* as well, but only in emic situations or when I am speaking of science in more of a phenomenological way. It is to this latter usage that I now turn.

## How Religion and Science Feel

When religious communities grapple with science, the convention has been to understand it as a kind of discursive work. This discursive work could be considered theology, and the religious figures that do the grappling could be considered theologians. Jonathan Edelmann, for example, has advocated that scholars of Hindu traditions adopt these terms as we strive to understand the work of Hindu intellectuals in their engagements with scientific discourses. Edelmann understands *theology* to be a useful term because it reflects the fact that Hindu intellectuals are engaged in the act of interpreting "scripture and tradition" and treat these sources of knowledge as foundational in their arguments.[21] There is certainly a kind of theological work going on in the Gayatri Pariwar's engagement with science as well. But conducting this research has made it abundantly clear that what happens when religion and science interact spills over beyond the tidy bounds of rational theological discourse and into the messily embodied realms of feeling, performance, and identity construction. Accordingly, while I will be describing the theological or discursive aspects of the Gayatri Pariwar's engagements with science, my analysis requires tools that will allow me to account for the non-discursive spillover of these engagements.

Affect theory—a field of theory that offers an alternative to the discursive obsessions of the humanities in the postmodern era—offers just the right set of tools for thinking about religion and science in non-discursive ways.[22] Affect theory draws our attention away from discourse and back to the body and the way it feels, offering a sort of critical phenomenology. This offers an intriguing opportunity for a study of how power—for example, in the form of scientific or religious authority—can flow in ways that are not exclusively tied to language and cognition.[23] It makes it possible to think about how these forms of authority might function on a non-discursive level—how it might make Gayatri parijans feel. And as if to wrap the whole package up with a bow, it provides a wonderful counterpoint to scientific rationalism and instrumentalism.

This potential of affect theory is particularly apparent in Donovan Schaefer's recent work *Religious Affects*, which argues that affect theory's rejection of the notion that language is the exclusive medium of power makes it a crucial resource for understanding religion as a material, embodied phenomenon rather than as a bundle of propositions and beliefs. Kathleen Stewart and Ann Cvetkovich illustrate how affect theory provides a framework for exploring a politics of everyday experience—not personal, but public—that is helpful in understanding Gayatri parijans' efforts to carve out a place for themselves amidst the moral crisis they see in their postcolonial, globalizing society.[24] Finally, Sara Ahmed offers great insight how affect helps to form communities and identities and how affect, which operates on a non-linguistic, non-cognitive level can nonetheless stick to signs and symbols.[25]

Written over twenty years ago, when the current wave of affect theory was in its nascent stage,[26] Ruth Behar's *The Vulnerable Observer: Anthropology that Breaks Your Heart* is also noteworthy for championing the importance of the emotions. Behar exhorts her readers to make themselves vulnerable, empathizing with the people they encounter in the field and later laying bare their hearts to their readers when they write up their ethnographies.[27] Well before I was exposed to affect theory, I had accepted this basic methodological imperative, and so the two have become deeply entangled in my understanding. In this project, I seek not only to understand how Gayatri parijans feel, but also to lay my own feelings bare. I seek to forge empathic connections between these sets of feelings, but without losing track of the radical disparities in power and privilege and how they give different shapes to the experience of living in Shantikunj. My hope is that the personal experiences I relay in this book, coupled with ample self-critique, provide deeper insight into the Gayatri Pariwar because of and not despite their lack of objectivity.

While affect theory does provide crucial framework for my argument in this book, it is by no means my only concern. As is the case with many ethnographers, I feel a certain obligation to relay the many fascinating anecdotes I gathered in the field. Given the dearth of literature on the Gayatri Pariwar, I also feel a certain need to provide as thorough an account of the community as possible. In accordance with the breadth of my field experiences and my interdisciplinary background, I deploy something akin to what Wendy Doniger called a "toolbox approach,"[28] adopting a variety of thematic and theoretical concerns so as to examine the Gayatri Pariwar from as many perspectives as necessary. Sometimes this involves threading my interest in affect through fields such as the anthropology of charisma (chapter 3), ritual studies (chapter 4), and spatial theory (chapter 6). At other times, it involves looking at how scientific authority helps to discipline the bodies needed for the project of building a postcolonial nation (chapters 1 and 6). Given the number of tools I have to work with, I will introduce each one in its own chapter as I prepare to use it rather than going into greater depth on all of them in this introduction.

## Historical Contexts

### Gayatri as Mantra and Goddess

As I consider what it means to recite the Gayatri mantra under a laboratory exhaust hood throughout this book, my focus is primarily on the modern period. But this question has a longer, far more complex answer if we consider the full sweep of Gayatri's history.[29] A detailed account of this history would be a massive undertaking in its own right, but a succinct overview will be helpful for framing my discussion of the Gayatri Pariwar.

The Gayatri mantra first appears in *Ṛg Veda* 3.62.10. Its name derives from the eight-syllable Gayatri meter in which it is composed, but it is also sometimes referred to as the Sāvitrī mantra for the deity it addresses: "Let us contemplate the great radiance of the deity Savitṛ; may it inspire our thoughts." The Gayatri mantra has been an important part of a ritual called *sandhyā*, which some high-caste Hindu men have considered obligatory to perform at dawn, dusk, and noon since at least the fourth century CE. These times in part reflect Savitṛ's sovereignty over the rising and setting of the sun in particular. The Gayatri mantra is recited during this ritual while offering handfuls of water in the direction of the sun. Vedic, epic, and Purāṇic literature provides a narrative rationale for the importance of this ritual in preserving the cosmic cycle. In short, the droplets of offered water that have been imbued with the power of the Gayatri mantra become *vajra*, or thunderbolts that help drive away the immortal demons that would otherwise destroy the sun during its transit between dusk and dawn.[30]

Another important ritual practice in which the Gayatri mantra has featured prominently is the *upanayana* ceremony, which has served as the life-cycle rite initiating high-caste Hindu boys into the study and practice of Vedic texts and rituals. The Gayatri mantra's association with this ritual appears to date back to the *Śatapatha Brāhmaṇa* (seventh to sixth centuries BCE). The role of the Gayatri mantra in this initiation is most closely associated with the Brāhmaṇa caste, with other mantras being preferred for members of the Kṣatriya and Vaiśya castes.[31] This ritualization of the Gayatri mantra reinforced its close association with Vedic orthodoxy and Brahminhood and helped it become a powerful symbol for Vedic and Brahminical tradition and authority.

This authority proved desirable for the authors of texts like the *Devī Bhāgavata Purāṇa* (circa eleventh to twelfth century CE), who were laying the groundwork for bringing goddess devotion into the mainstream. To this end, the twelfth *skandha* (book) of this text provides an extended discussion on the Gayatri mantra and its personification as a goddess, detailing the benefits of recitation, the esoteric significance of each syllable and the mantra as a whole, and the ritual norms surrounding its practice. Of particular note is an exchange in which the King Janamejaya asks the Vedic sage Vyasa about the proliferation of sects and deities in their time. The text describes the worship of the gods Vishnu and Shiva as non-Vedic, as opposed to the worship of the goddess Gayatri through her mantra as being clearly compulsory in the Vedic literature. In fact, we learn that sects such as those devoted to Vishnu and Shiva have strayed from goddess-worshipping traditions due to a horrific curse that caused them to incarnate in the Kali Yuga, having forgotten their Vedic obligations and preferring traditions that lacked Vedic sanction.[32] Once goddesses held such a Vedic pedigree, they could be freely identified with other goddesses who were external to the Vedic tradition.[33] One result of this process was that while Gayatri now functioned as a bridge linking Vedic orthodoxy and popular Purāṇic devotion.

But for all of its broad appeal, recitation of the Gayatri mantra was only sanctioned for high-caste men. This privilege eroded in the nineteenth century, with the Arya Samaj playing a particularly important role. Dayanand Saraswati (1824–1883), founder of the Arya Samaj, felt that gender and caste should not restrict one's ability to undergo *upanayana* and thereby be initiated into Gayatri recitation.[34] This fits with a larger project in which Dayanand Saraswati and other prominent Hindu intellectuals of his time engaged: universalizing and nationalizing high-caste Hindu traditions. This typically involved looking to classical sources practices and ideas that could function as the core of an authentic, standardized, and monolithic pan-Hindu identity. Women's and low-caste traditions were rarely if ever sources for inspiration for these formulations. Nevertheless, these revived and universalized traditions operated in tandem with the development of an Indian national identity and were part of an effort to find a thread that could bind together India's diverse quilt of traditions into a unified coherence. The Gayatri mantra was only one of a constellation of practices the Arya Samaj advocated in this context. But given its ability to span Vedic orthodoxy and popular devotional piety, one can appreciate why the Gayatri mantra in particular became the core of a movement like the Gayatri Pariwar.

## Indian Scientific Institutions

One afternoon while I stayed in Delhi to jump through one bureaucratic hoop or another, I found myself in the neighborhood of Jantar Mantar[35] and decided to pay it a visit. It was nearly closing time, but I had just long enough to marvel at this collection of massive astronomical instruments and read the Archeological Survey of India's helpful informational plaques. This facility was a perfect place to meditate on my research. Some contemporary critics of "alternative science" like Meera Nanda, whose book I was reading at the time, have suggested that precolonial India was marked by rigid adherence to traditional authority and an absence of empirical observation, rational thought, and intellectual innovation.[36] If that is the case, I could not help but wonder why Jai Singh II built this elaborate astronomical observatory in 1723.

Figure I.2. Replica of Jantar Mantar's Samrāṭ Yantra at DSVV.

As Sheldon Pollock has noted, much of the discourse on the changes India underwent during the colonial period has been haunted by a lack of familiarity with the historical period immediately before colonization.[37] This is perhaps the legacy of Orientalist scholars, who viewed India as having declined from a bygone glorious age, ultimately becoming static. If India had not done much noteworthy in centuries, why study its recent history? At least in theory, scholarship has been disabused of such foolish questions for decades, but our knowledge especially of the period immediately before colonization has yet to catch up. Pollock and his collaborators on the Sanskrit Knowledge Systems on the Eve of Colonialism project have been working to fill this gap, and the picture that has emerged of early modern India is in fact one of great intellectual dynamism. In *jyotiṣ* (astronomy), there was a new emphasis on empiricism and significant intellectual exchange with Persian and Arabic astronomers. In *alaṅkāraśāstra* (poetics and literary criticism), new discursive styles emerged. The Nyāya school of thought developed new terminology for describing the world and this terminology spread into other intellectual domains.[38] In the field of medicine, too, new treatments had emerged and there is evidence of intellectual exchange with Perso-Arabic and English medical systems.[39] And all of this happened as Sanskrit intellectuals in numerous fields had begun identifying themselves as "new" (*navya*) in contradistinction to the "old" (*prācīna, jīrṇa*) intellectuals who had come before them.[40] It is clear enough from all of this that Sanskrit intellectual traditions were moving forward even as they were exchanging ideas with other Eurasian intellectual cultures. It does not seem terribly provocative to read into all of this that something that might be called an Indian modernity had already begun to emerge well before colonization.

It is nonetheless painfully clear that the intellectual continuity of these traditions was disrupted as the British expanded their control over India.[41] Intellectual activity in and related to India during this period is well documented and has been subject to an incredibly robust postcolonial critique over the last few decades. Of particular importance is a discourse that focuses on the role that scientific institutions played in signifying British colonial authority through education, museums, medicine, transportation networks, and communication technology.[42] Beyond the symbolic power of such displays of the supposed superiority of Western scientific knowledge, the colonial government called upon scientific knowledge to help make sense of the populace in the hopes of better governing them by arranging them into manageable categories with definitive essences.[43] Other work raises important questions about who influenced whom in the intellectual exchange between the British and India; a great deal of what the British passed off as their own scientific knowledge they had in fact drawn from Indian sources.[44]

A decisive moment in the colonial displacement of Indian intellectual traditions (both Sanskritic and Perso-Arabic) by European intellectual traditions came with the English Education Act of 1835, which introduced English-medium schooling as the gateway to a middle-class life. This was not just linguistic training, but also training in the literatures and intellectual traditions embedded in the English language. Thomas Macaulay famously offered the rationale for this legislation in his "Minute on Indian Education." The Sanskritic and Perso-Arabic canons had previously been the basis of education in India, but Macaulay derided these literatures at length in relation to "the intrinsic superiority of the Western literature"; for example:

> The question now before us is simply whether, when it is in our power to teach this language, we shall teach languages in which, by universal confession, there are no books on any subject which deserve to be compared to our own, whether, when we can teach European science, we shall teach systems which, by universal confession, wherever they differ from those of Europe differ for the worse, and whether, when we can patronize sound philosophy and true history, we shall countenance, at the public expense, medical doctrines which would disgrace an English farrier, astronomy which would move laughter in girls at an English boarding school, history abounding with kings thirty feet high and reigns thirty thousand years long, and geography made of seas of treacle and seas of butter.

They should not merely reinforce the "monstrous superstitions" of Arabic and Sanskrit literature, but rather seek to shape Indian culture through this new system of education:

> We must at present do our best to form a class who may be interpreters between us and the millions whom we govern, a class of persons Indian in blood and colour, but English in tastes, in opinions, in morals and in intellect. To that class we may leave it to refine the vernacular dialects of the country, to enrich those dialects with terms of science borrowed from the Western nomenclature, and to render them by degrees fit vehicles for conveying knowledge to the great mass of the population.

For better or worse, Macaulay's plan worked just as he had hoped. Within decades, English became the prestige language in India and its intellectual categories had rapidly changed the discursive landscape. For the new educated class of Indians, the Western canon provided the touchstones that would determine the worth of their extant traditions. This in turn led to the rise of "hybrid sciences" or "alternative sciences," which synthesize Western scientific knowledge and methods with extant Indian intellectual systems and an intensification and popularization of religious reform, with Hindu traditions newly reconfigured to suit English intellectual categories.[45]

Scholarship on postcolonial Hindus' use of scientific authority is comparatively less abundant and follows less clear trajectories. Meera Nanda's *Prophets Facing Backward* emphasizes Hindu nationalists' synthesis of Hindu thought with scientific authority. She attributes the sorry state of affairs to postmodern science studies scholars' insistence that science is no better than any other way of knowing.[46] Lola Williamson briefly describes the kinds of scientific claims Transcendental Meditation makes, although about a third of this description is reserved for criticisms of the movement's research practices and she does not consider the significance of their discourse beyond an attempt to integrate the material and the spiritual.[47] While focused primarily on language, Srinivas Aravamudan reserves the postcolonial "New Age" gurus for his final chapter, where he argues they utilize scientific rhetoric as a means to circulate their teachings globally rather than a means to bolster their nationalist pride like their colonial precursors.[48] C. Mackenzie Brown, after a much longer examination of the reception of Darwin in the colonial period, finds continuities in the postcolonial period, with evolutionary theory being integrated with and subordinated to Hindu ideas along established patterns.[49] Corrine Dempsey notes the important role scientific discourse can play for modern Hindu communities, especially those born in diaspora for whom traditional explanations for miraculous occurrences and ritual activity are less appealing.[50] Joseph Alter observes how the scientific rhetoric of colonial- and postcolonial-era yoga practitioners highlights the materiality of their tradition, becoming an epistemology that is tied to an extant ontology, but in a subordinate fashion. Science as an authoritative way of knowing is thus tied to extant yogic knowledges about the body and health.[51]

These works offer great insight on scientific authority in postcolonial India and have had a marked influence on my project. But with rare exceptions, I have found that they have not deviated much from the large and established literature on scientific institutions in colonial India. Many of them span both the colonial and postcolonial periods, treating scientific authority in postcolonial Hindu traditions as a continuation, perhaps with small variations, of an earlier colonial trend. It is important to highlight such continuities. I am glad that this work is being done, and it has been helpful in situating my project in larger historical patterns. My hope is that my project will contribute to this literature by noting how, with the liberalization of the Indian economy in the 1990s, the onset of globalization, radical changes in communication technology, and the educational and professional shifts signaled by the boom in India's IT industry, scientific authority integrates with Hindu traditions like the Gayatri Pariwar in ways that are deeply indicative of challenges that are new to contemporary India.

## Chapter Outline

I understand myself as having two major tasks in this book. First, I want to provide as comprehensive a picture of the Gayatri Pariwar as possible, both historically and in the ethnographic present. Second, I want to advance an argument about what scientific authority does for the Gayatri Pariwar and for contemporary Hindu traditions on a broader scale. Most of my chapters advance both of these agendas to some extent. In terms of larger structures, most of my historical material unfolds over the first three chapters. Odd-numbered chapters deal with the Gayatri Pariwar's leadership, whereas even-numbered chapters deal with the community at Shantikunj and their activities.

Chapter 1 is by far the most historical of my chapters. It deals with the formative experiences of Gurudev leading up to (but not including) the founding of the Gayatri Pariwar. My objective in exploring this these formative experiences is to better situate the Gayatri Pariwar in the landscape of modern Hindu traditions. I begin this process by examining the movement's hagiographical literature on Gurudev. Then I look for points of commonality and disjuncture with two key touchstones: the Arya Samaj and Gandhi.

Having introduced the founder of the Gayatri Pariwar, in chapter 2 I shift my focus to the community with which I lived in Shantikunj for seven months. After providing a bit more historical background on how Shantikunj came to be founded, I take a particular interest in how permanent Shantikunj residents came to live in the ashram. Pursuing this interest by examining life histories of a number of residents, I isolate a particularly fascinating group, whom I call upwardly mobile but disillusioned. Growing up in a provincial setting, they pursued an education in a lucrative field, but upon entering that field in post-liberalization India, they experienced disillusionment and came to reside in Shantikunj in their search for deeper meaning. The differences between their attitudes toward labor and consumption and those of older Shantikunj residents are rather stark, and clearly reflect changing social contexts in neoliberal India.

Chapter 3 focuses on the transition from the charismatic leadership of Gurudev to the leadership of Doctor-sahib. After setting the stage with some recent institutional history, I think comparatively about the leadership of these two figures, arguing that Doctor-sahib's scientific credentials take the place of Gurudev's more conventionally cultivated religious charisma. I end by speculating about how scientific authority might function in ways that are rather similar to charismatic authority, maintaining a certain sense of vitality and dynamism in a movement's post-charismatic phase.

The movement's ritual life becomes central in chapter 4, where I focus on ritual discourse and practice in the Gayatri Pariwar. Synthesizing ritual studies with Sara Ahmed's notion of "affective economies," I understand ritual as facilitating the circulation of objects of emotion that form identities and communities. Since Gayatri Pariwar ritual discourse draws so heavily on scientific authority, science becomes such an object in Gayatri Pariwar ritual practice. Ritual practice backed by scientific authority becomes a site where upwardly mobile but disillusioned Hindus can reconcile their dual identification with scientific rationality and traditional ritualism.

Each generation of leadership in the Gayatri Pariwar has been a husband-wife pair. Explicit discourse from the movement emphasizes the leadership of the husbands in both generations, and there is comparatively less material to work with in understanding the role of the wives, Mataji and Jiji (Hindi terms for "mother" and "big sister," respectively). In chapter 5, I note that extant material on these women often focuses on their motherly roles in establishing a family-like atmosphere in Shantikunj. Although Shantikunj residents don't always explicitly attribute this family-like atmosphere to the female leadership, they are somewhat consistent in noting that it is one of the most important features that differentiate the Gayatri Pariwar from other movements. From this it becomes quite apparent that the affective work of the female leaders is central to the movement's success. They transform Shantikunj into an extended domestic space. This eases the dislocations of India's new economy. It also pulls the ritual activity in Shantikunj into the domestic sphere, safeguarding it against the affective inadequacies of professional, public, priestly ritual styles.

The Gayatri Pariwar's eschatological hopes come, appropriately enough, at the end. Chapter 6 is structured around the Gayatri Pariwar's notion that *satyug*, "the golden age" as their translations have it, will not be revived in some sort of thunderbolt event. Rather, it will ripple outwards from individuals to families and then to communities, nations, and finally to the whole world. I use this motif of an eschatology that expands slowly outwards to think about how the Gayatri Pariwar situates itself in space at different scales. Starting with the ashram itself, a microcosmic utopia, I move outwards to the pilgrimage and tourist circuits of the Garhwal Himalayas, then to the contentious identity politics of the Indian nation, and finally to the world as a whole, where communication technologies and transnational migration offer distinct glimpses of how the Gayatri Pariwar's eschatology might reach its final, global stage.

## CHAPTER 1

# Gurudev

In order to better understand the Gayatri Pariwar and its vision for the Indian nation and the world, I want to consider some of the major forces that went into shaping its ideology. In addition to providing useful historical contexts for the movement, I will tease out certain elements of the ethos of the Gayatri Pariwar that will illustrate where it is situated in the larger field of modern Hindu movements. In this chapter, I will primarily be considering what I, along with certain members of the movement, see as Gurudev's major influences: Mohandas K. Gandhi and the Arya Samaj. While the Gayatri Pariwar's interest in reviving Vedic ritual might lead some to view the movement as functionally the same as the Arya Samaj, this chapter will show that the Gandhian connections run deep and are crucial for understanding the Gayatri Pariwar's larger social vision. I will develop this point first by providing a brief biographical sketch of Gurudev before moving on to a more specific consideration of how his encounters with the Arya Samaj and Gandhi might have affected his mission later in life.

## Gurudev's Formative Experiences

The precise details of Gurudev's life are somewhat difficult to pin down. Although two of his most important books, *My Life: Its Legacy and Message* and *Companions in Solitude*, have primarily autobiographical content, both are relatively succinct and focus on his day-to-day spiritual life, his visions of an incorporeal guru figure, and his lengthy pilgrimages into the

Himalayas—in other words, their content is primarily aimed at providing inspiration and instruction to his followers rather than providing a detailed account of his life. Although there are many alive today who can speak of his later years when he was established as the head of the Gayatri Pariwar and residing at Shantikunj, relatively few are left who can speak of the formative experiences he had earlier in his life. Perhaps unsurprisingly, these senior Gayatri parijans share Gurudev's tendency to focus primarily on discourse about spiritual practice rather than on biographical details, although I was able to get some extremely helpful pieces of information from them. In addition to these oral sources, *Odyssey of the Enlightened*, written by Doctor-sahib and Jyotirmay, that attempts to describe Gurudev's life more thoroughly. But this text itself begins with a caveat that in the course of their research about Gurudev's life, they struggled with a shortage of source materials.[1] Despite these shortcomings, this hagiography provides the most comprehensive information, and is particularly helpful because the formative experiences it describes go a long way toward explaining the distinctive blend of ideas in Gurudev's thought.

Shriram Sharma was born on September 20, 1911, in a small village near Agra, Uttar Pradesh, called Anwal Khera. Although his autobiographies start in his later youth, Pandya and Jyotirmay treat Gurudev's birth as the culmination of certain political and religious omens. It is no accident, we are to understand, that Gurudev was born in the same year that the partition of Bengal, which had been one of the galvanizing incidents of the Indian nationalist movement, was undone. The authors also suggest it is significant that this was the year that the British government moved the capital to its location in independent India, Delhi. This was particularly meaningful because Delhi was the site of the last celebration held in honor of a new British emperor.[2] Pandya and Jyotirmay also view Gurudev's birth as fulfilling a prophecy made by Annie Besant that an important spiritual leader would be born in 1911. This prediction was evidently an elaboration on those of two earlier Theosophists: Henry Steel Alcott, who believed a "bodhisattva" would soon be born, and Helena Blavatsky, who claimed that Himalayan rishis (from *ṛṣi*, seer) would establish a human agent who would "inspire India towards fulfillment of her destiny as spiritual guide of humanity."[3]

Pandya and Jyotirmay's intentions in framing Gurudev's birth through these events are admittedly transparent, but it is worth taking note of them explicitly here, as they represent an aspect of the Gayatri Pariwar's self-perception that will continue to be important throughout this book. Although Pandya and Jyotirmay never go quite so far as to explicitly put Gurudev on the level of the major leaders of the Indian nationalist movement like Gandhi or Nehru, we can see very clearly that they perceive Gurudev, and by extension the Gayatri Pariwar, as serving a central role in building the Indian nation. But Gurudev will not just help to answer the question of what it means to be Indian—he will also raise India to a place of esteem on the global stage. Indeed, the authors continue to portray Gurudev's religious and political sensibilities as deeply entwined.

Pandya and Jyotirmay assert that at the age of eight Gurudev's formal *upanayana* (initiation) into Hindu traditions took place at the hands of Madan Mohan Malaviya,[4] a prominent member of the independence movement with strong ties to an early Hindu nationalist group called the Hindu Mahasabha. But according to Gayatri Pariwar literature, Gurudev experienced a more momentous initiation when he was fifteen. Gurudev writes that he had a vision of an effulgent, incorporeal Himalayan yogi who offered him instruction and revealed to him that his past lives had included such highly revered religious figures as Kabir, Samarth Ramdas, and Ramakrishna.[5] This yogi, who continued to guide Gurudev for many years, informed him of his calling to work for the good of society through participation in the independence movement; he also asked that Gurudev take up some relatively demanding religious practices, including four arduous pilgrimages into the Himalayas.[6]

Although Pandya and Jyotirmay emphasize that Malaviya was Gurudev's actual guru, it is noteworthy that the Gayatri Pariwar presents him as receiving much of his spiritual instruction at the feet of this incorporeal being. Indeed, Pandya and Jyotirmay may have seen the need to focus on Gurudev's *upanayana* at the hands of Malaviya as necessary to establish Gurudev as a legitimate initiate into Gayatri recitation. This is because historically in Hindu traditions, a guru's religious authority is dependent primarily on the lineage of gurus to which he or she belongs. The idea of establishing oneself as authoritative on the basis of an incorporeal being is not unique to Gurudev, but bears comparison to numerous other modern gurus.

The incorporeal yogi was clear that Gurudev should continue to take part in the independence movement, and it seems that this injunction was enthusiastically received. According to Pandya and Jyotirmay, Gurudev was active in the independence movement from at least the age of twelve,[7] and only increased his involvement after this point. By the age of sixteen he had found employment writing for a revolutionary newspaper called the *Sainik* (*Soldier* or *Warrior*) and was spending much of his time participating in various demonstrations, eventually landing in jail in 1932.[8]

This aspect of Gurudev's encounter with his incorporeal guide further solidifies the impression that the Gayatri Pariwar views political and social change as being inextricably linked with personal spiritual development. By asserting the necessity of his participation in India's struggle for independence, this transcendent being turned political engagement for the sake of social change into a spiritual imperative for Gurudev, and by extension all of his followers. This theme continues to run throughout Gurudev's life as well as this chapter.

In the early 1930s, Gurudev undertook several trips during which he would encounter religious, cultural, and political figures and institutions that would have a substantial influence on the development of his thought. The first and perhaps most impactful of these journeys took place in 1931, when Pandya and Jyotirmay tell us Gurudev spent several days at Gandhi's Sabarmati Ashram. Although Gandhi was quite busy, the text describes a brief conversation he had with Gurudev. After hearing that Gurudev wanted to serve the nation, Gandhi asks how he can help. Significantly, the authors have Gurudev reply, "I want to become like you."[9] According to Chinmay Pandya (popularly known as Chinmay-bhaiya), son of Jiji and Doctor-sahib and his probable successor as head of Gayatri Pariwar, it was not just Gandhi's personality that affected Gurudev deeply; the very notion of an ashram that survived on the basis of volunteer service would influence Gurudev's social vision and the way in which he would eventually organize Shantikunj.

In 1933, shortly after his release from prison, Gurudev traveled to Shantiniketan, where Rabindranath Tagore had established Visva-Bharati University. Gurudev was evidently impressed by the relative independence enjoyed by this privately founded university, which no doubt served as a model for Gayatri Pariwar's more recently established university, DSVV. He was also intrigued by Tagore's sense of the importance of villages in the independence movement and his efforts to organize them.[10] This was of course also a strategy that Gandhi regularly employed, and one that would eventually become the greatest strength of the Gayatri Pariwar.

The next year, he traveled south to the ashram of Ramana Maharshi. It seems likely that this ashram served as an important model for Gurudev, a sense Pandya and Jyotirmay give when they describe his fascination with the ashram's orderly caste-integrated dining hall,[11] which is also a prominent feature at Shantikunj. During his return trip to Agra, Gurudev would reflect on Ramana Maharshi's ashram in comparison with Sabarmati, wondering if it would be possible for an ashram to reconcile the meditative tranquility of the former with the worldly engagement and brisk activity of the latter.[12] The authors also present some conversations between Gurudev and Ramana Maharshi that continue to develop the recurring theme of spiritual discipline and nation-building as interconnected. For example, when Gurudev explained that he was "awakening the masses about the glory of our nation and culture," he was told that he must in addition "awaken inner strength [and] develop inner effulgence."[13] Later, the authors describe a private audience in which Ramana Maharshi told Gurudev, "your ambition for freedom of the country and dedicating your efforts for that is also *sādhanā* (spiritual practice)."[14] Here we see the continuation of the important notion that work for the benefit of society, in this case through participation in the independence movement, is itself a form of spiritual practice. In this case, it is presented in a particular way that seems to suggest an old Hindu idea—that action undertaken selflessly and for the benefit of others is a method of self-cultivation.

After returning from this trip, Gurudev began working to improve the status of the "Harijans,"[15] following Gandhi's lead.[16] Although he was frustrated that Gandhi was not giving enough attention to the independence movement in the mid-1930s, expressing his criticisms in the *Sainik,* he continued to support Gandhi's programs. In particular, Gurudev participated by "adopting" a village with the intention of improving education and public cleanliness as a way of bringing about grassroots social change.[17] Clearly, his encounters at Sabarmati and Shantiniketan were already bearing fruit—Gurudev had understood the importance of empowering the villagers to achieve meaningful change, and now he was getting valuable hands-on experience in how to make it happen.

Although the exact extent and duration of his involvement remains unclear, Gurudev was associated with both the Arya Samaj and the Theosophical Society.[18] Pandya and Jyotirmay describe these two organizations in glowing terms, asserting that they were revitalizing "Sanatan Dharma."[19] He goes on to praise their progressive positions on issues such as caste and gender, but is more critical of their rejection of a number of popular Hindu practices, including idol worship.[20] It seems that Gurudev broke from the Theosophical Society completely when they curtailed their efforts toward Indian independence in the wake of Annie Besant's death in 1933.[21]

Despite his association with the group, it is rather difficult to gauge the extent of the Theosophical Society's direct influence on Gurudev. This is partly because the Theosophical Society developed its doctrine largely from extant romantic Orientalist tropes that were trafficked widely in the world of reform Hindu traditions. Nevertheless, the notion that Gurudev received instruction from an incorporeal being from the Himalayas bears resemblance to a trope that was also used by Helena Blavatsky, founder of the Theosophical Society, who had claimed initiation at the hands of a yogi from a secret group of Himalayan masters in the late nineteenth century. Given the authors' interest in presenting Gurudev as fulfilling prophecies of Theosophical Society members, there is also some reason to believe that these prophecies had some influence on Gayatri Pariwar eschatology.

As for the Arya Samaj, it is clear that Gurudev was invited to lead its Mathura branch in 1941,[22] although he probably had contact with the movement much earlier at a less visible level. When questioned about Gurudev's association with the Arya Samaj, Chinmay-bhaiya emphasized his Gandhian social vision and spiritual originality before saying that Gurudev "grew up in an Arya Samaj environment," thus distancing Gurudev from the movement somewhat. Perhaps this has to do with the fact that by the mid-1940s, Gurudev broke with the Arya Samaj because they vehemently opposed his advocacy of image worship.[23] According to Vireshwar, one of Gurudev's oldest living followers, Gurudev believed that the Arya Samaj was thinking too narrowly in placing a restriction on such a common Hindu practice, and that he could do the same work for a wider segment of society if he did away with those kinds of limitations. Clearly, Gurudev had already taken some of Gandhi's lessons to heart.

Without denying Gurudev's Arya Samaj association, Pandya and Jyotirmay do not dwell on it long; they seem more interested in discussing Gurudev's reasons for leaving than his reasons for joining. My conversations with Chinmay-bhaiya and Vireshwar had a similar tone. Meanwhile all of these sources clearly felt more comfortable discussing Gurudev's Gandhian credentials at greater length. At the very least this makes it quite clear that the Gayatri Pariwar prefers to represent itself as associated with Gandhi's legacy rather than that of the Arya Samaj. The remainder of this chapter will be dedicated to exploring the extent to which this representation holds with the actual ideology of the Gayatri Pariwar.

## The Arya Samaj

Founded in 1875 by Swami Dayananda Saraswati, the Arya Samaj has been one of the most important Hindu reform movements. Although the Arya Samaj shares numerous characteristics with other reform movements of the time, such as a critique of idolatry, polytheism, and traditional Hindu views on caste and gender, it was in many ways a reaction to what Dayananda perceived as an excessive embrace of Western culture by reform Hinduism.[24] Also unlike other reform movements of the day, the primary focus of the Arya Samaj was in the revival of rituals of offering described in the ancient Vedic texts rather than on meditation and philosophies of non-dualism intended to extricate the soul from the cycle of reincarnation.

With that background information in place, I would like to proceed with a more detailed comparison of the Gayatri Pariwar and the Arya Samaj. One helpful tool for understanding the Arya Samaj's is a set of ten *niyamas* (principles), which Arya Samajists have been following from very early in the history of the movement. Although certainly not comprehensive, they will serve as a helpful organizational tool for seeing where the Gayatri Pariwar deviates from the Arya Samaj and where they seem to be aligned.

1. The original source of true knowledge and whatever is known through it is the highest Lord.

2. The Lord is the very essence of truth, consciousness, and bliss, formless, almighty, just, merciful, unborn, without end, changeless, without beginning, unparalleled, the basis of everything, lord of all, omnipresent, pervading all, ageless, deathless, fearless, permanent, pure, and the creator of the world, only he is worthy of worship.

3. The Veda is the book of true knowledge. To study the Veda and to teach it, to hear and expound it is the highest dharma of all Arya Samajists.[25]

These first three *niyamas*, taken together, express the Arya Samaj's basic theological and epistemological views. They assert that there is one deity who is without attributes, thereby rejecting the notion espoused by many Hindus that deities can have a form and that there may be more than one.[26] One of the fundamental upshots of this principle is that it completely invalidates image worship—if the only real deity worth worshiping is a formless one, there can be no images of deities to worship. I have already described how Gurudev parted ways with the Arya Samaj over this issue, so this is obviously a major point of disjuncture. But to further elaborate on Gayatri Pariwar practices in this area, it is worth noting that their attitude toward polytheism, deities with attributes, and image worship is not just begrudgingly tolerant but rather openly encouraging. Gurudev and his followers have tended to worship the Gayatri mantra personified in the form of a goddess. Part of the compound at Shantikunj is a small temple to Gayatri Mata that functions much like any other Hindu temple, complete with well-attended *ārati*[27] services at dawn and dusk.

As for epistemology, the Arya Samaj holds that the Vedas are infallible sources of religious authority that originated from their formless deity. They do accept certain other Hindu texts as being authoritative so long as they are consonant with the Vedas, but they reject a fairly large body of Hindu literature, including the widely popular Purāṇas, as being corruptions of the Vedic religion. Again, the Gayatri Pariwar appears to deviate fairly significantly from the Arya Samaj here. While the Gayatri Pariwar, like most Hindu movements, treats the Vedas as authoritative, they have a different account of their origins. Rather than seeing the Vedas as being a revelation from a deity, the Gayatri Pariwar understands the Vedas to be the recorded results of experiments conducted by rishis in ancient times. For the Gayatri Pariwar, it is this supposed scientific origin that makes the Vedas authoritative. The Gayatri Pariwar is more permissive when it comes to which texts they consider valid, including the Purāṇas, and furthermore they claim to be open toward continued religious innovation, so long it is scientifically grounded to their satisfaction.[28]

4. All should always be ready to accept truth and reject untruth.

8. All should destroy ignorance and increase knowledge.[29]

These *niyamas* seem to reflect the Arya Samaj's opposition to "superstitious" practices that many Hindus supposedly accept on the sole basis of tradition. They reflect a certain rationalist orientation, perhaps even a scientific temper, which is common among reform Hindu traditions, including the Gayatri Pariwar. Gayatri Pariwar discourse often speaks pejoratively of "superstition" and "blind faith" as opposed to what they call "scientific spirituality." They sometimes speak more specifically about practices such as dowry and caste discrimination as being among these practices they are trying to eradicate. Their basic position is that people should not take up practices purely based on tradition—rather, they should seek to understand the practices first and should only accept them as part of their lives if they have observable benefits. While this attitude is similar to the one Dayananda expresses in *niyamas* 4 and 8, it is worth taking into account that for the Arya Samaj, the scope of concepts like "truth" and "knowledge" is quite a bit narrower than for the Gayatri Pariwar because there are so few authoritative sources of knowledge in the Arya Samaj.

> 5. All should perform every action consistent with dharma, that is, after reflecting upon truth and untruth.
>
> 6. Doing good for the world is the chief goal of this society, that is, improving it physically, spiritually, and socially.
>
> 7. One's behavior towards all should be appropriate, consistent with dharma, and loving.[30]

These general ethical guidelines are also accepted by the Gayatri Pariwar. Although *niyamas* 5 and 7 are broad enough to be shared by many Hindus, *niyama* 6 represents a fairly distinctive core value for both the Arya Samaj and the Gayatri Pariwar. While some religious movements might advocate a withdrawal from the troubles of the social and political spheres to pursue inner peace, both Gurudev and some members of the Arya Samaj were highly active in the independence movement. It is worth clarifying that Dayananda himself took no active role in the independence movement other than rejecting the rule of "men ignorant of the Vedas."[31] But a number of Dayananda's followers participated in the Indian National Congress, which was central in India's movement toward self-rule.[32] In more recent times, the Gayatri Pariwar has been engaged in a variety of humanitarian efforts, such as mobile eye camps in areas where there are inadequate medical facilities. As suggested by Gurudev's biographical sketch and numerous conversations with Shantikunj residents that I will relay in the coming chapter, Gayatri parijans do not typically see a distinction between their spiritual lives and their work for the welfare of society.

9. Each should not be satisfied with his or her improvement alone, rather the improvement of all should be understood as one's own improvement.

10. All people should be bound in maintaining social principles which affect the welfare of all, and everyone should be free in the principles which affect the welfare of the individual.[33]

Although these *niyamas* might seem unobjectionable from the perspective of a movement that is oriented toward social change like the Gayatri Pariwar, they actually reflect a key difference in the way the two groups think about their mission. The Arya Samaj seems to have a very top-down view of social change—a trickle-down system, if you will. *Niyama* 9 is essentially enjoining Arya Samajists to look after the needs of others as a means of self-development. But in order to do this, an Arya Samajist would have to be in a sufficiently privileged life situation with enough financial stability and free time to pursue such philanthropy. This may well have been a deliberate move on the part of Dayananda, who was particularly interested in offering instruction to the Indian nobility.[34] The majority of Arya Samajists indeed come from the right kind of background to work for the well being of society in this way.[35] The Gayatri Pariwar, on the other hand, promotes a rather different form of social engagement. The core concept in Gurudev's plan for transforming Indian society and the world as a whole is that if individuals begin to change the way they act, they will automatically elevate those around them with their good influence, eventually transforming society through a sort of ripple effect. Consequently, there is no distinction made between improving one's self and improving society, as in *niyama* 9. By allowing Gayatri parijans to pursue social change by focusing on their individual problems, the Gayatri Pariwar promotes a kind of grassroots social change that requires no special privilege to pursue.

There are several other points of comparison that are worth considering, and the foremost among them is the role of *yajña* in the movements. This is perhaps the most visible similarity between the two movements—very few reform-style Hindu movements emphasize *yajña* to such an extent. But it is the basic type of ritual expressed in the Vedas and therefore fundamental to the Arya Samaj's practice, taking place during weekly meetings.[36] Although Gayatri parijans tend to consider recitation of the

Gayatri mantra as their core practice, they describe *yajña* and the Gayatri mantra as the mother and father of "Bhāratiya Dharma" (Indian dharma),[37] and perform it every morning around dawn in Shantikunj. It is not just their emphasis on this practice that is noteworthy, but also their shared belief that participants do not need to be high-caste males.

Caste is another significant area where the Arya Samaj and the Gayatri Pariwar are similar. In fact, their core positions are almost identical: both groups believe that caste should be determined not by birth, but rather by one's personal qualifications.[38] They furthermore regard the modern system of caste-by-birth as a corruption of an earlier, better system with more authoritative roots.[39] But in some ways, the Arya Samaj still has a more conservative view of caste than the Gayatri Pariwar. This is most clear in their acceptance of proscriptions against sharing food and cooking utensils between castes, aimed at the prevention of interdining.[40] In fact, the practice of interdining was one of the major criticisms Swami Dayananda leveled against other Hindu reform movements.[41] Meanwhile, the Gayatri Pariwar has embraced interdining with their large, communal dining hall with shared utensils, which seems to be based on what Gurudev observed in the ashram of Ramana Maharshi.

Another intriguing feature of the Gayatri Pariwar is their clear eschatological views. Through their spiritual and social efforts, they believe they can effect a global change in consciousness and usher in a new *satyug*.[42] On the other hand, the Arya Samaj believes that the durations of the *yugas* are cosmological constants that cannot be changed. Dayananda does believe that the right kinds of human action are able to make the Kali Yuga better,[43] but their attitude toward this project lacks the eschatological characteristics that color the Gayatri Pariwar's efforts toward reviving *satyug*. In other words, while Dayananda allows for the possibility of humans improving the experience of living in the Kali Yuga, he does not give any sense that there is a definite final end toward which he is propelling humanity. Conversely, Gurudev sees the revival of *satyug* as a definitive endpoint that his teachings are aimed at bringing about.

Since both movements are to some extent bound up with the project of nation-building, it is worth considering the different ways in which they articulate their identities and how that relates to the way they imagine the Indian nation. The Arya Samaj is in some senses a precursor to the Hindu nationalist movement that would develop in the twentieth century.[44] Its practice of utilizing a ceremony called *śuddhi* (purification) to "reconvert"

Indian Muslims and Christians back into the Hindu fold[45] continues to be a major tool for modern Hindu nationalists who view themselves, as did Arya Samajists, as embattled against missionaries. The Arya Samaj evinced a fairly militant attitude toward all other religious groups in India—not just Muslims and Christians, but also more traditional Hindus and reform Hindus whom they perceived as too Westernized—and struggled to stigmatize these outsiders.[46] Its vision of an Indian nation was ultimately an Arya Samaj utopia in which all outsiders were eventually assimilated into the movement, and in which the Hindu nation was "regenerated" by the Arya Samaj interpretation of the Vedas.[47]

Although the Gayatri Pariwar has a similar utopian vision for India, it is not constructed in such narrow terms, and I found no trace of the sort of militancy associated with the Arya Samaj in any of its literature or in my interactions with Gayatri parijans. The Gayatri Pariwar's utopian vision for the Indian nation, and indeed the entire world, is one in which people are able to retain their religious identities but ideally they also perform *yajña* and chant the Gayatri mantra. The Gayatri Pariwar regards these practices as "spiritual" and therefore compatible with whatever religious identity a person might have—a complicated claim to which I will return in chapter 6. From a Western perspective this might seem a bit far-fetched, but it is important to take into account that in India, the lines that separate traditions are not so hard and fast and people will often borrow elements from other traditions if they find them appealing. In practice, I struggled to find non-Hindus at Shantikunj; I encountered only two during my time there. Regardless, the fact remains that the Gayatri Pariwar is not participating in "reconversion" drives or treating Muslims and Christians in India as interlopers who are not truly part of India's cultural heritage. Thus, it seems that there is at least some room for diversity in the Gayatri Pariwar's vision of a nation unified by Gayatri Pariwar practices.

Finally, and perhaps most importantly for the purposes of this book, it is important to acknowledge that there are precursors to the ways in which the Gayatri Pariwar uses scientific authority in the Arya Samaj. As Gyan Prakash suggests in his influential work *Another Reason*, Dayananda's engagement with Western intellectuals necessitated this approach to justifying his beliefs because his opponents were able to utilize their position of social power to frame their debate in Western cultural terms.[48] So, according to Dayananda, the Vedas were based on the laws of nature, and thus their worldview could be developed through scientific authority. One way in which he accomplished this was by framing Vedic practices like *yajña* as having tangible public health benefits.[49] Dayananda would also occasionally deploy scientific authority as a tactic for dismissing traditional Hindu practices that he found undesirable, such as *śraddhā* (ancestor worship), astrology, and image worship.[50]

The Gayatri Pariwar's use of scientific authority runs parallel to the Arya Samaj's in a number of ways. The Gayatri Pariwar does not really find itself in need of defense from critiques by Western intellectuals as was the case during the colonial era, but the Gayatri Pariwar is not just carrying on the Arya Samaj's use of scientific authority because it is an established cultural pattern. The Gayatri Pariwar faces a similar concern as it struggles to spread its teachings across cultural boundaries. Even though it is setting the terms of this transnational conversation, power relations have not changed in a meaningful enough way that the Gayatri Pariwar can impose Hindu epistemologies, which rely substantially on textual authority, upon its global target audience.[51] The Gayatri Pariwar is a bit more circumspect when it comes to utilizing scientific authority to critique other traditional Hindu practices, especially where the traditions in question are not causing any immediate harm. But its teachings do frequently suggest that people should abandon religious practices that they are doing purely out of tradition and without any perceivable tangible benefits. In addition to these points of comparison, it is worth noting that there is a difference of scale in the use of scientific authority between the two groups. Whereas the Arya Samaj would deploy scientific rhetoric selectively but primarily focus on the intellectual authority of the Vedas, the Gayatri Pariwar consistently emphasizes the scientific basis of its mission and conducts laboratory experiments to verify the efficacy of its practices. Textual authority has some role to play for them, but it never seems to be adequate and is always in need of supplementation by scientific authority.

## Gandhi

Mohandas K. Gandhi is one of the best-known figures in Indian history and scarcely needs an introduction. Briefly, he was born in the town of Porbandar in 1869, studied law in London, and ran afoul of the British authorities while agitating for the rights of Indians in South Africa in the early twentieth century. Upon returning to India, he rose to prominence in the independence movement, which was already underway, mobilizing large segments of the population for a series of civil disobedience actions. In early 1948, mere months after the independence movement achieved success, he was assassinated by a Hindu nationalist.

Like many educated Indians of his day, Gandhi struggled to reconcile his Indian cultural heritage with the deep impact Western culture had upon his life through his experiences of growing up colonized and being educated abroad.[52] While there is no denying that his approach to this problem was distinctive, it is also clear that he was not the first Indian to face this struggle, and that elements of his religious and political ideologies are similar to a number of reform movements like the Arya Samaj. For example, Gandhi was critical of prevailing ideas about caste and gender and argued for the reform of those systems, albeit in a limited and somewhat problematic way. He is well known for his attention to widowhood, and he understood women as having an important but highly gendered role in the independence movement—they were not suited for any political action where arrest was a possible outcome.[53]

Caste was a major topic for Gandhi. He considered himself an advocate of the untouchable communities, whom he called Harijans (Children of God). Although he wanted to eliminate untouchability, his tendency to regard Harijans as belonging politically and religiously to the caste Hindu community put him at odds with B.R. Ambedkar, a leader from within the untouchable community.[54] Gandhi supported a system of four castes as being crucial to the stability of Indian society, but became increasingly critical of traditional Hindu notions about caste as his life went on, eventually working to eradicate its hierarchical and hereditary aspects by requiring his high-caste followers to do work normally reserved for the lower castes and encouraging interdining and intermarriage.[55]

Although Gandhi's discourse about gender and caste is primarily sociopolitical whereas Dayananda's is primarily socioreligious, both advocate a similarly moderate program of movement toward greater social equality while preserving distinctive social roles. But it is worth noting that Gandhi was somewhat more radical on the matter of intermarriage and interdining, bringing him closer to the Gayatri Pariwar on that point.

Gandhi's ideas about gender and caste form part of a larger constellation of ideas about what a free Indian nation should look like.

Although Gandhi at times evinced a limited identification of Hinduness with Indianness, the India he imagined was at least in a certain sense pluralist. Very early in his career, Gandhi articulated a vision that Hindu-Muslim unity was not only possible because religious difference did not trump national identity, but also necessary for overthrowing the British. He understood the Indian nation to be primordial and capable of absorbing or assimilating different religious and cultural traditions that have come its way throughout history without losing its essence. He blamed the disunity of his day on the British policy of "divide and conquer," and he suggested that Hindus and Muslims must work together, returning India to a state of integral wholeness, if they were to free themselves of the yoke of empire.[56] The shortcomings of Gandhi's tendency to oversimplify the differences between Hindus and Muslims in an effort to conceptualize a coherent nation-state would eventually lead to his difficulty in comprehending the Muslim League's demand for the creation of a separate Islamic state. Nevertheless, Gandhi's conciliatory efforts toward Muslims enraged Hindu nationalists, who made multiple attempts on his life because they felt that his work toward empowering and mobilizing Muslims was contrary to Hindu interests and had made the partition of India inevitable.[57]

Seen in a certain light, the parallels between Gandhi's vision for India and the Gayatri Pariwar's are striking. Like Gandhi, the Gayatri Pariwar sees a place for both Hindus and Muslims in India, and in so doing distances itself from Hindu nationalist conceptions of Indian identity. But both share a sense of a shared, primordial Indian culture, which in the Gayatri Pariwar's case is manifest in the Gayatri mantra and *yajña*. The Gayatri Pariwar's notion that these practices can and should be adopted widely by non-Hindus evinces a similar sort of idealism to Gandhi's notion that the differences between Hindus and Muslims were a British invention that could be easily overcome.

The gulf between Gandhi and the Gurudev is perhaps widest on the topic of religious practice. This is well represented by a conversation between the two that the authors relay in *Odyssey of the Enlightened:*

> Bapu [Gandhi] said, "Preparations for the morning program might be going on. Did you participate in the prayer?" Shriram nodded his head.
>
> Bapu asked—"Which part of this program did you like?"

> "Everything was fine," said Shriram, "but the mantras of the Eeshavasyopanishad impressed me very much. I will repeat that prayer daily."
>
> "What is the use of repeating the prayer?" Bapu questioned. No answer could be given to this.[58]

Gandhi went on to emphasize the importance of a simple lifestyle,[59] presumably as a sort of contrast to Gurudev's interest in daily ritualized religious practice. Gandhi had a marked disinterest in the outward trappings of Hindu traditions, but was nonetheless deeply concerned with religion, and especially with the ways it could contribute to a healthy, free India. Gandhi was thus particularly interested in elements of religions that could contribute to personal moral development, including nonviolence, celibacy, and fasting.[60] For Gandhi, these practices became obsessions because they were inextricable from the independence movement, since moral bodies were healthy bodies, and healthy bodies were the cornerstone of the nation.[61]

Gurudev was never persuaded by Gandhi's dismissal of daily ritualized religious practice, and he and his followers have continued to view such practices as being important to cultivating healthy, moral bodies capable of further refining the Indian nation. Indeed, in this respect Gurudev may have more in common with rural Hindus than Gandhi did. But Gurudev does seem to agree that a life of self-disciplined simplicity and moderation has a major role to play in reforming society as well. Gurudev encouraged his followers to take up regular fasts and to avoid non-procreative sexual activity. At Shantikunj, residents must live a simple, quasi-monastic life in which they are permitted to have families but are expected to wear the same simple clothes, eat the same simple food, and live in similar simple quarters—regardless of what kind of volunteer work they contribute to the community. Consequently, ritual activities aside, Gurudev's ideas about how an individual's lifestyle relates to his or her capacity to advance the Gayatri Pariwar's social mission bears strong resemblance to Gandhi's.[62]

Gandhi's skillful integration of religious signifiers into his social and political discourse was key in his ability to mobilize large portions of India's villages who may have felt they had little in common with the other urban, educated, Westernized leaders of the independence movement. This is not to say that Gandhi was the only leading Indian nationalist who recognized the significant role that villages must play in building a coherent independent Indian nation,[63] but rather that he was particularly successful in his ability to draw them into the struggle. Despite his origins in a larger town and his time spent in London, Gandhi advocated a populist discourse in which rural India was the most "authentic" India. As a result, he was able to focus the attention of the elite on the plight of the villagers.[64] His colleagues were consequently compelled to head out to rural India to organize the villages at a grassroots level. By leading villagers in Champaran and elsewhere in actions aimed at redressing specific local social injustices, Gandhi ultimately positioned himself as a hero who would improve the lot of the rural poor as a whole.[65]

In my biographical sketch of Gurudev, I have already described how the Gayatri Pariwar presents him as having been involved with Gandhi's project of village empowerment. I want to argue that this experience was absolutely essential to the development of Gurudev's ideas that eventually took form in the Gayatri Pariwar. One of the features of the Gayatri Pariwar that make it noteworthy among modern reform Hindu movements is its appeal in rural areas and with less-educated segments of the population. Like Gandhi, Gurudev's articulation of a Hindu modernity is tempered by a distinctly populist sensibility. This sensibility is perhaps most clearly visible in his rationale for leaving the Arya Samaj—he recognized that their rejection of polytheism, image worship, the Purāṇas, and other widely popular Hindu traditions was inherently tied to the elitist world of urban Hindus with Western-style educations and was therefore unlikely to gain traction in rural India. Gurudev's experience with organizing in village settings also helped him understand how a network of local leaders working to engage villagers at the grassroots level might be a more effective way to spread his movement rather than the trickle-down approach taken by the Arya Samaj.

Although Gandhi, with his populist orientation toward indigenous tradition, is not especially associated with scientific rhetoric, he did on occasion deploy it in ways that warrant brief consideration. As part of his obsession with the relations between morality, health, and the nation, Gandhi made significant use of scientific rhetoric, and especially the notion of experimentation (it's no accident his autobiography is entitled *The Story of My Experiments with Truth*) to describe his activities and to exhort others to join him. For Gandhi, an ashram like Sabarmati or even a body like his own could function as a laboratory, as capable of establishing objective, transcendental truths through direct, personal experience as its brick-and-mortar equivalents could through their elaborate instruments.[66]

It is difficult to imagine that there is no meaningful connection between Gandhi's discourse about personal experience as experimentation and the Gayatri Pariwar's discourse about only accepting practices which have tangible results and its emphasis on conducting laboratory experiments on the efficacy of its practices. The connection becomes even clearer when considering how this is bound up with their shared discourse on the interconnectedness of morality, health, and social reform and their shared interest in mobilizing the rural poor. Through their discourse about experimentation, Gandhi and Gurudev empower people of any means to use their bodies as laboratories through which they can discover new lifestyles that allow them to live healthier lives in greater harmony with their communities. Of course, Dayananda's use of scientific authority to link *yajña* with public health anticipates this in some ways, but his discourse was not so fixated on the notion of experimentation because his epistemology was so centered around the authority of the Vedas. Nor did he have a particularly solid sense of how to appeal to less-educated rural Indians.

While I understand the temptation to notice the Gayatri Pariwar's program of moderate social reform in conjunction with the Vedic revivalism they demonstrate in the relative centrality of *yajña*, these areas of influence seem superficial indeed when considered in comparison to the interconnected epistemological, medical, social, and political ideas described above. This certainly does not mean that the Arya Samaj's contribution to Gurudev's thought is negligible—ultimately, I think of the Gayatri Pariwar as translating the Arya Samaj's Vedic revivalism through a Gandhian populist grammar, and that goes a long way toward explaining how it has had such success spreading reform Hindu traditions in rural India.

CHAPTER 2

# Coming to Shantikunj

One of the most fruitful questions I asked Shantikunj residents was how they came to live in the ashram, and the journey of a man named Gyaneshwar from provincial Uttar Pradesh to Shantikunj via Moscow was easily one of the most dramatic. His story starts in Deoria district, where he grew up in a family whose piety and interest in the Gayatri Pariwar he did not initially share. This all changed when he traveled to Moscow for medical school. Disconcerted by Western lifestyles, he suddenly appreciated the value of Hindu traditions. Guided by a priest in his hometown, Gyaneshwar took up Gayatri recitation to protect himself against his colleagues' apparent moral dissolution. This new practice was accompanied by a study of Gurudev's literature, the rhetoric of which resonated with Gyaneshwar's scientific mindset, moving him deeply. He intensified his practices, finding them more and more rewarding, and finally resolved to visit Shantikunj. After visiting, he deepened his study of Gurudev's teachings, and finally resolved to live out his life in Shantikunj to better dedicate himself to the Gayatri Pariwar's mission.

The drama of Gyaneshwar's story derives not only from the geographical distance he traveled, but also from the resulting conversion from a self-described skeptical atheist to a devoted Gayatri parijan. But for all of its drama, it shares certain themes with the life stories of a number of other Shantikunj residents. These themes—a traditional upbringing in provincial India, a STEM education that provides an initiation into India's new global middle class, and an experience of disillusionment with contemporary middle-class life that is mitigated by moving to Shantikunj—are crucial to understanding the place of the Gayatri Pariwar in contemporary

India. Taken loosely together, they are indicative of a group that I call "upwardly mobile but disillusioned." In this chapter, I identify the distinctive traits of these Shantikunj residents and argue that the experiences that brought them to the ashram represent a kind of middle-class moral crisis. Understanding this crisis will prove crucial for examining the role of scientific authority in Hindu movements like the Gayatri Pariwar in contemporary India.

I begin this task by providing a brief historical account of how the Gayatri Pariwar coalesced around Gurudev and came to be located at Shantikunj that provides necessary context for understanding the Gayatri parijans whose stories I am considering in this chapter. I then shift my focus to Gayatri parijans' life histories with particular attention to the circumstances under which they moved to Shantikunj. After imparting a sense of the multigenerational community that lives at the ashram, I highlight stories of the upwardly mobile but disillusioned and note how they reflect contemporary India's political economy and the resulting moral crisis. I then move on to examine Gyaneshwar's story in detail, since it was one of the most extensive and compelling narratives of upward mobility and disillusionment I recorded. Finally, I conclude with a discussion of how these Gayatri parijans' experiences represent a kind of moral crisis, and I point to some of the ways in which the Gayatri Pariwar's use of scientific authority helps to resolve this crisis.

## Founding the Gayatri Pariwar

In the last chapter, I presented historical material that dealt primarily with Gurudev's personal history and especially his formative experiences up through his split with the Arya Samaj in the mid-1940s. Here, I shift into the Gayatri Pariwar's institutional history. Starting in 1938 just before Gurudev struck out on his own and ending around 1971 with the founding of Shantikunj, this history serves as a bridge from the historical, pre-institutional concerns of the previous chapter with the Shantikunj-based ethnographic concerns of the rest of my project while providing necessary context for understanding the people who live in the ashram. The founding of Shantikunj is by no means the last important event in the Gayatri Pariwar's institutional history, but subsequent events are much more closely tied to themes I will explore in the next chapter.

The first watershed moment in the Gayatri Pariwar's institutional history was the creation of a periodical called *Akhand Jyoti* (*Eternal Light*). In 1938, after several years of grassroots organizing in village India, Gurudev decided that it was time to shift his focus from the kind of political journalism he had done at the *Sainik* to more religious publishing endeavor. Or, to put it in Pandya and Jyotirmay's terms, Gurudev's journalistic focus shifted from facilitating "*swarājya*" to facilitating "*Rāmrājya*."[1] The Gandhian tones here suit the populist sentiments the Gayatri Pariwar attributes to *Akhand Jyoti*: in comparison to other elitist spiritual magazines that existed, this was to be "a magazine that presented a practical spirituality for the villagers of India."[2] Just as *Akhand Jyoti* retains this Gandhian populism, it also retains a focus on nation-building. It promotes a spiritual revolution to go along with the political revolution, working toward a nation whose continued independence will be guaranteed by the morality and health of its citizens. No doubt these aims were easy to empathize with for literate peoples of the day, and this publication together with Gurudev's other writings plays a role for the Gayatri Pariwar's upwardly mobile but disillusioned followers.

The outbreak of World War II provided logistical challenges for the founding of *Akhand Jyoti*, making publication somewhat irregular at first. But by 1946, Gurudev's Mathura-based press had begun to publish *Akhand Jyoti* regularly.[3] It is perhaps no accident that this was happening the same year that he parted ways with the Arya Samaj over its elitist attitudes toward *mūrti* worship. Although the authors present no explicit chronology and do not describe a causal connection between these two events, this timing is impossible to overlook. One possible reading of this situation is that Gurudev increased the volume of his publication as he struck out on his own from the Arya Samaj in order to assert his institutional independence. But the reading I favor would be that the end of World War II made it easier for Gurudev to publish more regularly, and that the increased publicity of his thought on *mūrti* worship is what created the rift with the Arya Samaj. Another major factor was likely his marriage to Mataji, who from early on performed important emotional labor that was crucial for the Gayatri Pariwar's eventual success—a topic to which I will return in detail in chapter 5. In any event, this publication served to establish Gurudev's reputation with broader audiences, and according to some senior Gayatri parijans, *Akhand Jyoti* was the first precursor to the Gayatri Pariwar. Gayatri parijans consider *Akhand Jyoti* to be a core component of their mission to this day, and claim that it has over 1.5 million subscribers.[4]

In the early years of India's independence, *Akhand Jyoti* became increasingly popular, and by 1950 Gurudev had established a center for his growing mission in Mathura called Gayatri Tapobhumi. Although Gayatri Pariwar literature does not particularly emphasize the occasion of its founding, there was an event held at Gayatri Tapobhumi in 1958 which many Gayatri parijans consider quite significant. This was a massive *yajña* performed simultaneously at 1024 fire altars. Under protest from "orthodox" Hindus, Gurudev invited everyone, regardless of caste or gender, to participate in ritual practices that were normally reserved for Brahmin males. The movement estimates that as many as 400 thousand participated in this *yajña* and listened to Gurudev's nightly lectures. Attendees at this event were among the first to receive initiation from Gurudev, and so this seems to be the moment at which the movement began to take on a more concrete shape.[5] This highly public universalist religio-political statement writ in the language of *yajña* was quite important for the movement, its daily ritual life, and its public image, especially for educated, cosmopolitan Gayatri parijans, in ways that will become clear over the course of this book.

The next major event for the Gayatri Pariwar took place in 1971. The movement invested in a large piece of land in Haridwar, which would become the new headquarters of the movement, Shantikunj. Biographical literature seems to imply that this move was prompted by a desire to be closer to the Himalayas, where Gurudev was about to travel for a lengthy pilgrimage on foot.[6] Additionally, the movement was beginning to outgrow its small space in Mathura. And as I will argue in greater detail later, Haridwar—a city traditionally understood as being situated at the exact spot where the Ganges flows out of the Himalayas and into the North Indian plains—carries important symbolic resonances for a movement whose mission is to bring the wisdom of ethereal Himalayan sages to the masses of India.

Shantikunj started off as no more than a "small two-story building that would house [Gurudev's] wife and family."[7] This likely included not only his wife and daughter, but some of his "spiritual" family as well. Shantikunj became the site of "training camps" aimed at preparing volunteers to revive India's golden age.[8] As these camps increased in popularity, the ashram expanded by adding residential buildings for guests and permanent community members, a lecture hall and a dining hall, each suitable for about a thousand occupants, three pavilions for *yajña* altars, a temple for Gayatri Devi, and many other buildings for various special functions.

## Gayatri Parijans

Now that I have provided a sense of how Shantikunj came to be founded, I can move on to how its residents came to call it home. It is important to bear in mind the scope of this project as outlined in my introduction. The Gayatri Pariwar is incredibly socioeconomically diverse and Gurudev's Gandhian populism clearly pulls in an audience that is not typically associated with reform Hindu movements, but my focus here is on the middle-class residents of Shantikunj. As this chapter and much of the rest of my project will make clear, this focus on the middle class provides an important window on religion in India after the IT boom.

### Children and the Elderly

With this clarified, I'd like to proceed by describing some of the groups I encountered at Shantikunj before moving onto my discussion of the upwardly mobile but disillusioned residents who are of particular interest to me. Fascinating as I find them, there was another subset of residents whose presence at an ashram was, in a certain light, more surprising: children. Shantikunj residents are expected to marry and are encouraged to have children, although having more than about two is frowned upon. Ashram children attend school at Gayatri Vidya Peeth, a nearby school that is run by the Gayatri Pariwar and staffed extensively by volunteers. When school is not in session, the sounds of children playing, including the occasional game of cricket, reverberates through Shantikunj's residential areas, making it easy to forget that one is in an ashram and not a particularly close-knit neighborhood.

At the opposite end of the age spectrum, Shantikunj has a substantial population of elderly people. Unlike the children, the presence of the elderly at an ashram is not particularly surprising. They have been the target demographic for ashram life for about as far back as Hindu literature goes—for men, at least, renunciation is the last of the traditional stages of life. Of course, modern ashrams like Shantikunj have a large population of younger residents as well. This is why I was intrigued to learn that many of the senior residents I spoke with, despite being followers of Gurudev since the early days, had not moved into the ashram until relatively recently.

A.K., for example, was born in 1936 in Madhya Pradesh. The son of a doctor, A.K. followed in his father's footsteps. He first learned about Gurudev while he working on a government medical board in 1960, when his brother lent him a copy of *Gayatri Mahavigyan*. As a doctor, he was intrigued by Gurudev's ideas about consciousness, which was a concept he felt was underexplored in the medical science of the time. A.K. arranged to meet with Gurudev, and told me of the encounter: "He was so nice to talk to that I was practically mesmerized, you know. But still, I was a medical doctor, a man of science, a scholar of science, so I told him that I wanted to ask some questions on this science of consciousness." Gurudev's answers persuaded him, and he and his wife became followers, changing their lifestyle by studying the movement's literature, attending functions regularly, and adopting a vegetarian diet. Nonetheless, something else in his life had to change before he would be ready to move to Shantikunj: "In 1984 I decided with my wife that I should resign from the board. By that time both of my sons were practically set. One became an engineer with a BE and an MA. Another went to the US with my younger brother, who had already been there for the last 15 or 20 years. So I was practically free. Then I left the job and joined Shantikunj." For A.K., then, the crucial factor in deciding to move to Shantikunj was the sense that his job as a father was done. The level of commitment to the Gayatri Pariwar needed to want to move into Shantikunj may have been there already, but he does not seem to have thought of it as a viable option while the work of securing his sons' future was incomplete.

Mahesh's story is not terribly different. Born in the mid-1940s, he lived for most of his life in Nepanagar, Madhya Pradesh. This small industrial town near the Maharashtra border is dominated by a large newsprint manufacturing facility, where Mahesh worked as a mechanical engineer. He first learned about the Gayatri Pariwar in about 1984 from an acquaintance who shared some of Gurudev's literature with Mahesh and his wife. But circumstances prevented him from moving to Shantikunj for some time:

> I took my retirement from the service life. Till then, I was serving the organization and it was my duty to serve the organization fully. I had the maintenance department under me, and

> it was a bit of an old plant, so there were many problems at that factory. So I could not find more time till my retirement. But since retirement, we have devoted our full time. We came to Shantikunj in 2001 or so. . . . But while I was in service, I devoted my full time to my job because it was my primary responsibility to attend my job.

Here we see that Mahesh felt a certain sense of obligation to dedicate himself fully to his work, and he could only dedicate substantial time to the Gayatri Pariwar once he was satisfied with the service he had rendered to society as a mechanical engineer.

Naturally, there are a few elderly Gayatri parijans who have lived in Shantikunj for quite a long time. One such person is Vireshwar, who from what I could tell was the most senior Shantikunj resident I had the honor of interviewing. Like many other senior Gayatri parijans, when Vireshwar walks through Shantikunj, he frequently has to stop to let community members touch his feet. While I usually prefer to conduct interviews privately, in this case it was not possible to do so, as several nearby residents were interested in hearing him speak. Vireshwar was an electrical engineer working in Jhansi, Uttar Pradesh, in 1954 or 1955 when he heard of a public *yajña* Gurudev was planning that would be open to all. Intrigued, he attended the event. He found Gurudev's social vision, which he called "yug nirman yojana" (plan for changing the era), particularly appealing. This concept, as Vireshwar explained it to me, is that, "As you think, so you do. So if your thoughts are purified, your actions will be purified. Purifications of your thoughts and emotions that is Gayatri. And purification of your karm, that is *yajña*." In 1967, several years before the founding of Shantikunj, Vireshwar quit his job and dedicated himself to Gurudev's mission full time.

It is clear that the senior generation of Gayatri parijans has some members like Vireshwar, who left behind their careers well before retirement age. Nonetheless, it is intriguing that quite a few members of this generation, like A.K. and Mahesh, waited so long before joining the movement. Given the preponderance of young and middle-aged adults in Shantikunj now who dropped their careers just as they were starting to join the community, I cannot help but wonder why the senior generation, generally speaking, did not seem ready to join the ashram at younger ages. A.K. mentions seeing his children as well established as a precursor to retiring to Shantikunj—why didn't he want to raise them in Shantikunj, as seems to be the case with younger generations of Gayatri Pariwar parents? Meanwhile, Mahesh felt a deep obligation to his work as a mechanical engineer, framing it as "service." Why did he find his job so fulfilling, while many younger Gayatri parijans had quite the opposite experience?

Evident in the narratives of Mahesh and A.K. is a traditional Hindu sensibility about the stages of life. During early adulthood, one is a *gṣrhasthā*, or householder, and one is expected to contribute to society while looking after one's own family. Later on in life, one retires and withdraws from familial responsibilities, perhaps moving to an ashram or living in the wilderness as a world renouncer, or *saṃnyāsin*, before the end. But these narratives also reflect a Nehruvian middle-class moral sensibility about work that prevailed before the Indian government began the process of liberalizing the economy in 1991. Morality has historically been a central concern of the Indian middle class, who during the colonial period built their social status in part through claims to moral respectability.[9] During what Sanjay Srivastava terms the "postcolonial stage" of the Indian middle class, opposition to continued Western influence and a commitment to serving the needs of a newly independent India become central.[10] It is in this context that what I am calling a Nehruvian middle-class moral sensibility forms. Moral respectability remains important to securing middle-class status in the postcolonial stage, but this moral respectability derives in part from participating in any of the numerous large-scale public sector undertakings that Jawaharlal Nehru created early on in India's independent period.[11] This Nehruvian middle-class moral sensibility treats participation in the project of serving the needs of the new Indian nation and helping it develop as a kind of selfless moral duty.

## Upwardly Mobile but Disillusioned

Senior Shantikunj residents' embrace of Nehruvian middle-class moral sensibilities provides an excellent contrast to the younger generation of Shantikunj residents. As I will show, these Gayatri parijans follow a different trajectory, viewing their careers as being about the accumulation of wealth and its associated luxuries. This conforms to what Srivastava terms the "postnational" stage of the Indian middle class, in which the needs of India and resistance to Western power become less important while participating in globalization and consumerism become more central to middle-class identity.[12] This shift in attitudes between the generations is consistent with expectations for and observations from India's developing neoliberal society—a society generated by economic deregulation and marked by a number of interrelated phenomena such as widening income inequality, growing corporate influence, powerful transnational trade networks, and perhaps most importantly, commodity consumption as a primary basis for identity and community formation.[13]

It should now be clear why I am so interested in upwardly mobile but disillusioned Gayatri parijans. In a certain sense, they reflect a changing society in India after economic liberalization opened the doors wide to the forces of globalization. Their flight to Shantikunj is made in pursuit of an alternative to this status quo. Consequently they connect with the question that precipitated this research: why does scientific authority seem to be foregrounded now more than ever in Hindu-based religious movements? By positioning themselves so clearly in relation to India's contemporary political economy, upwardly mobile but disillusioned Hindus represent an important subset of the population of Shantikunj for me to explore this question.

There are, of course, variations within the life narrative that distinguishes upwardly mobile but disillusioned Gayatri parijans. If Gyaneshwar's story is among the more dramatic, Ashutosh's story is quite a bit closer to an ideal type for this segment of the Shantikunj population. Ashutosh was thirty at the time of our visit, and it was apparent to me that he commanded a great deal of respect for a man of his age. He was quite busy as he taught computer science at DSVV and was also involved in automating the registrar's office, but nonetheless he was able to take some time out of his workday to speak with me. Born in Pipariya, Madhya Pradesh, Ashutosh mostly grew up in an industrial town called Korba, in Chhattisgarh, where his father worked as a supervisor at the National Thermal Power Corporation. His mother, who worked as a schoolteacher, was particularly interested in the Gayatri Pariwar during Ashutosh's childhood through the medium of Akhand Jyoti, and she eventually brought her family for a short trip to Shantikunj in 1999.

Ashutosh was, for the time being, intent on pursuing a career in information technology and so, the following year, he moved to Bhopal to obtain his BE. After graduating, he worked for about two years in Mumbai at a software company called I-Flex Solutions, of which Citigroup held a controlling interest. Ashutosh was not far into his career when he began to have doubts:

> When I was in Bombay, when I just joined my first job, we worked for five days, and during the weekends we used to wander here and there. We used to go to malls and it was difficult for us to pass our time. This is what I went through. There was a void in my life, which made me think I'm not fully utilizing my time for something good. So that void led me to an organization called ISKCON, which is the International Society for Krishna Consciousness. It is also spread worldwide. So that organization attracted me, and probably I had some spiritual seeds in me I was more inclined toward that institution. And slowly, my association with that institution grew further, and when I was associated with them and visiting regularly with them in Bombay, that is when I thought that I won't continue my career for a very long time. I will just try to earn sufficient enough so that I don't feel any financial scarcity and probably move on for something which I would like to pursue in my life, which is some spiritual pursuit.

Ashutosh had not quite reached that point by the time he left his first job. Around the time that Citigroup's shares of I-Flex Solutions were purchased by Oracle, Ashutosh moved to Bangalore, where he worked for Goldman Sachs India as an analyst and developer for three years. This move rekindled his connection with the Gayatri Pariwar, which has a strong presence in the city:

> I was associated with Gayatri Pariwar in childhood and in Bangalore I got associated with more Gayatri parijans there. And we started work there and I was more involved with them in Bangalore and that was how destiny was written for me. So I had moved to Bangalore and eventually I asked the head of the All World Gayatri Pariwar here, Dr. Pranav Pandya ji, about coming here [to Shantikunj] so that I can devote my life, the rest of my time here. So he told me to wait for a couple of years, and then I finally came here in 2009.

It was not a sort of intense culture shock that gripped Ashutosh, although the move from Korba to Mumbai was no doubt quite a shift. Rather, it was the sort of generalized ennui that comes from having money and time to spend, but little of value to spend it on. Nor is there any sense, as with older Gayatri parijans, that his work for I-Flex Solutions and Goldman Sachs India was particularly satisfying on its own merits. While Ashutosh says he was simply waiting until he had saved enough money to dedicate his life to spiritual pursuits, it is worth noting that very soon after starting his new job and reconnecting with the Gayatri Pariwar, he was already asking permission to live in Shantikunj. This makes me suspect that the timing of Ashutosh's eventual decision to leave his career behind was not about having enough money, but rather about some particular appeal that the Gayatri Pariwar had over ISKCON. Both may have integrated traditional lifestyles with modern rhetorics, but the Gayatri Pariwar had a stronger association with his upbringing, which may have made it more desirable.

Ashutosh's boredom, his feeling that he was waiting, and his concern with how he would "pass his time" bears comparison to phenomena discussed in Craig Jeffrey's *Timepass*. Jeffrey's concern is with educated Jat men at universities in Meerut who are stuck waiting for employment seemingly without end. Descended from wealthy farmers, these young men pursued an education in the hopes of retaining a competitive edge in the post-liberalization economy. But their expectation that they would find professional work after completing their education turned out to be a false hope.[14] Jeffrey locates these young men in the "lower-middle class," and notes that India's liberalization undermined the economic strategies that had been key to their success. Conversely, he notes that the "upper-middle class" is more optimistic about the changes to the Indian economy. Since IT professionals in major metropolises generally fall into the latter category, one might expect that Ashutosh's experience of liberalization should be poles apart from the experience of the Meeruti Jats in Jeffrey's study.[15] Given a choice, I think almost anyone would take Ashutosh's situation over that of an unemployed Jat in Meerut, and yet the nearly identical sets of feelings experienced by both point to a kind of double bind that faces some members of the middle classes of neoliberal India: the sense that one is living a meaningful life is in short supply regardless of one's employment status.

The story of Chandrakala differs in a few details, but should already seem familiar in certain ways. She was also thirty at the time of our conversation, and she grew up in Jamshedpur, a planned industrial city in Jharkhand built around Tata Group's oldest and largest steelworks. Her father, an employee of Tata Motors, had been associated with Gurudev since the 1960s and visited Shantikunj frequently. Chandrakala was about nine years old when she was first able to accompany her father to Shantikunj, but by that time Gurudev had already left his body. Nonetheless, her encounter with Mataji, who was the head of Shantikunj at that time, left quite an impression on Chandrakala.

Chandrakala went on to pursue a master's in computer applications in Gwalior, and planned to balance her career goals with her commitment to the Gayatri Pariwar by working for five to ten years, then taking two or three years off to do volunteer work for the Gayatri Pariwar. She explained in some detail why she wound up moving to Shantikunj permanently instead:

> *I used to think that when I am doing my job*[16] and I'm earning money, what is the use of that money? Am I doing something for society? Then the answer from my viewpoint, is no, I'm doing nothing. Because this money also only makes me want to buy something for me. For me only! Or for my parents or for my siblings. But for the society? No.

Chandrakala did not elaborate on some experience of ennui or disgust stemming from contemporary Indian professional lifestyles. Rather, she seemed to have an assumption that voluntary service with the Gayatri Pariwar was a more effective way to contribute to society than pursuing a conventional career. The personal wealth that would be generated by such work was problematic for her, because it would only tempt her to spend it selfishly, thus turning her attention away from the needs of society. It was this sense that she could only truly serve society if she were not being paid that led her to move to Shantikunj and work as a volunteer, thereby taking personal material gain out of the equation.

Divyesh expressed similar sentiments. A man of forty-four, he had lived in Shantikunj for about twelve years at the time that we spoke. His father, a banker, and his mother, a housewife, read *Akhand Jyoti* and prayed the Gayatri mantra at home with their family, but did not frequent Shantikunj or do much volunteer work for the mission. Despite the fact that Gurudev himself conducted Divyesh's *annapraśāsan* and *vidyārambh* ceremonies[17] when he was visiting his family's home in Agar, Madhya Pradesh, Divyesh told me that as a young man, he was a "non-believer." After receiving his BE in Indore, he pursued a career as a mechanical engineer for five years at the Oil and Natural Gas Corporation, which he proudly described as a Fortune 500 company.

When I asked him what happened to change his attitude and bring him to Shantikunj, he said,

> Actually in 1990, I came to Dehradun for my interview with ONGC. At that time I saw, I had darshan, I had a glimpse of Guruji. He used to sit there and people from the ashram, they used to come in a queue and they could have a glimpse of him. So I saw him at that time, and I came to know about his mission. Before that, I was aware that there was some person who is like a divine *siddhapuruṣ*, and *in our home*,[18] he gave us lot of boons and all of our family is indebted to him for all of these things. But still, I was not in his fold, and I did not know what his mission was. After I came to Shantikunj, I came to know about all his literature and all his teachings basically. Then I tried to read more and more about him, and slowly-slowly I got the feeling that what is essential in life is choosing your aim and choosing your ideals to the best available to you. So what I was doing in my job was not giving me any satisfaction, so I was, we were given this alternative, where we have this grand personality of Guruji to follow and the grand aim of his mission for the transformation of the world. We can work for the upliftment of humanity, and peace of mind and self-development are the byproducts.

While Divyesh does not articulate Ashutosh's ennui with hanging out in malls or Chandrakala's frustration with the temptations associated with disposable income, he does express a lack of satisfaction with his job that should be all to familiar by this point. This is coupled with a sense that working as a volunteer at Shantikunj would be more fulfilling, perhaps because "peace of mind and self-development" would be his wages. Additionally, he is slightly older than Chandrakala and Ashutosh, and came to Shantikunj a bit earlier, in 1995, but by this point the economic reforms had already begun to have an effect on Indian society.

I could continue providing such examples, but the pattern to which I am trying to draw attention should be quite clear at this point. Shantikunj residents represent a wide cross-section of Indian society, but the ashram seems to have a special appeal with a group that reflects social changes in post-globalization India. This group, whom I am calling upwardly mobile but disillusioned, tends to come from provincial towns and small industrial cities, where their families had some measure of contact with the Gayatri Pariwar, ranging from a somewhat passive interest in the movement's publications and major events to a deep commitment to Gurudev and his teachings. These upwardly mobile but disillusioned Gayatri parijans pursued an education that set them on a career path that was generally more lucrative than that of their parents. But when it seemed that their careers could not provide them with the life satisfaction they desired they ultimately moved to Shantikunj.

Upwardly mobile but disillusioned Shantikunj residents were experiencing what Jarrett Zigon would call "moral breakdown." Zigon developed the concept of moral breakdown as part of his effort to develop an anthropology of morality that regards morality as a dynamic product of human agency rather than as a static, habitual product of predefined social norms. Moral breakdown occurs when everyday life is subject to a form of disruption that requires people to develop new tactics to solve new problems.[19] The collapse of Nehruvian socialism and its large public sphere has created a kind of moral breakdown that has had a profound effect on the upwardly mobile but disillusioned Shantikunj residents I met.[20] This state of affairs has required that these Gayatri parijans fashion new moral selves that are equipped to handle the problems of post-liberalization India.

Their explicit reason for moving to Shantikunj was that it seemed to offer more life satisfaction through the opportunities it created to serve society in a way that seemed unambiguously selfless. Members of the older generation were able to fulfill their moral sensibilities by pursuing public sector careers. In the Nehruvian milieu, a background in science and technology was instrumental because it made it possible to participate in tangible ways in the development of the country. The younger generation felt that they had no such opportunity because the public sector had contracted so drastically after liberalization. Science and technology careers were no longer about helping India develop, but about personal enrichment. In this sense, even scientific pursuits may seem to lose moral legitimacy from the vantage point of the upwardly mobile but disillusioned.

Contemporary India's middle class have adapted to these changes in a number of ways. Upwardly mobile but disillusioned Shantikunj residents suggest through their characterization of contemporary middle-class lifestyles that India's young urban professionals have simply lost interest in moral respectability as a defining feature of their social status. This characterization aligns with scholarly observations about the increased importance of conspicuous consumption for post-liberalization India's new middle class.[21]

Of course, it would be too simplistic to assume that this moral breakdown could only be solved by moving to Shantikunj—there are other opportunities to express middle-class moral respectability through participation in social reform projects. One such possibility is described in Joanne Waghorne's discussions of temple patronage in Chennai in the mid-1990s. Using the wealth brought to them by their upward mobility, middle-class Hindus build and renovate temples as a way to impose their own norms of order, cleanliness, and respectability on these spaces, thus advancing their agendas for society.[22] Given the availability of alternative means of engaging in projects that express middle-class moral respectability, it is clear that other factors helped to draw upwardly mobile but disillusioned Shantikunj residents to live at the ashram. No doubt, it is also a factor that in every case, their parents were involved in the Gayatri Pariwar, at least to some extent. This is especially clear in Ashutosh's case, where ISKCON was able to provide him with some satisfaction, but it was not until he fell back in with the Gayatri Pariwar that he was ready to leave his job. Their earlier encounters with the Gayatri Pariwar likely primed them to reject the lifestyles of India's new middle classes and to turn instead to the Gayatri Pariwar's moral projects, with their links to older ways of expressing middle-class identity. But such ties to their upbringing are not entirely sufficient in appealing to Gayatri parijans. In the next section and in much of the rest of this book, I will demonstrate that this subset of the community also sees something of their new selves—educated, professional, and cosmopolitan—in the scientific rhetoric used to justify the ritual practices at the core of the Gayatri Pariwar.

## Gyaneshwar's Story

My interview with Gyaneshwar took place in his office in the polyclinic located at DSVV, where he worked as a diagnostician and faculty member in the school of Yoga and Health. Listening to my recording of our conversation, I hear the whimsical strains of the bansuri[23] playing on his stereo over the monotonous drone of the ceiling fan and am reminded of the atmosphere of tranquility it engendered. This atmosphere was further enhanced by Gyaneshwar's calm, measured, thoughtful speech—traits that suggested an excellent bedside manner. Nonetheless, his passion for the topics I asked him about was evident in the astonishing detail he would go into as he answered my questions:

> D: Could you tell me a little bit about where you grew up? Your family, your hometown, those sorts of things?
>
> G: My name is Dr. Gyaneshwar Mishra, and I'm a physician in medicine. I worked in a cardiac surgery department in Delhi. I have taken my medical degree from Russia, from Moscow. After that, I came here in 2004, passed the examination in India, then I worked for two and a half years at New Delhi Cardiac Center, in cardiology and then cardiac surgery. I worked in cardiac surgery for six months, participated in more than more than eighty operations, such as bypass and valve transplantation.

Within the constraints allowed by his humble demeanor, Gyaneshwar starts by describing some impressive accomplishments from his professional life before coming to Shantikunj. He highlights the prestige of pursuing an education abroad and at a major hospital in a cosmopolitan city. By emphasizing these achievements, Gyaneshwar was affirming at the outset, even before talking about his upbringing, his membership in a globalized professional class. It is a fitting way to start a narrative of upward mobility in the new Indian economy: one that emphasizes a connection to global flows and urban spaces as well as achievement in a prestigious STEM-related field.

> Since my medical graduation, I was very much influenced by my master, Vedmurti Taponisht Pandit Shriram Sharma Acharya, who is the founder of the All World Gayatri Family. So since that time, my life's mission has been to dedicate my service, to do whatever I can for my master. So in 2007, in September, I voluntarily resigned from Delhi Ganga Ram hospital, then I came here in this university working as a volunteer of the Gayatri Pariwar, working in this polyclinic as a consultant and faculty in the school of Yoga and Health, where I lecture on

pathology and modern clinical diagnostic tools and methods.

After introducing himself, Gyaneshwar immediately moves to cover the crucial transition from Delhi to Shantikunj—a transition that occurs without ever losing track of his professional identity. He still utilizes his medical training, only now it reflects Gurudev's influence and accordingly is in service of a higher purpose. The move to Shantikunj is not a turn away from his professional identity; rather, it is a relocation (from Delhi to Shantikunj) and sublimation (from the mundane to the spiritual).

> That's my professional background. About my family background, my father was a tax inspector in the state government and my mother was a housewife, my wife is also a housewife, and I have one child.

Following his more extended "professional background," Gyaneshwar offers a relatively brief account of his "family background"—perhaps its brevity signals a sense that his professional and spiritual pursuits are more central to his identity than his upbringing, although he is happy to elaborate on his family as I ask him for more information.

> D: What is your family's religious background? Were you aware of the Gayatri Pariwar or any other . . .
>
> G: My parents were, my family, we subscribed to the *Akhand Jyoti* monthly journal, we used to, my parents, participate in rituals and programs of the Gayatri Family that were local to my district, Deoria, near Varanasi. But I did not believe in these things up until 1997. Although in my family there was a good spiritual atmosphere, everybody used to practice—they used to go to the temple, they'd chant mantras, they'd do havans—but I had no interest at all. You could say that I was an atheist. And being a science student, I did not believe in these kinds of rituals and the prayers. I was thinking it was a waste of time. But when I came to know about Gurudev, when I went through his literature, his way of presentation, his way of explanation, that influenced me a lot and that initiated me into the spiritual life.

This confession of erstwhile disbelief was a fascinating and surprising turn to our conversation. In his hindsight, Gyaneshwar speaks positively of his family's religious activities, Gayatri Pariwar or otherwise. The connection he makes between his skepticism and his identification with science is rather noteworthy. Just as his identity as a medical professional remained intact when he moved to Shantikunj, his identity as a scientifically minded person would also have to remain intact as he embraced the Gayatri Pariwar's practices. This sets up a situation in which Gyaneshwar had to be reconciled to his family's piety through the Gayatri Pariwar's scientific rhetoric.

> D: What about his literature and his presentation that was so compelling to you, to make such a dramatic change?
>
> G: First of all, what happens in my life which has changed me from an atheist to a theist is that I grew up in a very middle-class family and we were following all the norms and the culture of the Indian traditions—Hindu tradition rather—but when I went to Russia as a medical graduate scholar, it was the first time I was exposed to Western culture. I have never thought about, imagined, or had any information that in Western culture, people do certain things.

Just after contrasting his family's piety with his own scientifically-based atheism, Gyaneshwar makes his family the basis of a second contrast—their adherence to middle-class Hindu traditions was radically different from what he experienced of Western culture in Moscow.

> What was inconvenient for me there was that the younger generation, they drink alcohol and smoke. Their eating habits are also very much not acceptable for me. They were eating meat, eggs, and fish. And the worst of all was that the culture, the lifestyle of the girls—the young girls, 18 years old, 16 years old, 25 years old—they don't have any norms, you know? There was . . . The girls come into the hostels, prostitutes come, the boys and girls are. . . . One girl, I know her, she's my colleague. Yesterday I have seen her with one guy, then after one month with some other, after two months with some other. So these things were very agitating for me and I was not comfortable

> with this atmosphere. I was afraid for myself, I was afraid of my surrounding. What was frightening for me was that I have seen medical life in India, how the Indian students, the medical students, how they're working, how they're working hard, how they're maintaining their character, how they're maintaining their culture, how they're purely living. And if they had relations with any girls, they're maintaining it purely; they have relations with only one of them. So I was born into this atmosphere, and when I have seen that I thought that I may spoil myself. These surroundings may spoil me. I was young and I was thinking I can also fall prey to these things, like alcohol or the flesh or . . . this kind of culture of enjoying the girls, which from inside, I thought okay, better not to be a doctor. I will not continue my medical education in this culture; I will go back.

Other upwardly mobile but disillusioned Gayatri parijans tend to focus on the shallow consumerism and selfishness of new urban professional lifestyles as the source of their disillusionment and sense of moral crisis, but for Gyaneshwar it is a sort of profound personal moral discomfiture brought on especially by the sexually liberal environment in Russia. A move from Deoria to Moscow is an even deeper dislocation than a move from, say, Pipariya to Mumbai because liberal European moral cultures are a more radical departure from the popular, traditional values of provincial North India. The stormy seas of moral difference threaten to drown Gyaneshwar's sense of who he is—a student of science and a skeptic, perhaps, but also a man with certain principles. The only way he saw to buoy these principles was to swim clear of the choppy transnational flow into which he had strayed.

> And then I realized in Moscow—what is India? Although we are not much, although we do not have such a high hygienic level, although we don't maintain hygiene—Russia is very clean and very well established, while India is not—but then India, the culture, I have come to know what India is, what the culture is, what the norms are, what the significance of family values is, the social values, the way we live in India. Then I thought, better to go back to that because I may spoil my life here. My

> senior colleagues were also suggesting to me that if you do not develop friendships with Russian girls, how you can learn the Russian language? If you cannot learn the Russian language you cannot learn the medicine for which you have come here. But then too, I thought "Okay, it is better not to be a doctor, but I will not involve myself in these things."

Like many Hindus who find their piety deepened by life outside of India,[24] Gyaneshwar's experience of difference in Moscow made it impossible for him to take traditional Indian morality for granted. The way in which he frames this newfound appreciation for his homeland—Russia's superficial cleanliness but lack of moral purity contrasted with India's abundance of moral purity and lack of hygiene in the material realm—bears a curious resemblance to the classic and widespread Orientalist trope of the "material West" and "spiritual East." For Gyaneshwar, this is reflected in Moscow's impressive glitz that is ultimately rendered empty by his perception that its people lacked deeper moral refinement. Gyaneshwar's experience of this dichotomy led him to abandon not just his plan to attend medical school in Moscow but his professional aspirations altogether—perhaps the unpleasant loss of morality that he associated with upward mobility was not entirely localized in Moscow.

> Anyhow I passed six months there, and then I returned back. I explained my frustration to my parents, and to one of my, you can say, "priests," who used to come to my house to guide us, performing puja, *yajña*, many of the rituals, Vedic rituals. I told him about my frustration, I shared my frustration with him as well, and he gave me confidence. He told me that no girl will forcefully pour alcohol in your mouth, no girl will forcefully come in your room and ask to live with you, uh, to pass the night with you if you yourself do not show any wish or if you yourself do not want to do this. So he told me if you want to protect yourself, you take this Gayatri mantra. And I was born in a Brahmin family—although I was not by karma Brahmin, but I was born in a Brahmin family—so he told me you are born in a Brahmin family, you should practice Gayatri. Then I started practicing Gayatri and slowly, slowly, the morning and evening practice of Gayatri mantra gave me

> the confidence that whatever the situation, if I myself were not eager to be involved, then I can know nobody will destroy me.

Although Gyaneshwar has not yet spoken about how he reconciled taking up this ritual practice with his scientific skepticism, it is clear enough that his experiences in Moscow opened him to a new range of possibilities. Perhaps he was willing to put those reservations on hold as he began to explore his heritage as a Brahmin, and the notion that he was doing the practice for a sort of therapeutic value to affirm his own moral identity rather than out of a more conventional piety or hope for supernatural intervention made this shift possible. The result, as Gyaneshwar tells us, is that his principled self became less tenuous—Moscow's bacchanalian temptations no longer posed such a large threat to the integrity of his identity.

> So with this confidence I went back to Russia, and there I continued morning and evening Gayatri prayer, and incidentally, one of my [inaudible] gave me, when he came to know that I practice Gayatri, he gave me a book written by Gurudev, *Great Science and Philosophy of Gayatri.* I read that and the way of explanation, the way of presentation and the reasoning behind all these practices given by Gurudev influenced me a lot and I understood properly why we do all these things. Till then my understanding was that it's just mainly a ritual, they are performing superstitiously. Then I came to know what the scientific reason behind this is.

As I will describe in greater detail in chapter 4, *Great Science and Philosophy of Gayatri* (*Gayatri Mahavigyan*, later known in English as *Super Science of Gayatri*), one of the movement's crucial texts, presents Gayatri practice as following or working similarly to natural laws. Gyaneshwar had already decided, perhaps provisionally at first, to take up Gayatri practice, but perhaps it was troublesome to integrate his scientific worldview with his lived appreciation for his heritage and sense that Gayatri recitation carried him through his crisis. The scientific rhetoric of this text makes is possible for a scientist like Gyaneshwar to see that traditional ritual practice is compatible with his skeptical mindset. This is a further step in the formation of a new, integrated identity. On the one hand, there was Moscow, with its desirable science but undesirable moral values; on the other, there was Deoria, with its undesirable superstition but desirable moral values. Gyaneshwar had already seen how the Deorian practice of Gayatri recitation could protect him from Muscovite dissolution, and by reading Gurudev's work he now sees how he can maintain this Deorian practice without abandoning his developing Muscovite scientific sensibilities. The moral authority he associated with his heritage could be reconciled with the intellectual authority of the West.

> And that influenced me, then I became eager to go deep into the *sādhanā*, so I decided that once I had summer vacation I would go back to India and I would do a nine-day *anuṣṭhān*. You know *anuṣṭhān*? I performed this nine-day *anuṣṭhān* in my hometown in my family's home, and afterwards I felt a strong desire to perform it once again at the place where the Gayatri mantra has been practiced for many years. So that place was no doubt the Gayatri *teerth*,[25] Shantikunj. When I came here I practiced and I listened to the lectures of the disciples of Gurudev in Shantikunj, and that influenced me a lot and the atmosphere, everything influenced me a lot. And when I met with his holiness, Dr. Pranav Pandya ji and Her Holiness, they have given me love and parental care and guidance to me, and this relationship was also maintained when I went back to Russia.

With this second reconciliation in place, there was no longer a reason for Gyaneshwar to be ambivalent. His practice intensified as he took up *anuṣṭhān*, a nine-day period of partial fasting, celibacy, and simple living during which the Gayatri mantra is chanted 24,000 times. He began to align himself more closely with the Gayatri Pariwar—the institution that allowed him to integrate his Muscovite and Deorian selves, thereby resolving his moral crisis. The movement started to become a sort of surrogate family for him. His upbringing may connect him to Deoria and his professional life may connect him to Moscow, but in the Gayatri Pariwar he finds what is desirable about each place—science and morality—without the things that make them undesirable—superstition and debauchery.

> Then I listened to the lectures of Gurudev, when I was a second year—that was 1999. When I listened to his lectures,

> all twenty-four volumes, after listening to that, it was a break-through in my life. That changed my life completely and after listening to his lectures—his lectures were so challenging and so penetrating! And I thought in my heart and my feelings that I decided that I have chosen Pandit Shriram Sharma Acharya as my master, as my guru. Till now I was living according to my ambitions and my aims, and the aims of my family. But since I have adopted a guru, from now on I will live according to the will and wishes of my master. So for this reason, I decided to quit my medical education in my second year, and I did not take any examinations there. And then I came here, my parents were very angry with me that I decided so suddenly.

Gurudev's lectures proved even more powerful than *Great Science and Philosophy of Gayatri* and rendered Gyaneshwar's identification with the movement complete; the Gayatri Pariwar had become his new family and displaced his own. Thinking that his medical training must be sacrificed to the will of this new family, he resolved to quit, much to the consternation of his parents.

> When I came here in Shantikunj, Shraddheya Jiji, Her Holiness, sent me back once again, and you know [she said] if you want to work for Gurudev, you should be a good person. You should be a knowledgeable person. Then you can, if you have any knowledge, if you have any mastery in any direction then you can help with the movement of Gurudev in a much better way. Then I went back and I continued my medical education and I finished my degree there. And then I came in India in 2004, when I practiced, as I told you, in Delhi for two years. Then in September 2007 I came here.

But this decision on Gyaneshwar's part caused consternation for his new parents as well. It seems that Gyaneshwar's own aspirations were not so different from those of the Gayatri Pariwar in a certain sense. But this should not be surprising—how else would the Gayatri Pariwar have been so powerful in integrating Gyaneshwar's bifurcated identity?

Gyaneshwar's story has taken us far in understanding the upwardly mobile but disillusioned community that lives at Shantikunj. The moral values, ritual practices, scientific rhetoric, and sense of surrogate kinship that Gyaneshwar found in the Gayatri Pariwar are powerful sites for reconciling identities split by disillusionment with upward mobility. His old self was aligned with tradition, family, and morality. His new self was aligned with reason, science, and personal freedom. His old self feared consumerism, moral dissolution, and displacement. His new self fears superstition, provincialism, and stagnation. These two selves, initially seeming at odds for Gyaneshwar, were the source of a moral crisis for Gyaneshwar. But the Gayatri Pariwar mended his split self, assuring him that you can value science and technology without turning away from tradition and morality. Tradition without superstition; science without rootlessness. Freedom without chaos; stability without stagnation.

## Conclusion

The story I am telling in this chapter is one in which young Indians perceive in science an opportunity to participate in a middle-class project. Their disillusionment comes when this project turns out not to be what they expect: rather than feeling that they are building a better India like previous middle-class generations, they feel that their STEM careers bring them into contact with morally troubling transnational flows—Western moral dissolution in Gyaneshwar's case or the consumerist materialism of India's new globalized political economy in the case of my other contacts at Shantikunj. The younger generation's disappointment in contradistinction to the relative satisfaction of the older generation points to a change in the relation of science to the moral, social, and political projects of the middle class. The Nehruvian vision of science and engineering as tools to actualize middle-class projects is harder to see after liberalization; instead, these professions strike the younger middle-class Shantikunj residents I spoke with as merely a means to personal enrichment with little social benefit.

As I will demonstrate in subsequent chapters, the Gayatri Pariwar restores the moral legitimacy science enjoyed in pre-liberalization India through their intense application of science to their middle-class project of religious revival and social reform. This reconciliation of the moral authority of Hindu traditions with the intellectual authority of science operates not just at the individual level, with the Gayatri Pariwar's scientifically legitimated rituals functioning as a site for moral refinement. It also operates in society at large, where Gayatri parijans, morally refined through these ritual practices, can project their values out to the rest of society.

CHAPTER 3

# From Gurudev to Doctor-Sahib

Tears had begun to well up in Javanika's eyes, and I felt responsible. My question had not been insensitive, but it had brought up a painful memory: Javanika had never been able to meet Gurudev. She had read his books, seen his pictures, and met regularly with an Auntie-ji who conducted *yajña* with her and informed her about the Gayatri Pariwar. In 1988 at one of Auntie-ji's gatherings, she met her future husband, Mehul. That very year, Mehul insisted that Auntie-ji take him to Shantikunj, where she introduced him to Gurudev. But Javanika did not go, and soon the possibility of meeting Gurudev slipped away forever.

Javanika, a woman of forty with two children, aged seven and ten, had agreed to take some time out of her busy day at the Gayatri Pariwar's school, Gayatri Vidyapeeth. Although she was in the midst of an extended stay at Shantikunj, I originally met her not at the ashram, but by chance when she brought her children for a voice lesson with Rajeev-ji, who was teaching me sitar. Although she and Mehul had moved to the United States before her first child was born, she had taken to bringing her children to Shantikunj regularly for increasingly lengthy trips to help them connect with their culture and to make sure their easy American lives did not spoil them too much. Although she had a master's in computer science, her children inspired her to pursue a degree in education at California State University. At Gayatri Vidyapeeth, her role was to mentor local teachers in Western educational methods, though her colleagues felt that the benefits of such training were dubious.

The cheerful hubbub of children learning in nearby classrooms was a sharp contrast with the growing strain in Javanika's voice as she struggled to maintain her composure. "In 1990, when Gurudev left his physical body I was absolutely not convinced that *he* would go without meeting *me*." Her emphasis contained a trace of self-parody, painting her very legitimate pain and resentment as almost narcissistic. But her effort to maintain this ironic detachment from her feelings quickly faltered as her grief began to overwhelm her. "How can you go without . . . I didn't see you yet, you just met Mehul, and how are you going now? And I cried a lot that time that he didn't see me but he saw Mehul and kind of that was inner . . . Like we are all so much having this ego . . . And I was like crying that . . . I have to meet you." Again, she expressed guilt about her feelings, but her last attempt to suppress them failed, and her voice broke as she heart-wrenchingly asked of her absent Gurudev, "You have to tell me what I have to do in my life and how can you go?"

Recovering from this painful memory, Javanika began to recount her subsequent marriage to Mehul two years later. Against the protestations of Mehul and his family and against Gayatri Pariwar norms, Javanika's family had provided a substantial dowry. Javanika and Mehul felt that the moral way to handle this situation would be travel to Shantikunj together after their wedding to donate this dowry to the Gayatri Pariwar. Although Gurudev was gone, the experience of being in a space filled with material objects associated with Gurudev was still emotionally intense. But in contrast to her recollection of Gurudev's untimely departure, Javanika spoke fondly of this experience as testament to Gurudev's abiding power:

> It was time for us to go for darshan, for Akhand Deep,[1] and Gurudev's room, and meeting Mataji, before meeting Mataji, we went to Gurudev's room, and when we just entered, Daniel, you won't believe. I mean you can even put a bucket I started crying *that* much in '92. I don't know what happened and what kind of energy. Any first-time comer will feel that and I just noticed it from everybody—I think whoever enters that room for the first time, I mean, has to have some emotional touch from that place. And I was kind of just trying to take all my bad karmas or like give me some more tough times or challenges in my life or whatever he was preparing me for. It was kind of like an invisible surgical process which was hap-

> pening and I just started crying a lot, a lot. And that was like, that was a moment for me!

In this chapter, I consider the circumstances—linguistic and material—that fostered the intense emotions Javanika associated with Gurudev and the role these emotions serve in solidifying Gurudev's religious authority. In parallel, I explore the superficially different sets of feelings associated with Gurudev's successor, Doctor-sahib. As I will illustrate, Gurudev's status derives from his charismatic authority, while Doctor-sahib draws most strongly on scientific authority to establish his legitimacy as a successor. If the continued expansion of the Gayatri Pariwar under Doctor-sahib is any indication, his use of scientific authority has eased the normally difficult process of routinizing charisma. This is because scientific authority as it is deployed in the Gayatri Pariwar retains some of the affective resonances of charismatic authority such as a sense of perpetually unfolding revelation, a feeling of hope for revolutionary change, and an experientially oriented epistemology.

In pointing to the affective intensity of science in this chapter, I am developing a crucial piece of my framework for thinking about the role of scientific authority in the Gayatri Pariwar and in Hindu traditions more broadly. In order to understand this role, my contention is that it is not adequate to simply assume that science sets bodies in motion through compelling logic and evidence alone. Rather, as I will show in this chapter, science moves bodies at least partly through its capacity to instill feelings like confidence and even wonder. Understanding this affective capacity of science is crucial for understanding how it comes to be linked to the Gayatri Pariwar's moral project and the appeal of this project for the movement's disillusioned STEM professionals.

In order to better contextualize the themes I am interested in that relate to the routinization of charisma, I will begin with an overview of some salient events that have taken place since the founding of Shantikunj. I will then move on to situate my understanding of charismatic authority in the extant literature before relating my own thoughts on the concept. Having established this groundwork, I will comparatively consider the bases of authority for Gurudev and Doctor-sahib to tease out their differences. I will conclude by arguing that despite their differences, there are substantial continuities that have helped keep the Gayatri Pariwar strong in its post-charismatic stage.

## A Changing Family

I have covered most of the history of the Gayatri Pariwar in previous chapters, but there are a few remaining details that will be important for understanding the movement's post-charismatic transition and more recent history. Information on Gurudev's later life and the post-charismatic stage of the movement is even sparser than for Gurudev's earlier life.

My running history of the Gayatri Pariwar left off with the founding of Shantikunj in 1971, and the explosive growth the movement experienced thereafter. While new residential spaces continue to be constructed on the grounds of Shantikunj up through the time of my fieldwork, it seems that the originally purchased property was not enough to serve all of the movement's needs. The Gayatri Pariwar has since opened two nearby satellite facilities, a research center and a university, which set the stage for the transition from Gurudev to Doctor-sahib nicely.

The first of these satellite facilities, named Brahmavarchas Shodh Sansthan ("Light of Brahma" Research Center), was opened in 1979, only eight years after Shantikunj. Gurudev believed that the practices he was advocating were ancient but that their scientific basis was lost to the ravages of history. The research conducted at this center was to rediscover this scientific basis by exploring the physiological, psychological, and "parapsychological" effects of Gayatri Pariwar practices.[2]

While I tend to associate the use of scientific authority most strongly with Doctor-sahib in this book for reasons that will become clearer by the end of this chapter, it is worth pausing here to note that Gurudev clearly laid the groundwork for this trend. I have already described in chapter 1 how Gurudev's scientific rhetoric bore a certain resemblance to that deployed by leading Indian modernists, especially Gandhi and to a lesser extent Dayananda Saraswati. The fact that Gurudev founded this research institute so soon after opening Shantikunj further reinforces a sense that he saw scientific authority as playing a valuable role for his movement.

Nonetheless, Gurudev was trained as a journalist, not a scientist, so someone else would have to lead the research efforts at Brahmavarchas. The man he appointed for this task was his son-in-law, a medical doctor named Pranav Pandya, who has since come to be known as Doctor-sahib. Biographical information on Doctor-sahib is scarce, but it is likely that he was intended as a successor for Gurudev from early on. It is perhaps unsurprising that a householder guru-led movement would pass leadership through family. But the case of Doctor-sahib is somewhat more interesting because he is not a direct descendant of Gurudev and Mataji but rather their son-in-law. This may suggest that Doctor-sahib was already in some sense chosen as a successor when he was accepted as a match for Jiji. It also suggests that he was being groomed for his current role of head of the movement, and that this likely started quite early. My contention in this chapter is that Doctor-sahib's appointment as director of Brahmavarchas Shodh Sansthan began this process of grooming, and I will show that holding this position became a major source of authority for him in his current role.

On June 2, 1990, Gurudev's leadership of the Gayatri Pariwar ended. According to his "Last Message," he voluntary departed from his body, which had become something of an encumbrance and was not necessary for him to continue his life's work—a claim to which I will soon return.[3] At this point, according to a brief biographical sketch available on the Gayatri Pariwar's website, Doctor-sahib's life began an "even more significant phase," perhaps implying that his leadership of the movement began at this time.[4] A parallel biographical sketch of Mataji suggests that she was in charge of the movement between 1990 and her death in 1994.[5] It is clear enough that Mataji was in charge during this brief period from a plethora of accounts of visits to Shantikunj during this period, including those of Javanika and Chandrakala, both of whom speak wistfully about Mataji's darshan, and that of Lise McKean, who describes Mataji as running the movement as of the early '90s. Perhaps Doctor-sahib's biography can be reconciled with these other texts if we assume that, given Mataji's advanced age, the years between 1990 and 1994 were a transitional period, with leadership responsibilities gradually shifting from Mataji to her son-in-law and daughter as she lived out her last years.

Regardless of where we mark the beginning of their leadership, it seems that under the Pandyas, the Gayatri Pariwar took on its "All World" characteristic, with the movement attributing the establishment of centers in over eighty countries to him. Despite the fact that many successors to charismatic religious leaders struggle to maintain a following, the Gayatri Pariwar under the Pandyas became more popular than ever.

Perhaps one of the clearest indicators of the movement's continued growth under the Pandyas is that in 2002, the Gayatri Pariwar opened its second satellite institution, Dev Sanskriti Vishwavidyala. This deemed university is a short walk from Shantikunj, and its faculty and staff are predominately Gayatri parijans who receive "only a subsistence allowance."[6] While it has its own residence halls and is open to the general public, it seems that many of its students are part of the movement and have family at Shantikunj. Doctor-sahib serves as the chancellor at DSVV, although this seems to mostly be an honorary position. Gayatri Pariwar literature frames Doctor-sahib's accomplishments in relation to the founding of DSVV as mostly administrative, not visionary per se. Rather, Doctor-sahib was merely carrying out an extant vision of Gurudev.

The Gayatri Pariwar constructs a sort of mythology for DSVV that frames it as an extension of Brahmavarchas Shodh Sansthan, thereby also tying it to the personality of Gurudev. During the inaugural ceremonies of Brahmavarchas, Gurudev is said to have entered a trance. Upon emerging from this trance, he relayed to those around him a need to depart from the modern university model "where we mass-produce specialized workers for keeping the complicated and stressful modern life, which is blindly hurtling towards the abyss of 'no where.' "[7] Gurudev wanted to return to a model that focused on moral development in a way he thought comparable to pre-modern institutions like Nalanda and Takshashila. Such an institution would also be able to carry out research on an even larger scale than at Brahmavarchas Shodh Sansthan. The Gayatri Pariwar thus presents DSVV as the fulfillment of Gurudev's vision under the administration of Doctor-sahib.

## Theorizing Charisma

### Charisma, Affect, and Emotion

With this historical background established, I would like to move forward by articulating how I understand charismatic authority ahead of my larger analysis of how it relates to scientific authority in the Gayatri Pariwar. Academic discourse on charismatic authority has a long history, but its origin is most closely associated with the work of Max Weber. Weber famously offered a tripartite schema of social authority: legal, traditional, and charismatic.[8] Legal authority has involved a bureaucracy built upon a set of coherent rules that constituents have agreed on and that typically have a rational and instrumental basis. This typically includes such bodies as constitutional states, corporations, scientific institutions, and in some cases even certain religious organizations.[9] But it is perhaps more common in religious organizations for traditional authority to dominate. This involves a social order on the basis of what has been handed down from the past. It is oriented less toward a set of rules than toward an authority figure who is selected by traditional means to represent tradition.[10] Those subject to charismatic authority are also beholden to a person, but the basis and scope of that person's authority are not defined by what has been done in the past. Rather, it derives from "a certain quality of an individual personality by virtue of which he is set apart from ordinary men and treated as endowed with supernatural, superhuman, or at least specifically exceptional powers or qualities."[11] Weber was clear that these three types of authority are not necessarily mutually exclusive, but often mix to some extent.[12]

Because charismatic leaders are only authoritative to the extent that they possess these exceptional qualities, they must maintain a group of followers who perceive them as being somehow more than human. A continued emotional connection between followers and charismatic leader is thus needed for the maintenance of charisma. The bond established by this shared emotional connection becomes the basis for a community of voluntary followers built around the personality of the charismatic leader. This community typically breaks from the mundanity, rationality, and instrumentality of traditional and legal authority, giving charisma a certain revolutionary character.[13] And at least in the Anglophone tradition, Weber is interpreted as thinking that the emotional character of charismatic authority marks it as irrational and doomed to fade in the modern era.[14]

It should be no surprise that history and historiography have not been kind to this vision of charisma's diminished role in a modern rational public order, but this makes the notion of charismatic authority all the more useful as an analytical tool. Following Edward Shils, Clifford Geertz applied the notion of charismatic authority to elucidate the "inherent sacredness of sovereign power."[15] Noting the shared attributes of gods and kings—a connection which is explicit in traditional Hindu religio-political contexts—Geertz suggests that this connection is still alive and well in modern political systems. Any kind of political system contains symbolic forms that express authority and allow leaders to embody power so long as they adhere to aesthetically appropriate performances.[16]

While Geertz has several proof cases of his own, it may be worth briefly considering how Gandhi manifests his charisma as a political leader, especially since Gandhi served as an important model for Gurudev's work. Gandhi already had some political clout upon his return to India as a result of political action in South Africa, of course. But this accomplishment alone was not enough to render him a major player in the Indian nationalist movement. One of Gandhi's first moves upon arriving in India was to travel around the country, ostensibly for the sake of understanding "authentic" Indianness. He then proceeded to take up a simple lifestyle that embodied this authenticity. While many of his colleagues in the independence movement adopted Western bourgeois affectations in an attempt to render themselves powerful, Gandhi adopted the affectations of village India to the point of personally embodying them. In so doing, he came to possess a tremendous affective resonance with the people of India and achieved a prominent role in the independence movement.

A more recent proponent of charisma as a scholarly term is Charles Lindholm, whose work *Charisma* has done a great deal to revitalize anthropological interest in the concept. Expressing his shock at the momentary irrationality of rioting students in the '60s and the more protracted lapses of reason he saw in followers of Guru figures, Lindholm applies comparative anthropological analysis to !Kung shamans and three well-known charismatic leaders and their followers: Adolf Hitler, Charles Manson, and Jim Jones.[17] He ultimately suggests that the emotional intensity and hope for revolutionary change involved in following a charismatic leader are more appealing than ever for the escape it offers from alienation, oppression, and the supposedly dull disenchantment of modernity.[18] Lindholm's affirmation that emotion has some role in the modern period is a step forward from the Anglophone Weberian tradition, and goes a long way toward clarifying the appeal of charismatic authority. But it still seems to reify the notion that rationality is the norm in the modern period, and emotion the deviation.

Although there are a number of more recent works dealing with charismatic authority, I want to call particular attention to the work of C. Julia Huang-Lemmon, which builds upon the insights of Charles Lindholm and Thomas Csordas to develop a theory of charisma that is viable for ethnographic study after the corporeal turn. Huang-Lemmon views charisma as involving powerful experiences circulated between bodies and emphasizes how it reveals the importance of emotion and nonverbal corporeality for theorizing practice and formulating systems of meaning.[19] Huang-Lemmon further articulates a "three-body model" that is helpful for keeping track of the flows of affect that circulate through the kinds of corporeal networks formed around charismatic leaders. The first of these is the leader's body. It performs personal magnetism and in exchange receives the adoration of its followers. The second is the follower's body, which is the locus of intersubjective experience and is moved by the charisma of the leader but must be disciplined in accordance with the will of the leader. Finally, there is the collective body, which is transformed into a structured community through the action of charisma.[20]

My understanding of charisma also integrates insights from the burgeoning field of affect theory. Since affect theory understands power as flowing between bodies in ways that do not rely exclusively on verbal language, it instead redirects our attention to some of the fundamental elements of charisma—body language, vocal inflection, and material objects can all carry this form of power called "affect." According to Sara Ahmed, affect can become sticky and attach to signs and symbols, including those within the realm of language, but even in this case, affect moves us in ways that do not rely upon cognition. As affect circulates between bodies it intensifies in a process that Ahmed calls an "affective economy." Affect leaves impressions on bodies, shaping identities and eventually communities as bodies that have been shaped by similar affects come into alignment with one another.[21]

Affect is helpful for understanding charisma: a form of power that flows between bodies building identities, relationships, and communities, but is not processed through rational cognition. But its utility should not be limited to understanding charismatic authority just because it is obviously emotional—affect theorists urge us to see affect as a vector of power with broad implications for understanding human behavior in everyday life.[22] Even when humans seem our most rational, even when behavior seems to stem from cognitive dispositions, it is desirable to dig deeper to see how affect may still be at work.

Given the wide-reaching implications of affect theory for understanding how power operates on non-cognitive levels, I conceive of charismatic authority as necessarily having a basis that is primarily affective, but I would also contend that other forms of authority are also rooted at least partially in their emotional resonances. As such, I question the tendency in discourse about charisma to treat emotion as so distinct from other forms of authority such as—in the case of the Gayatri Pariwar—scientific authority. It might be more rigorous to suggest that one distinctive feature of charismatic authority is the fact that its emotional qualities are overt and often explicitly acknowledged as the basis for the bodily networks it sustains and the practices it motivates. Meanwhile, where other forms of authority predominate, the role of emotion is obfuscated, often through some form of rationalization.

Aside from the intense affective qualities of charisma, I consider one of the telltale indicators of charismatic leadership to be an ability to break away from established conventions and to point followers toward new ways of being. Charismatic leaders may or may not regard themselves as being bound by traditional or rational-legal authority structures, but their followers typically do not view them as bound by these external forms of authority. Because they are not bound by extant conventions, charismatic leaders can thus be harbingers of innovation and change solely on the basis of the emotional impact they have on their followers.

## *Aucitya* and the Drama of Charisma

I understand the ability of charismatic leaders to inspire their followers as arising from their ability to embody culturally defined ideals that represent the most dearly held values and aspirations of their followers. Charismatic leaders achieve this embodiment by performing these ideals and by surrounding themselves with objects that are charged with these ideals' emotional intensity. This may be a calculated move in some cases—a form of deliberate crowd manipulation—but I am not so cynical as to believe this is always true, nor is it my intent to imply that this is the case with Gurudev.

My particular view of the kinds of performances that generate charisma is indebted to Leela Prasad, and less directly to discussions of aesthetics in the Sanskrit literary canon. In her book *Poetics of Conduct,* Prasad deploys the concept of *aucitya,* or dramaturgical propriety, to understand what makes a type of formal sermon on moral conduct called an *āśīrvāda* (lit. blessing) persuasive. According to *rasa* theory, the value and purpose of poetry and other forms of art is an ability to instill emotions in an audience. Like most other theoretical literature in the Sanskrit canon, *rasa* theory is not descriptive, but prescriptive. *Rasa* theory is concerned with telling authors exactly how they should go about writing literature that evokes emotional responses in their audiences. In the context of *rasa* theory, *aucitya* involves being sure that the elements in a poem cohere emotionally. More importantly, in a dramatic presentation *aucitya* requires that not only must the dialog be appropriate to the intended *rasa*, but also the non-linguistic elements: props, costumes, vocal inflection, and body language.[23] While considering her informants' comments about what makes an effective *āśīrvāda*—"choice of speaker, idiom of delivery, selection and range of illustrations, content and length of the *āśīrvāda* exegesis"—Prasad finds the aesthetic concept of *aucitya* helpful in understanding what makes for a persuasive lecture about moral behavior, especially when a good *āśīrvāda* is supposed to induce in its audience a state of devotion to dharma.[24]

The same analysis Prasad deploys to understand what makes a compelling *āśīrvāda* applies easily to considerations about what makes a person charismatic. In a charismatic figure, a number of elements—life story, clothing, rhetorical style, body language, and surroundings, to name a few—come together harmoniously in a culturally defined way to induce powerful emotions in followers and instill in them a desire to change their behavior.[25] In pointing to the ways in which linguistic and non-linguistic components intermingle in making a person emotionally compelling, the concept of *aucitya* is of great utility in thinking through the multiple levels on which charisma operates.

## Routinizing Charisma

The death of a charismatic leader provides a movement with a variety of challenges and opportunities, requiring them to eventually disband or look for some way to persist in the absence of charisma. This process, which Weber called the "routinization of charisma," may be accomplished by seeking out a successor whose charisma may or may not be comparable to that of his or her predecessor, by embracing traditional or legal authority, or some combination of these strategies. This generates controversy among followers, especially if the leader did not establish a clear and effective plan before his or her demise.[26]

A number of examples could illustrate the difficulties movements face while routinizing charisma. The well-known case of ISKCON, or the Hare Krishna movement, is telling of these difficulties. The founder of ISKCON, Bhaktivedanta Swami, hoped that his movement would remain coherent after his death if he created an appropriate institutional structure to take his place. The Governing Body Commission—a name which may have been borrowed from the Indian Railways' board of directors—was to serve this function. Working from *Robert's Rules of Order*, they were to settle the administrative responsibilities required by the movement according to rules established by Bhaktivedanta Swami before his death.[27] This attempt to establish a legal-rational authority structure alongside Bhaktivedanta Swami's charisma had immediate consequences, including an emphasis on financial issues, increased hierarchy among devotees, especially in relation to gender, and of course increasingly widespread corruption. Despite Bhaktivedanta Swami's best efforts, ISKCON was wracked by controversy after his death as senior disciples vied for leadership while holding questionably to norms of moral conduct that are important to the movement. This cost the movement a great deal of its vitality in the West, although it is still somewhat popular in India.[28]

Bhaktivedanta Swami seemed to believe that his body of teachings coupled with a self-regulating bureaucracy would be enough to maintain the coherence of his movement. He underestimated the important role that his bodily presence played in sustaining his movement, especially outside of India, where his followers had been asked to undergo an especially radical departure from their cultural background.[29] Bhaktivedanta Swami's body, along with the narratives entangled with and performed by that body, carried an affective intensity that compelled his followers to behave in accordance with ISKCON norms. The movement's Governing Body Commission simply lacked the affective intensity to sustain these behaviors.

The Siddha Yoga movement took a rather different approach to routinizing charisma. Swami Muktananda, a charismatic guru who is credited with spreading the movement globally, put a great deal of effort into grooming his successor, Swami Chidvilasananda. She met Muktananda when she was quite young, and starting in her teens was around him almost constantly. He would speak positively of her to his followers and eventually selected her as his English-language translator, thereby building up her mythos as someone with a deep connection to him. Her brother, Nityananda, followed a similar trajectory, and after they had been initiated as a *sannyāsī*, or renunciant, they were announced as Muktananda's successors. But after about three years of leading the movement together, Nityananda left the movement, claiming he had broken his vow of celibacy.[30] The movement took another blow as allegations of sexual abuse under Muktananda intensified. As for Chidvilasananda, she continues to lead by force of personality, suggesting she is herself a charismatic leader. But her charisma does not seem to have held up to these scandals, as the movement's membership has long been in decline.[31]

Swami Muktananda's strategy differed from Bhaktivedanta Swami's in that he hoped to maintain a charismatic core for his movement. This is reminiscent of a phenomenon Weber and a number of more recent scholars covering the routinization of charisma describe as secondary charisma, in which the charisma of a leader like Muktananda rubs off on his successors, like Chidvilasananda and Nityananda, but is nonetheless derivative.[32] By presenting these two as his chosen successors, Muktananda utilized his own charisma to invest other bodies with the affective intensity needed to keep the bodies of his followers in alignment. But perhaps because it is derivative, this secondary charisma proved fragile. Whereas another charismatic figure like Osho could maintain his popularity after numerous scandals,[33] Muktananda's successors' secondary charisma shattered when the narratives with which their bodies had been invested were called into question by outside forces.

As these examples illustrate, the routinization of charisma is no easy feat to accomplish. Without a leader who is able to instill in followers a sense of commitment to the community and to motivate the intense discipline needed to realign one's body with the body of the charismatic leader, controversies easily tear post-charismatic movements apart as followers stray from the path. And as was the case with ISKCON, even before such scandals emerged, the process of creating a bureaucratic apparatus detracts from the revolutionary feel of the movement.

## Charismatic Authority and Scientific Authority

### Names and Titles

As I have already noted, the continued vibrancy of the Gayatri Pariwar sets it apart from these other movements. Over the course of the next few sections, I would like to examine some of the strategies the movement deploys in routinizing Gurudev's charisma, which will allow me to illustrate how Doctor-sahib's scientific authority fills this difficult void. I start my analysis by considering the provocative differences between how Gayatri parijans refer to these leaders before considering how their stories are narrated and finally examining the ways in which Gayatri parijans express reverence and respect for these figures.

In more formal settings, Gurudev is styled as Pandit Shriram Sharma Acharya. The title *pandit* (*paṇḍit*) here suggests that Gurudev has mastered the Hindu corpus in a traditional Indian intellectual context. *Acharya* (*ācārya*) expands on *pandit*, suggesting that he is actively engaged in sharing his knowledge of scripture with others. These titles may appear to indicate a basis for Gurudev's religious authority purely in tradition and text rather than in charisma, but I would argue that these modes of authority function alongside and feed into Gurudev's charismatic authority. These titles thus contribute to an integral aesthetic whole that instills a feeling of *bhakti*, or devotion, in Gurudev's followers. In order to generate the right kind of *aucitya*, charismatic figures must marshal extant cultural concepts like being a pandit or an acharya to situate themselves in a way that establishes their social relevance. But the ends toward which charismatic figures draw on these seemingly traditional concepts is distinctive. Gurudev's authority is not deployed to sustain Hindu traditions as they have existed during his lifetime. Rather, it sustains an eschatological hope that he will revive *satyug*. As such, the traditions and texts that are marshaled under these titles point not to Gurudev's associations with social continuity, but rather to his capacity to bring about a rupture with the present and a return to this glorious, bygone golden age.

While "Pandit Shriram Sharma Acharya" seems to suffice in most formal contexts, occasions that call for particularly flowery language see him styled "Yugrishi Vedmurti Taponishth Pandit Shriram Sharma Acharya." These more ornate epithets point to Gurudev's charisma more clearly. In attributing the title "Vedmurti" (*vedmūrti*, embodiment of the Vedas) to Gurudev, the Gayatri Pariwar suggests that he personally embodies religious knowledge rather than simply being informed by it. Meanwhile, "Yugrishi" (*yugṛṣi*, seer of the era) connects Gurudev to the rishis who recorded the Vedas while pointing to his eschatological function, that is, his role in bringing about a radical break with the current *yuga* and ushering in a new one. Finally, "Taponishth" (*taponiṣṭh*, established in austerity) brings to mind Gurudev's arduous Himalayan pilgrimages—a feat few ordinary people could imagine themselves performing—while simultaneously drawing a parallel with the great ascetics of Hindu literature. We see then that the various performative elements that generate Gurudev's *aucitya* inhere in his body and are further signified by his titles.

Of course, in most informal situations, Sharma's followers simply refer to him as "Gurudev." *Guru*, like *acharya*, suggests "teacher," and indeed this term can often have a relatively mundane meaning in Indian cultural contexts. But "dev" complicates this picture by suggesting not a mundane teacher but rather one who is "radiant" or "divine." With these titles, his followers go well beyond suggesting that Gurudev has mastered Hindu religious and intellectual traditions or even that he embodies them, suggesting that he possesses a divine authority that transcends humanity. This title strongly gestures to Gurudev's charisma, as it marks him as someone who is perceived as superhuman and worthy of being followed and emulated on the pure basis of his radiance or divinity.

On the other hand, I have struggled unsuccessfully to find a written document in which Pandya's name appears without the title "doctor." My sense of this title's importance for his followers is reinforced by the fact that in conversation, he is often referred to as "Doctor-sahib," which I would gloss roughly as "respected doctor" or perhaps more literally as "Mr. Doctor." But however one translates it, it is clear that he is not Dr.

Figure 3.1. Veneration of Gurudev, Shantikunj, Basant Panchami 2012.

Gurudev or even Doctor-acharya. Followers stop short of calling him a guru (even after death, this title belongs to Gurudev), coming no closer than English words like "mentor" and "guide."

Although the honorific *-sahib* is fairly widespread in contemporary South Asia, it may be worth noting that it was once the honorific most closely associated with British colonial authorities. The variety of contexts in which *-sahib* is used nowadays leaves me hesitant to push this point too hard. But since the title "Doctor" associates Pandya with the affective resonances of Western intellectual authority, I am also hesitant to overlook the possible connection. Perhaps it is not too bold a point if I suggest that in their shared postcolonial context, many of Doctor-sahib's followers might experience "Doctor" and "-sahib" as possessing mutually reinforcing affective resonances that impart a sense of Western-style authority that has been hybridized with Indian authority.

In addition to the association Doctor-sahib's title creates with Western-style intellectual authority, it reinforces his personal link to medical science. If Doctor-sahib had pursued a PhD with a focus in quantum mechanics, it might well make him an authority for segments of society who are in a sufficiently privileged position to value a relatively abstract branch of science. But as a medical doctor, Doctor-sahib has a scientific background speaking to a broader concern: health. The Gayatri Pariwar's populist bent is at work here—if the movement hopes to mobilize rural India in support of its social vision, speaking to their interest in maintaining or improving their health is likely to be more successful than informing them that the Vedic sages had discovered quantum mechanics long ago.

Doctor-sahib's status as a medical doctor is also important to his urban middle-class followers. As I have already shown, many members of the post-liberalization middle class at Shantikunj are committed to the movement because it allows them to work for the betterment of society in ways that private sector jobs do not. Doctor-sahib's ability to authorize claims about the medical benefits of Gayatri Pariwar practices helps sustain a feeling for these middle-class community members that they are engaged in such a project. And finally, Doctor-sahib's title also links him to some of the Gayatri Pariwar's charitable medical projects, including mobile eye camps, in which poor rural people can have their practical concerns taken care of while middle-class community members find fulfillment in bettering society. Thus, Doctor-sahib's title signifies not just Western-style intellectual authority, but also his ability to tend to the practical needs of the poor and to the humanitarian impulses of the middle class.

Gayatri parijans do not see Doctor-sahib as having the authority to break with the past and create new doctrine, as would be the case with a charismatic leader; rather, they view him as being charged to continue carrying out Gurudev's vision—we have already seen this clearly in the rhetoric surrounding the founding of DSVV. Thus, although his titles gesture strongly to his identity as a medical doctor and suggest that he embodies scientific authority in the same way that Gurudev embodied traditional authority, this does not render him charismatic.

Figure 3.2. Doctor-sahib, speaking from behind a lectern at DSVV.

## A Hagiography and a CV

Another indicator of the different kinds of authority Gurudev and Doctor-sahib possess is in the radical differences in their life stories. Charismatic leaders often have quite compelling life stories that emphasize their uncanny, extraordinary personalities while perhaps aligning them with charismatic leaders of the past. It is rather common for these life stories to be written and published by the leader as an auto-hagiography. One classic auto-hagiography that has become a paradigm for this genre is Paramahansa Yogananda's *Autobiography of a Yogi*. Yogananda recounts his remarkable life as a sort of spiritual odyssey, starting with his preter-natural memories of infancy. He tells readers of his youthful visions of the Himalayan yogis he wished to join. After many years of encountering numerous religious figures, he is visited by one such Himalayan yogi, an immortal guru named Babaji, who had been silently setting the stage for Yogananda to bring yoga to the West.[34]

Gurudev has written two such texts: *My Life: Its Legacy and Message*, which was written in 1988 and covers much of his spiritual life, and *Companions in Solitude*, which is a travelogue compiled from materials written in 1960. While they are unique and original works in many ways, they very much fit aspects of the paradigm *Autobiography of a Yogi* established. For example, the Gayatri Pariwar places great emphasis on his instruction at the hands of an incorporeal Himalayan yogi, starting with a vision at the age of 15.[35] This encounter is the first biographical detail presented in the preface of *Companions in Solitude* and the first life event that Gurudev discloses in *My Life* in any substantial detail, suggesting its significance for him and his desire to emphasize it to his readers. This vision and his lifelong interactions with these incorporeal yogis bear some resemblance to aspects of *Autobiography of a Yogi*, as mentioned above. Of course, Gurudev and Yogananda are not the only two gurus who have claimed such a lineage—Jaggi Vasudev and Sri Sri Ravi Shankar have similar stories. The idea of lineage invoked by these figures seems to suggest an authoritative basis in tradition. Historically speaking, being part of a reputable lineage is an important basis for the authority of religious figures in Hindu contexts. But because the incorporeal figures from whom these lineages derive are not knowable by ordinary people, only by the superhuman guru, this invokes a sense of sublime wonder that operates on an affective level, and is still well within the realm of charisma, albeit again one that nods to extant traditions even as it supersedes them.

One of the commands of this incorporeal yogi for Gurudev was that he would have to take a series of arduous pilgrimages into the Himalayas. Traveling on foot, he would arrive at Nandanvan, a meadow at an altitude of over 14,000 feet, after passing Gangotri, traditionally considered the source of the Ganges; Gomukh, at the foot of the glacier that serves as one of the river's physical sources; and Tapovan, a high-altitude meadow beyond the glacier traditionally associated with ascetics. At Nandanvan, he would live among rishis, whose company would prepare him to continue their mission with his own life.[36] The detail in which these pilgrimages are described and their relative prominence in the book's organization again suggest that Gurudev wanted to emphasize these experiences to his followers as an aspect of his story that renders him authoritative.

This intention is reinforced by the fact that almost the entirety of *Companions in Solitude* is dedicated to recounting a lengthy pilgrimage that took place around 1960. In it, Gurudev describes in detail a wide variety of miraculous occurrences on the pilgrimage trail. He presents the character-building that occurred during his difficult journey as evidence of divine guidance. Of course, *Companions in Solitude* is more than a mere description of these experiences; it is a didactic text. These stories serve to establish Gurudev as an intermediary figure. He has undertaken pilgrimages so intense that only a saintly person would undertake them. He survived their dangers and developed as a person because of a special divine interest in his life. And now, he can offer the fruit of those travels to his followers.

Moving from these formative experiences to Gurudev's death, Gayatri parijans hold that he voluntarily shed his mortal body to continue his work unencumbered by physical constraints. This notion is not unique to the Gayatri Pariwar, but rather is a fairly common motif in Hindu descriptions of the passing of saintly figures; it is one way in which religious movements routinize charisma. By emphasizing Gurudev's continued ethereal presence, followers are able to continue sensing his affective echoes and thus feel that his charismatic leadership is not completely lost. Not only should it be possible for followers to sense his presence themselves, but they can also take comfort in the notion that his will still guides Doctor-sahib, who serves as a sort of steward, and the movement as a whole. Javanika's story demonstrates the effects of this discourse well—she was deeply saddened by the fact that she will never meet Gurudev corporeally, but is comforted when she feels his lingering affect when she visits Akhand Deep.

When I first arrived at Shantikunj, my primary contact in the movement told me as part of my orientation that *My Life* and *Companions in Solitude* should be the first Gayatri Pariwar books I read. Later, as I met more Gayatri parijans and began the process of conducting interviews, I was given the clear sense that many Shantikunj residents accept that these texts are the key to understanding the movement. The fact that two autobiographical works should have such significant status for the movement is an indicator of Gurudev's charismatic status. Even after his death, Gurudev—and not his successor—remains the heart and soul of the movement. And it is not just his ideas—which are recorded in countless other publications—that are essential to understand, but rather the set of experiences that he as a person embodied. If his body is no longer present to bring about intense emotional states in his followers, one may still be able to understand what he represented to his followers, to glean the affect that sticks to his life story by reading his experiences. The stories that relay these experiences contribute to the integral whole, the *aucitya*, which projects Gurudev's charismatic authority. His arduous pilgrimages and guidance from incorporeal beings at Nandanvan solidify the image, signified again and again by his titles, that he is Taponishth and a Yugrishi.

In stark contrast, I have not been able to find any publications describing Doctor-sahib's life in detail, despite the fact the he is himself quite the prolific author. The Gayatri Pariwar's website does provide something of a written profile for him, but it reads less like a hagiography or even a biography than it does like an academic cover letter and CV.[37] The profile starts by mentioning his relationship with Gurudev and outlining his major achievements:

> A close and direct disciple of Pandit Shriram Gurudev Acharya, Dr. Pranav Pandya is renowned world over as a pioneer of scientific spirituality. As the Head of the Organization, he disseminated the message of Indian culture, in its true spirit, across the globe and established branches of Gayatri Pariwar in over 80 countries. Under his dynamic leadership the Dev Sanskriti University at Haridwar is establishing new milestones and reforming the face of modern education.[38]

This "cover letter" portion of his profile then goes into greater detail about his educational, medical, and scientific achievements before elaborating on his role and the positions he holds in the Gayatri Pariwar.

His profile moves onto a CV-like "Chronology of Life Events," detailing the years he met Gurudev, received his degrees, held biomedical research positions, and finally took charge of important offices in the Gayatri Pariwar:

- 1963: Came in contact with Gayatri Mission . . .
- 1972: M.B.B.S. from M. G. M. Medical College Indore, India.
- 1975: M.D. from M.G.M. Medical College, with gold medal.
- 1975–1976: Worked with eminent medical scientists in the Departments of Neurology and Cardiology at M.G.M. Medical College . . .
- 1976–1978: Served as a physician in Bharat Heavy Electrical Limited hospitals in Haridwar and Bhopal . . .
- 1978: Received lucrative job offers in U.S.A . . .
- Since 1979: Serving as Director of Brahmavarchas [Research Center], Haridwar
- Since 1994: Editor of the monthly magazine Akhand Jyoti (Hindi) . . .
- Since 1995: Serving as Head of All-World Gayatri Pariwar . . .[39]

The CV-like portion of his profile ends with a chronological listing of his "accolades and honors:"

- Participated in conferences and delivered exclusive lectures at Cambridge University, Oxford University, Harvard University . . . and other Universities.
- Addressed a joint session of [Parliament] in London in February 1992.

- Presented scientific aspects of Indian Culture to the World Parliament of Religions held in Chicago in 1993 and in Cape Town in 1999.
- Honoured by NASA, in 1996 as a distinguished scientist and reformer for worldwide dissemination of scientific aspects of Indian Culture.
- Conferred the 'Hindu of the Year' 1999 award by Federation of Indian Associations and Federation of Hindu Association for dissemination of Indian Culture abroad.[40]

The implications of this presentation of Doctor-sahib's life should be clear: this is no hagiography. The details of his life do not impart a sense of saintliness to him. Unlike Gurudev, he does not come across as someone whom his followers should aim to emulate or as someone whose life experiences could be spiritually instructive. Rather, his profile presents him as someone who is suited to the task of leadership in an institution in which charisma must be routinized. His contact with Gurudev and earlier achievements within the movement should be adequate to prove that he is qualified to continue the mission. But why the emphasis on his biomedical achievements? How might this information make followers want to "hire" him as Gurudev's successor? Even without articulating how Doctor-sahib's scientific experiences are relevant to the religious context of the Gayatri Pariwar, the scientific authority projected by the experiences he embodies is palpable. As a "man of science," he is empirical, rational, and reliable. This seemingly emotionally detached way of narrating Doctor-sahib's life and framing his achievements instills in followers a sense that he is a trustworthy authority figure, even in a religious context.

Although little ink has been spilled over it, there is a place in Doctor-sahib's life that is perhaps as important in generating his religious authority as the Himalayan retreat inhabited by rishis was for Gurudev—his *yajña* laboratory at Brahmavarchas Shodh Sansthan. At the center of this laboratory, there is a traditional fire altar located beneath a large exhaust hood. At this altar, Doctor-sahib performed the traditional fire offerings that are central to Gayatri Pariwar ritual life for the sake of conducting various experiments. For example, he would collect the smoke given off by the fire pit as various substances were offered into it through an exhaust hood situated just overhead. He would then expose various pathogenic cultures to this smoke in order to argue that this practice would cure diseases and improve one's health.

The notion that these practices are good for your health is not new. This was a presumption of Gurudev that was shared by Dayananda Saraswati, founder of the Arya Samaj, among others. Nonetheless, the fact that Doctor-sahib actually performed the process that proved the veracity of these claims generated substantial religious authority. This laboratory space, with all of its associations with scientific authority, is a place where Doctor-sahib's experiment-performances sustained and solidified the legitimacy of Gayatri Pariwar practices. By embodying scientific authority, Doctor-sahib becomes an effective post-charismatic leader because he has a capacity to continue legitimating Gayatri Pariwar practices.

## (Post-)Charismatic Places

On several occasions I was asked to go for audience with Doctor-sahib and Jiji. On the mornings when this happened, I would line up with hundreds of other followers outside of the building in which Gurudev once lived. After the tightly packed queue emerged from a narrow staircase, I found myself in the space Javanika described at the beginning of this chapter: Gurudev and Mataji's old apartment, in which their furniture and other material possessions were on display. These rooms struck me as being in equal measures temple and museum, as the items on display—a couch, a bed, sandals, various religious artifacts, and other ordinary items from Gurudev's life—were present both as objects to be venerated for their spiritual value and objects to be preserved for their historical import.

The items on display were rather humble, and suggested the simple lifestyle that Gurudev was said to live. By signifying the simplicity that Gurudev embodied, these items took on some of the affective resonance associated with Gurudev's charisma. Followers expressed their reverence to Gurudev through these objects, lovingly touching their forehead to the spot where his feet might have been while he slept, sprinkling flower petals on his couch, and offering silent prayers to the objects he once worshiped.

The climax of this tour is a glimpse of the shrine where Gurudev did the majority of his practices. Followers are not allowed into the shrine itself, but stay outside and offer their prayers and prostrations from a distance. It is common for the inner sanctum of a Hindu temple to place such a requirement on visitors, but this is rather unusual for a domestic shrine.

And indeed, this is no ordinary domestic shrine. It is rendered sacred in a way that is more extraordinary than would be the case if the objects and actions associated with it were connected with an ordinary person. The space as a whole becomes an object of reverence by its association with Gurudev.

Perhaps the most important item in this shrine is an oil lamp to which devotees like Javanika offer particular reverence. Indeed, even on mornings when Doctor-sahib and Jiji are not giving audience, visitors will still line up for what is called "Akhand Deep darshan." This lamp, which Gayatri parijans say has been kept burning continuously since 1926 by Gurudev and his followers, signifies Gurudev's preternatural ritual diligence. Many of the material objects that fill Gurudev's old quarters have a relation of *aucitya* to Gurudev's charisma because they project a saintly simplicity for which his followers can strive in their day-to-day lives. Akhand Deep also has a relation of *aucitya* to Gurudev's charisma, but is highlighted because it speaks to Gurudev's saintly excess—something his followers might only dream of achieving.

After winding through these spaces I emerged into a large room that serves as sort of audience chamber in which Doctor-sahib and Jiji meet their followers. In keeping with tradition for meeting religious leaders in India, I touched my head to the ground in front of Doctor-sahib's feet. He then usually asked, in the manner of a concerned host, if I was comfortable, how my research was progressing, and other basic questions about my stay at Shantikunj. After a brief exchange, I moved over and offered the same respectful greeting to Jiji before receiving some sweets to signify the generosity of my hosts and being ushered out of the room.

The fact that the Pandyas receive this kind of reverential greeting in a highly ritualized environment should not undermine the sense that Doctor-sahib is a post-charismatic leader. Consider the fact that followers have audience with them only after winding their way through a collection of the material artifacts that remain from Gurudev's life—not those associated with the Pandyas themselves. This treatment frames the Pandyas as being worthy of reverence not inherently, but rather because they are successors or representatives of the saintly Gurudev. And it presents them, again, as stewards of the immortal, incorporeal Gurudev. To a certain extent, this is reminiscent of the notion of "secondary charisma," as discussed in my treatment of the routinization of charisma in the Siddha Yoga movement, above. But the Pandyas' status as authority figures in the Gayatri Pariwar is not so fragile as the status of Chidvilasananda and Nityananda was in Siddha Yoga. Doctor-sahib has an additional layer of external authorizing via his medical-scientific credentials just as his wife, Jiji, creates an additional bond of kinship with the Gayatri Pariwar's charismatic origins.[41]

The closest equivalent to the Gurudev's apartment for Doctor-sahib would have to be his *yajña* lab. When I first visited Brahmavarchas Shodh Sansthan, the resident researcher gave me a tour of the facilities after answering a few of my questions about his work. He guided me through a series of laboratories oriented around a center courtyard—a common architectural style in India—describing the kinds of research that could be done in these labs, most of which involved taking various biometrics from practitioners to look for changes in their physiological state. These rooms, as Lise McKean notes in her brief discussion of the Gayatri Pariwar, had a certain museum-like quality,[42] especially since research activities had shifted to DSVV by the time of my visit.

The sense of being in a space that was as much a museum as a temple, like the one I got in Gurudev and Mataji's apartments, did not resurface until the conclusion—and climax—of the tour. At this juncture, my guide brought me into a small freestanding structure situated in the middle of the courtyard. Some of the groundskeepers, working in the picturesque gardens of medicinal herbs that surrounded this freestanding structure, stopped their work and joined us inside. While my companions stopped short of standing with their palms pressed together, their body language changed as they entered this space even as my guide's vocal tone softened, leaving behind the confident tones of a professional researcher at work and taking on a reverential quality. This shift in mood finally put us in an affective space reminiscent of Gurudev and Mataji's apartments.

There was no sense that Gayatri parijans worshiped this space. No jostling queue of devotees clogged the walkway leading up to the *yajña* laboratory. This space and the objects in it—fire altar, exhaust hood, and other laboratory instruments—nonetheless constitute the inner sanctum of Doctor-sahib's post-charismatic authority. The religio-scientific activities Doctor-sahib carried out in the *yajña* laboratory circulated a kind of sticky affect that remains in this space, as illustrated by its effects on the bodies of my guide and the groundskeepers who accompanied us. This affect is also stuck to Doctor-sahib's body, reinforcing his position of authority in the Gayatri Pariwar.

## Conclusion

In these examples, I have illustrated how the Gayatri Pariwar frames the authority of Gurudev and Doctor-sahib quite differently. Gurudev embodies Hindu tradition, seems to transcend ordinary humanity, and has a compelling life story that puts him in the company of other saintly figures while marking him as someone to emulate. Conversely, Doctor-sahib seems to embody the idea of science and is marked by his educational and research achievements not as someone to emulate, but as someone who is qualified to present accurate information. This portrayal may be somewhat unconventional for the leader of a religious movement, but I want to suggest that Doctor-sahib's ability to embody scientific authority and signify it to his followers is part of the reason that the Gayatri Pariwar has been so successful in its post-charismatic stage.

One of the factors that may make charismatic authority appealing is the possibility that the movement will not stagnate but will be continually renewed by the maverick tendencies associated with charismatic leadership. Gurudev was able to fulfill his followers' desires for a perpetually unfolding revelation not only through his engaging lectures but also through his prolific work as a writer—achievements his followers frequently emphasize. But scientific authority also brings with it the promise of continuous renewal, and so by embodying scientific authority, Doctor-sahib keeps followers feeling like it is possible for the process of revelation to continue.

Scientific and charismatic authorities are appealing not only because they represent this tendency toward perpetually unfolding revelation, but also the possibility of revolutionary change. This is well illustrated in Gayatri Pariwar eschatology. Gurudev has played a role in bringing about the coming golden age by following the guidance of incorporeal yogis and subsequently exerting his will on the world after death. But the Gayatri Pariwar also presents the scientific authority Doctor-sahib embodies as crucial in their eschatology because only with adequate proof will enough of the human population change their behavior in the ways needed to bring about this golden age.

Finally, charismatic leaders like Gurudev are authoritative in part because of their ability to produce powerful affective responses in followers. These intense, immediate bodily sensations are perhaps the most crucial basis of charismatic authority. Because recognition of charismatic authority is located so specifically in the body, the bodies of charismatic followers become touchstones for evaluating religious authority. Although there are a number of intense feelings associated with acceptance of scientific authority, I hesitate to make such an easy comparison in particular because such feelings are so quickly and easily rationalized. Rather, I want to consider a particular point in the scientific rhetoric of the Gayatri Pariwar. While experiments like those performed in a brick-and-mortar laboratory by Doctor-sahib certainly play a role in their scientific rhetoric, this is only one of the senses in which the Gayatri Pariwar deploys the idea of science. If I may borrow an image from Joseph Alter, they also treat the body as a flesh-and-blood laboratory, capable of discerning the validity of Gayatri Pariwar practices through experience. Because the Gayatri Pariwar's scientific rhetoric emphasizes bodily experience in this way, followers are able to maintain the bodily orientation they had under Gurudev. Their bodies still remain touchstones for evaluating religious authority; only now the ways in which they are presented with religious authority has changed.

Given the argument I have presented in this chapter, it might seem that it would make more sense to conclude that Doctor-sahib is every bit the charismatic leader that Gurudev was. Whereas the charisma of the latter was rooted in a traditional saintly lifestyle, the charisma of the former was rooted in modern narratives about the universal power of science that have been present in India since the colonial era. But this interpretation of Doctor-sahib's authority fails because it does not adequately account for the ends toward which Doctor-sahib directs his authority—maintaining the teachings of Gurudev. While the current era of Gayatri Pariwar history is certainly marked by careful adaptation to the processes of liberalization and globalization that began unfolding right around the time of Gurudev's death, it is all done within the framework of his teachings. His ideas about nation-building are now framed by his larger project of ushering in a new *satyug*, or golden age, for all of humanity. His tendency to draw on science as a source of metaphor is now less emphasized than the data generated by the research institution he founded. Even the most noteworthy achievement of the Gayatri Pariwar under Doctor-sahib's leadership, the opening of the movement's university, is treated as the realization of Gurudev's vision rather than Doctor-sahib's personal achievement.

As I have suggested in my discussion of charisma, one of the key distinguishing features of charismatic authority is an ability to reject accepted conventions and favor of some bold new direction. While Doctor-sahib's scientific background allows Gayatri parijans to feel that at any moment, there could be a breakthrough that changes everything, no such breakthrough has happened and there has been relative continuity with the past. If Doctor-sahib were wielding independent charismatic authority, we would expect to see bold changes in the Gayatri Pariwar rather than a cautious approach rooted in the legacy of Gurudev. Doctor-sahib may be able to stir intense emotions in his followers, but those emotions lead to different ends than those stirred by Gurudev—adherence to established principles rather than the production of new principles. On these grounds, I would resist the notion that Doctor-sahib's ability to lead through affective intensity could accurately be described as charismatic authority. Rather, it illustrates the potential affective intensity of non-charismatic forms of social authority.

While I maintain on this basis that there is a valid distinction to be made between the kinds of authority wielded by Gurudev and Doctor-sahib based on the different outcomes of their authority, the more important point I wish to make on the basis of the evidence I have presented in this chapter is that scientific authority and charismatic authority can function in astonishingly similar ways. Even if Doctor-sahib has not made any radical departures from the precedents set by Gurudev, he has successfully utilized the intense emotions his followers have toward the idea of science to maintain those precedents where other post-charismatic leaders have failed to do so.

CHAPTER 4

# Ritual-Experiments

The recorded sound of Mataji's voice announced many of Shantikunj's daily ritual activities, reverberating throughout the premises via an extensive network of speakers set up outdoors and indoors, in public spaces and private quarters. Of these many activities, my favorite was easily the *nādyog* meditation, which took place at 6 p.m. At this time, everyone in Shantikunj was expected to stop what they were doing, remain still and silent, and listen to the bansuri for about fifteen minutes. On rare occasions, someone would be so oblivious to the stillness that descended over Shantikunj that they would continue about their business. Residents would sometimes become quite angry, their shouts of chastisement momentarily breaking the quietude, if only to enforce it.

On most days I would sit in my room and turn on its PA speaker so I could hear it with maximum clarity. For much of my fieldwork, I thought that my enjoyment stemmed mostly from my appreciation of music. I would often pull out my sitar to practice afterwards, inspired and wanting more. After several months of hearing the same prerecorded bansuri improvisation every day, this sense wore thin. It ceased to be about the bansuri for me, and more about the silence behind it that made it so easy to hear. The bansuri's delicate flight highlighted the silence in its background created through our collective inaction. Even if we weren't interacting, even if not everyone was together in public, even if we weren't performing any act other than to simply listen, this was the one time a day when everyone in Shantikunj was doing the same thing—ritualized nothing. My Dutch Reform grandmother may well have seen this as an example of idle hands doing the devil's work, but the effort that went into establishing our collective idleness was in reality quite productive, as it was a kind of affective work. It reinforced the desired affective state of *shanti*, or peace, in Shantikunj, and the universal collaboration required to effect this state brought us together. Perhaps in our idle togetherness, we rejected not only my grandmother's Dutch Reform ethic but also contemporary India's spirit of neoliberal alienation.

Daily rituals like this *nādyog* meditation are a crucial part of the ethos of Shantikunj. Given this importance, ritual comes up in a number of contexts in this project, but here I want to give sustained attention to the community's ritual practices and the ritual discourses the movement deploys to justify and impart meaning to these practices. My specific interest in considering ritual in Shantikunj is framed by my analysis of upwardly mobile but disillusioned residents in chapter 2. In that analysis, I offered some general thoughts about how life in Shantikunj might help such Gayatri parijans reconcile their two senses of self through a close reading of Gyaneshwar's conversion narrative. Here I will draw on ritual studies and affect theory to offer a more specific sense of the Gayatri Pariwar's appeal for the upwardly mobile but disillusioned middle class. In conversation with these theoretical literatures, I analyze ritual as a tool for forming personal and communal identities that are aligned with both moral virtue and scientific rationality.

Many other Hindu groups might understand ritual practices like Gayatri recitation and *yajña* to be moral obligations rooted in ancient texts and intend specifically for high-caste men. But the Gayatri Pariwar departs from this understanding. They present these ritual practices not as moral obligations but rather as moral technologies that inscribe virtue upon the bodies of their practitioners, thereby helping to fulfill upwardly mobile but disillusioned Hindus' middle-class moral yearning. They also present these ritual practices not as particularistic and rooted exclusively in textual authority, but rather as universal and scientifically verifiable, thereby conforming to upwardly mobile but disillusioned Hindus' post-Enlightenment mindset. Gayatri recitation and *yajña* in the Gayatri Pariwar thus help to form and reinforce identities that are oriented toward intertwined notions of morality, scientific rationality, and universalism—what the movement calls "scientific spirituality."

As in much of the rest of this project, I am focusing on the contemporary period in this argument, but I must note at the outset that the problem of reconciling Hindu traditions with scientific rationality is not new, nor for that matter is it a struggle that is unique to the Hindu context. It has been common for Hindu reformers who encountered Western secular intellectuals and Protestant missionaries in the nineteenth century to view ritualism as empty, superstitious, and inauthentically Hindu, leading them to deemphasize such practices in favor of meditation and philosophical speculation based on modern interpretations of yoga and Advaita Vedānta.[1] We have already seen this attitude in action in Gandhi's dismissal of Gurudev's interest in ritual. But we have also seen that the Arya Samaj, in reaction to the perceived excesses of other Hindu reform movements of the day, embraced *yajña*, worked to justify it in modern terms, and made it the center of their religious practice. Considering the fact that Gurudev split from the Arya Samaj because he considered their rejection of *mūrti pūjā* elitist, the Gayatri Pariwar can be seen as a further reaction against branches of Hindu reform that might be perceived as too Western and too out of touch with popular Hindu piety.

I now move to a discussion of the details of the ritual life of Shantikunj. Ritual is a broad concept in scholarly discourse that encompasses far more than ritualized worship practices like *yajña* and Gayatri recitation. In many ways, ritualization pervades life at Shantikunj. With rare, slight variations for major holidays, the ashram follows the same schedule every day, which flows nearly uninterrupted from 3:30 or 4 a.m. (depending on the season) to 9 p.m. But most of these events are not required of ashram residents, and so unsurprisingly very few people follow this rigorous schedule. Even less surprisingly, I generally did not follow it so rigorously either; indeed, as a night person I often struggled to attend each morning's compulsory events.

I will start with a brief section on Shantikunj's morning and evening *ārati*. While this practice is less important to the Gayatri Pariwar than Gayatri recitation and *yajña* and it has accordingly generated less ritual discourse, *ārati* merits consideration because it distinguishes the movement from the Arya Samaj and ties it to popular Hindu tradition. The next two sections will cover Gayatri recitation and *yajña* in detail on the basis of ethnographic evidence and critical readings of the Gayatri Pariwar's literature. Finally, rather than look at each other ritualized aspect of daily life in Shantikunj in detail, I will pull back to provide a sense of the ashram's schedule as a whole and reflect on its connections to the Gayatri Pariwar's scientific rhetoric.

## *Ārati*

Shantikunj's small Gayatri Mata Mandir is located on a raised white marble platform, adjacent to a courtyard ringed by statues of the rishis. This *mandīr*, the Gayatri Mata *mūrti* it enshrines, and the ritualistic worship conducted there, brings Gurudev's conflict with the Arya Samaj into focus. The Gayatri Pariwar's advocacy of this form of ritualized worship is not exclusive to Gayatri Devi. Nonetheless, it is noteworthy that this particular deity is subject to ritualized worship in Shantikunj. For a reform-oriented Vedic revivalist movement that wishes to connect with the religious lives of ordinary Hindus, there is a certain coherence to the choice: the Gayatri mantra is perhaps the quintessential Vedic mantra, and one of the few that still has widespread currency in modern India. This is not coincidental with the existence of a goddess with established iconographies who is seen as a manifestation of the mantra. By making Gayatri central to the movement, the Gayatri Pariwar is consequently able to seamlessly bind together Vedic ritual and temple ritual without ever working outside of the religious grammar of modern Hindus.

The evening *ārati* is certainly the better attended of the two daily ceremonies. The courtyard next to the raised platform on which the temple is built fills to capacity with hundreds of residents and visitors to the ashram, who watch from the side as an elderly woman performs a fairly standard ārati in sync with a recording of Mataji's voice leading the group in the associated songs and chants over the ashram's PA system. When she finishes, we line up to offer our individual *praṇāms*, and to receive *prasād*. The priestess who tends this *mandīr*, in some sense likely a proxy for Mataji herself, is informal and welcoming, as each devotee approaches her individually for a sip of the water used in the *ārati*. In this sense, she is perhaps more like the attendant of a local village shrine than some orthodox temple priest.

*Ārati* is subject to much less ritual discourse than Gayatri recitation and *yajña*, and so there is little to say here in terms of what it has to do with science. It is nevertheless clear enough that it serves an important role for upwardly mobile but disillusioned Hindus. This is because *ārati* to Gayatri Mata, especially in the particular manner in which it is conducted at Shantikunj, provides a connection to popular ritual activities of provincial India without ever straying from the Vedic revivalist message of the Gayatri Pariwar.

Figure 4.1. Gayatri Mata Mandir, Shantikunj.

## Gayatri Recitation

### Practice

There was one span of time in particular when I made a concerted effort toward intensive Gayatri recitation. Prior to my arrival at Shantikunj, I had heard that it was possible to take a nine-day program as an introduction to Gayatri Pariwar practice. Although I asked Somnath to let me undertake this program early on in the course of my fieldwork, he suggested that it would be particularly difficult to be awake during Haridwar's cold winter mornings. When the weather started to become more pleasant, I reminded him of this conversation and he suggested that there were some conferences happening soon at DSVV, then it would be Holi, so I should wait a little longer still.

Once Holi had come and gone, I spoke with Somnath again, and he recommended that I should do it during *Vasant Navarātrī*, since Gayatri parijans believe that the benefits of all of their practices are intensified during *Navarātrī*. This nine-day program turned out to be an *anuṣṭhān*, the same program that Gyaneshwar had undertaken at the last stage of his conversion experience. In short, it entails following the ashram schedule rigorously while remaining celibate, eating very plain foods, living simply, and perhaps most importantly, reciting thirty *mālās* (3,240 repetitions, roughly a four-hour process; a *mālā* is a string of 108 prayer beads) of the Gayatri mantra per day for eight days. I would do this over the course of three shifts between dawn and dusk, sitting in a different place for each shift. As a supplement to my interviews with Gayatri parijans about these practices, most of whom stuck closely to the movement's official discourse in their replies, I will interrogate my own experiences during Gayatri recitation as a way to better understand the practice.

During *anuṣṭhān*, Somnath encouraged me to recite about half of my *mālās* for the day around sunrise, and so I generally started the first of three sittings at 6 a.m. After circumambulating the outdoor *samādhi* (burial shrine) of Gurudev and Mataji, I found a spot nearby and began my first set of Gayatri recitations. Somnath had suggested the spot near the *samādhi* as a particularly good place to do this practice, and dozens of other Gayatri parijans were in the area doing the same. Sitting on the cool marble floor or on simple mats, the practitioners faced the *samādhi* and mouthed the Gayatri mantra in near silence. We each held a *mālā* in our right hand, generally hidden by a shawl, to keep track of our numerous recitations. With few exceptions, the assembled Gayatri parijans maintained an intense focus on their recitation; even if they were sitting with friends or family members, their mouths rarely stopped their recitation and their eyes remained either closed or fixed upon the *samādhi*. Even my presence, a rarity at an almost exclusively Indian ashram, did not provoke the usual curious stares from those who were engaged in Gayatri recitation.

Several days into the *anuṣṭhān*, a group of visitors arrived at the ashram and stood near the *samādhi*, taking in the sight of the practitioners

Figure 4.2. *Samādhi* (Memorial) to Gurudev and Mataji, Shantikunj.

who had gathered for their morning Gayatri recitations. One man in this group noticed me, broke away from his group somewhat spontaneously, walked toward me smiling, and reverently touched my feet. The ethnographer in me wanted to drop my *mālā* on the spot and ask the man why he had chosen to engage with me in this manner and not any of the other countless ashram residents nearby. But as my mind raced to process our encounter and considered how best to respond, the man moved on and the opportunity to question him slipped away. I suspect that this visitor found me to be a striking sight, my red beard and freckled complexion juxtaposed against the saffron *kurtā* and *dhotī* that all male ashram residents wear. The startling sight of a foreigner like me engaged in Gayatri recitation must have been charged with a greater emotional intensity than the far-less-surprising sight of Indians engaged in the same practice nearby.

I understand emotions like the one experienced by this ashram visitor to be a constructive force of ritual's capacity to structure identities and communities.[2] Sara Ahmed's notion of affective economies illustrates how this works. In an affective economy, an object of emotion circulates between bodies, molding these bodies to a particular shape in the process and aligning similarly disposed bodies together.[3] I understand ritual activity as a kind of labor that establishes an affective economy, structuring the selves of ritual actors as their bodies experience the objects of emotion embedded in the framework of their ritual activity. I may have thought myself to have been simply engaged in an act of participant-observation, but by reciting the Gayatri mantra in that place, in those clothes, as a Westerner, I had inadvertently broadened the circulation of the Gayatri mantra, strengthening its affective currency in the process.[4]

The surprise that this ashram visitor experienced at seeing me engaged in Gayatri recitation is no doubt partially a result of the fact that I am very clearly not of a twice-born caste. There is no dharmic obligation for a non-Brahmin male like me to undertake this practice; moreover, this practice would have, from an orthodox standpoint, traditionally been verboten to someone of my impure ritual status. My ability to practice Gayatri recitation with no requirement for conversion or initiation reflects the Gayatri Pariwar's deep commitment to the idea that its practices, including Gayatri recitation, can be taken up at any time by anyone, regardless of caste, gender, or indeed, nationality. As such, the Gayatri Pariwar's efforts to revive Vedic-style ritual are broader in scope and more radical than those of the Arya Samaj, which were focused on Indians and involved a "reconversion" ceremony.[5]

On most days, I would do my afternoon Gayatri recitation around 11:30 a.m. sitting on my bed. During the morning session, it was clear how Gayatri recitation helped to circulate emotion because it was a public performance of piety. But I would suggest that even performing a ritual in private can add intensity to this affective economy. An academic reader might say that it was ridiculous for me to do this ritual practice in private—I wasn't really learning anything by watching or interacting with others in public as I performed the ritual, and I wasn't doing the *anuṣṭhān* out of any kind of earnest piety. What compelled me to keep working toward the full number of recitations, even though no one would have been the wiser had I skipped? I felt things. I felt respect for my host community, and a desire not to betray them. I felt a responsibility as an ethnographer to engage honestly with the ritual life of Shantikunj. I felt an obligation to them to strive sincerely to fulfill the vow I made at the beginning of the *anuṣṭhān*. Even when I was performing this ritual in private and as a participant-observer, the ritual bound me to the community through these feelings.

For my final evening session of Gayatri recitation, I would settle into one of the rishi shrines that ringed the courtyard near the Gayatri Devi temple at around 4:30 p.m. While I originally chose this location because it was close to the location of my afternoon *seva* and the evening's *ārati*, I found that I particularly enjoyed sitting in these spots, where I had more seclusion than I did near the *samādhi* but could still people-watch. Moreover, I liked sitting near the rishis' statues, especially if I could manage to squeeze into Yajñavālkya's shrine.[6] Yajñavālkya's sense of humor made him a favorite of mine,[7] and sitting in the presence of his image chanting a Vedic mantra, I could not help but feel a certain emotional connection with him, as a character, through the medium of his image. Thus, even with all of the baggage I carried along with me as an ethnographer, my ritualistic recitation of the Gayatri mantra established an affective economy, saturating Yajñavālkya with affect, creating a sense of affinity between, the statue, the character, and myself.

Despite seeming like an internal, personal practice, during each of my three daily sittings for Gayatri recitation, my attitudes and relations toward the people and objects around me came to the fore and were reinforced. This primarily had to do with my identity as an ethnographer, as sitting after sitting, hour after hour, I labored away at understanding the Gayatri Pariwar through this form of respectful engagement with a practice that they valued immensely. Whatever my motives, I participated in the same affective economy that other Gayatri parijans do when they recite the Gayatri mantra. Only, my ethnographic training became a sort of ritual discourse that shaped the way I participated in this economy.

## Discourse

My own experiences only go so far in understanding how ritual works for Gayatri parijans. When I asked community members about the ritual life of the community, they often pointed toward Gurudev's book *Gayatri Mahavigyan* (also called *Super Science of Gayatri* in translation) as the best way to deepen my understanding of the significance of Gayatri Pariwar practices. In my conversations with many residents of Shantikunj, this was one of the first texts I was told to read if I wanted to understand the movement—just after Gurudev's autobiographical works. This text also played an important role in the conversion narratives of a number of Gayatri parijans who emphasize their scientific temper. A.K., for example, was a medical doctor born in 1936 in Madhya Pradesh. When he read *Gayatri Mahavigyan* in 1960, he found its "science of consciousness" compelling because it went beyond the medical science of the day. He resolved that as a "man of science," he should meet with Gurudev to question him further on the text. Given the abundance of similar sentiments at Shantikunj, this text is an extremely useful source for understanding the way the movement understands Gayatri recitation as a universal technology of moral self-fashioning with a scientific basis.

*Gayatri Mahavigyan* serves as a relatively comprehensive discussion of the Gayatri mantra and its practice. It starts with a discussion of the origin (*utpatti*) of Vedmātā Gayatri (the Goddess Gayatri, understood as mother of the Vedas), enumerates the benefits of Gayatri recitation, explains the mechanics of these benefits, clarifies that it is a practice—contrary to popular misconception—that everyone can participate in, and details how the practice should be done. The role of scientific authority comes to the fore as Gurudev describes the benefits of Gayatri recitation and the mechanisms by which they accrue. I want to highlight some of the ways in which Gurudev deploys the idea of science in this text, simultaneously emphasizing the universality of this practice and its rationality. By working through this text, I will illustrate the range of meanings signified by these practices and why skeptical readers like A.K. might feel compelled to take these practices up.

Early on in *Gayatri Mahavigyan*, Gurudev describes how the Gayatri mantra activates twenty-four energy centers located in the body and in turn twenty-four related desirable personal qualities—in other words, it cultivates virtue. He treats this as a completely psychosomatic process rather than one that involves divine intervention, saying, "Once they understand that transformations are taking place as a result of their own *Sadhana* [effort, practice] they would realize that it is not by way of some unexpected gift from somewhere but is the result of a well organized scientific process of spiritual growth. *Gayatri Sadhana* is not based on blind faith but has a solid scientific basis."[8] The logic embedded in Gurudev's thought here seems to be that expecting Gayatri recitation to pay off through a divine boon amounts to blind faith, whereas regarding the practice to benefit one through psychosomatic mechanisms is scientific.

Gurudev likely recognized that his psychosomatic account of why the Gayatri mantra is effective might put him at odds with popular piety—which would run counter to his populist orientation. By treating

Gayatri recitation as purely psychosomatic, he removes the deity from the picture and risks falling into the hyper-rational elitist impiety like many other Hindu reform movements, thereby alienating his popular support base. Without deviating from his psychosomatic model of religious practice, he preempts such concerns by emphasizing "confidence coupled with faith," arguing, "Psychologists are well acquainted with the power of self-confidence. Instances have been cited in several of my books and articles to prove that only on account of imaginary fear people met untimely death and persons who were almost dead got new life on account of faith and confidence."[9] Faith here does not bring boons from deities; rather, Gurudev treats it as an orientation whose seemingly miraculous benefits are completely psychosomatic and accounted for by the field of psychology. Indeed, Gurudev later suggests that it is an orientation that is necessary to realize the benefits of Gayatri recitation because practitioners who have found Gayatri recitation efficacious

> do not subscribe to the scientific rationale that the miraculous looking boons are the reward of their own self-effort. They ascribe them to the Divine Mother's grace. Thus their egos are subdued. . . . Even though the benefits which *Gayatri Sadhana* provides are the result of an exact scientific method, it is necessary to have feelings of deep gratitude and devotion to the Divine Mother, whose manifestation in creation each soul is.[10]

Science and popular piety are thus reconciled. It is possible to understand the psychosomatic effects of Gayatri recitation, but desirable for the sake of personal development to continue regarding these effects as having an external, divine source. Through this logic, devotion itself is subsumed under the psychosomatic paradigm because it becomes a means to personal development and perhaps even a prerequisite for realizing the benefits of Gayatri recitation.

While articulating the power unlocked by Gayatri recitation, Gurudev shifts tactics, illustrating his points by way of analogy to established scientific concepts. According to Gurudev, at the base of our spine, an atom (*paramāṇu*) called *kūrma* is attached to the *brahmanāḍī*[11] at the base of the spine, where the *brahmanāḍī* coils around the *kūrma*, forming the kundalini.[12] After describing this subtle physiology, Gurudev argues that this feature of the human body is the key to unlocking limitless and powerful "vital energy" or *prāṇ* by way of an analogy with nuclear power. The text quotes physicist Arthur Compton at some length, as he waxes poetic about the seemingly limitless new possibilities harnessing nuclear energy will bring to human society.

The text offers surprising detail in pursuing this analogy:

> *Kundalini* centre is the most suitable location for breaking and uniting two living atoms and for transforming them, because living (*Chaitanya*) atoms at all other places in the body are round and smooth, whereas in *Kundalini* this pair clings together. In uranium and plutonium the interlocking of atoms is in an oblique, irregular manner so that their breaking-up is easy as compared to the atoms of other metals. In the same manner it is easier to regulate the movement of living atoms located in *Kundalini*, according to one's desire.[13]

Here we see that Gurudev not only draws on scientific authority to explain the results of Gayatri recitation, but also to explain the mechanisms by which those results are achieved. The text describes atoms in our subtle physiology as working according to the same natural laws as fissile materials. By presenting the results of Gayatri recitation and the mechanisms by which they are achieved as consistent with known laws of nature, this rhetoric persuades readers like Gyaneshwar that this practice is consistent with his identity as a man of science.

Not only does our subtle physiology offer possibilities similar to that of splitting the atom, it has been researched by an analogous methodology in the ancient world:

> Just as scientists of every country today are busy in doing research on physical atom, the spiritual scientists, *rishis* who had realized the truth, had conducted deep research in ancient times on living atoms in human body in seed form. . . . Research about *Kundalini* was done with the same precision in ancient times as scientists are doing these days in respect of material atoms.[14]

This is a central aspect of Gayatri Pariwar discourse. Indeed, within minutes of arriving at Shantikunj for the first time, I was told that the rishis were scientists and that the Vedas are the recorded results of their experiments. As such, all of the experimentation the Gayatri Pariwar conducts is about recovering knowledge that the rishis already generated rather than somehow displacing their work with new knowledge. It is easy for me to see how this reading could be compelling. A more traditional account of the origin of the Vedas says that they are simply woven into the cosmos as a fundamental component of the fabric of reality. In this scheme, the role of the rishis was not to receive the Vedas from some divine source, but rather to perceive and record them. This emphasis on the rishis as simply observing something in nature and recording it makes the idea of presenting them as functionally similar to modern scientists less of a leap and more of a short hop. As was the case with Gayatri Pariwar rhetoric reconciling popular piety with science, this subtle reconciliation of traditional authority figures like the rishis with scientific authority saves the Gayatri Pariwar's reformist rationality from straying too far from popular piety.

A third tactic for legitimizing Gayatri practice through scientific authority is closely related to Gurudev's discourse about the rishis as scientists. For a sufficiently skeptical reader, it might seem problematic to suggest that the rishis alone were capable of scientifically validating Vedic-style ritual practice. Their observations should, in the universalist rhetorics of the modern sciences, be repeatable by anyone. Perhaps anticipating such a concern, Gurudev suggests that they are indeed repeatable, but only with suitably well developed technology: "Sound waves, atoms or air, germs of diseases cannot be seen by the naked eye, still their existence cannot be denied. *Yogis* have seen these *Chakras* by their yogic vision and have gained miraculous knowledge, insights, and powers through investigations of the inner being of man."[15] Yogic vision thus becomes a desirable research instrument that may be used to observe firsthand the workings of one's subtle physiology. Admittedly, we are again working by analogy to science here, or more specifically to the scientific method. But there is an important distinction to be made: in this analogy, Gurudev speaks to the possibility that a sufficiently advanced practitioner can empirically confirm their subtle physiology. This promise of empirical proof thus represents a third way to call upon scientific authority to legitimize ritual practice.

In sum, Gurudev's discourse about Gayatri recitation in *Gayatri Mahavigyan* suggests that this practice will have the same positive effects on every body, regardless of caste, gender, religion, or culture, because we all have the same innate capacities built into our subtle physiology. Its positive effects can be observed by anyone, once again regardless of their identity. By presenting the results of Gayatri recitation, the mechanisms by which they are achieved, and the ways in which they are known as consistent with known laws of nature and empirical-rational epistemologies, this discourse allows readers who identify with the idea of science to experience Gayatri recitation as a practice that is consistent with their identity. In other words, this ritual practice is rendered coherent with their emotional investment in the idea of science.

My conversations with Gayatri parijans about Gayatri recitation engaged themes that were very similar to those found in *Gayatri Mahavigyan*. My conversation with Ashutosh illustrates these similarities well. After moving to Shantikunj to escape the unfulfilling life he had working for transnational firms in Mumbai and Bangalore, he found great fulfillment in the Gayatri Pariwar's efforts to revitalize society, and saw Gayatri recitation as the key to this process:

> So [the reform of society] can only be a divine wish, for which [Gurudev] is an instrument. And he chose the Gayatri mantra, which is a universal prayer; it is not confined to a specific sect or religion. . . . This he propagated throughout India and across the world. . . . He chose Gayatri mantra to elevate the intellect of the common masses so that they can rise above their very selfish lives and work toward their own spiritual good and also uplift the society as a whole.

Ashutosh's emphasis on the universality of this practice and its efficacy for instilling moral virtue reflects Gurudev's discourse very closely.

In terms of the scientific basis of these practices, Ashutosh told me that for his part, he was willing to take all of Gurudev's teachings on faith. But Gyaneshwar had a different experience. It is worth reexamining his discussion of *Gayatri Mahavigyan* in the context of the relationships between ritual, science, and emotion:

> I read that and the way of explanation, the way of presentation and the reasoning behind all these practices given by Gurudev influenced me a lot and I understood properly why we do all these things. Till then my understanding was that it's just mainly a ritual, they are performing superstitiously. Then I came to know what the scientific reason behind this is.

Gyaneshwar resolved to undertake an *anuṣṭhān* in his home village upon completing the book, and soon after repeated this process at Shantikunj. Gurudev's scientific discourse in *Gayatri Mahavigyan* changed Gyaneshwar's emotional orientation toward ritualized Gayatri recitation. Prior to reading this text, Gyaneshwar felt that there was a disjuncture between his identity as a scientific person and ritual practice. This disjuncture evoked Gyaneshwar's contempt for superstition. But reading *Gayatri Mahavigyan* and its presentation of Gayatri recitation as scientific changed Gyaneshwar's emotional relation to the practice, rendering it coherent with his identity. Gyaneshwar's body was aligned with the practice and eventually with the community of similarly disposed bodies at Shantikunj.

## *Yajña*

### Practice

*Yajña* starts at 5:45 and runs for about three hours, as groups pass through the ashram's three *yajña* pavilions one after another. No one group generally does the full *yajña*. Only the first group opens the *yajña*, kindling the fire and undertaking other preliminary steps. The last group into the pavilion is similarly responsible for extinguishing the sacrificial flame and closing the ritual. Bookended by these two groups performing slightly more extensive rituals, the many other groups who sit in their turn around the fire altar have a relatively short, five-to-ten-minute-long ritual to perform.

I did not just participate in *yajña* during my attempted *anuṣṭhān*. In fact, my very first morning I was awakened around 7 a.m. to participate in the ritual. Bleary-eyed, I was ushered through the frigid January twilight to a room near the *yajña* pavilions, where, confused but compliant, I was helped into a saffron *dhotī* by a small group of ashram men. We joined what seemed to be the shortest of the three queues outside the *yajña* pavilions. I could hear the dozens of worshippers packed into each pavilion chanting, progressing through the *yajña*'s multiple stages.

After what seemed to be quite a long time, but was likely only a few minutes, it was time to gather around the fire altar—a far more adequate source of warmth than my thin woolen shawl. There are eight fire altars in each pavilion, and about eight people sit around each altar—men and women, residents and visitors, Brahmins and non-Brahmins, friends, family, and strangers all intermixed. To the accompaniment of various mantras, I attempted to imitate those unfortunate enough to be sitting near me, but they often had to correct me. But several months later, by the time I was doing the *anuṣṭhān*, I had the motions—if not the mantras—down pat. The first few steps of the ritual are mostly about purification: sprinkling water on ourselves, sipping it, touching our moistened fingers to the back of our heads, where adult male Gayatri parijans have a small braid, called a *śikā*, observing breath control by breathing in one nostril and out the other, and finally touching our moistened fingers to our mouth, nostrils, eyes, ears, arms, and legs. The ritual actors then offer praise to the earth, anoint one another with sandalwood paste and rice, worship the fire altar, and recite some prayers to a variety of deities. The central part of the ritual involves chanting the Gayatri mantra:

> *oṃ bhūr bhuvaḥ svaḥ tat savitur vareṇyaṃ*
> *bhargo devasya dhīmahi dhiyo yo naḥ pracodayāt*

After each repetition, we say "*svāhā*," an utterance associated with offering as we deposit a mixture of herbs called *samāgrī*. After this offering, we say "*idaṃ gāyatryai idaṃ na mama*,"[16] which is supposed to dedicate the offering to the deity, not the ritualist's potentially selfish ends. This procedure is repeated numerous times,[17] with each repetition flowing into the next. After making a smaller number of offerings of *samāgrī* to other deities, we got up to allow the next group their turn.

There are two particularly noteworthy touchstones that help to shape the emotions and meanings that circulate during these ritual practices. The first of these was the massive public *yajña* Gurudev organized in 1958 as described in the opening of this chapter. Relatively few of Shantikunj's current residents were present at the event, but I would be surprised if any of the community's adult residents had not heard of it. The founding of Akhand Jyoti and later Shantikunj may have laid the institutional and material framework for the movement in ways that the 1958 *yajña* did not, but those events are not mythologized in the same way as this *yajña* because their relatively mundane accomplishments did not have such affective import.

The 1958 *yajña* was a large-scale public event with obvious religiopolitical import. A great deal of literature on Vedic-style rituals conducted in India in the last twenty years or so since the ascent of Hindu Nationalism focuses on such public rituals and their political significance. For example, in "Riots and Rituals: The Construction of Violence and Public Space in Hindu Nationalism," Peter van der Veer examines a series of *yajña* the Vishwa Hindu Parishad conducted in the 1980s. These rituals communicated a national unity under a Hindu banner, excluding non-Hindus from the nation just as they were excluded from the ritual.[18] Timothy Lubin describes an elaborate, multi-day *yajña* as being the center of a public spectacle in "Veda on Parade: Revivalist Ritual as Civic Spectacle." Observing that the social and political situation in contemporary India is quite different from the situation in the classical period, Lubin notes that this spectacle became an opportunity to propagate modern ideology.[19] In *Everyday Nationalism*, Kalyani Menon suggests that by being public, Hindu Nationalist *yajña* differentiate themselves from more traditional *yajña*, like that documented in Frits Staal's *Altar of Fire*, where non-Brahmins could not be present. In contrast, at a VHP *yajña* honoring soldiers who had died in the Kargil War, Menon notes that the ritual space was shared with non-Brahmins—Sikhs in particular. As with other VHP *yajña*, the ritual was for an explicitly public purpose, and anyone whom Hindu nationalists regard as Hindu—Sikhs, Buddhists, and Jains—were welcomed into the ritual space, while Muslims and Christians were excluded.[20] The public performance of *yajña* described by Menon, Lubin, and van der Veer communicate a range of ideologies while marking public space, and indeed the space of the nation, as Hindu.

Gurudev's 1958 *yajña* was performed in an earlier era, before the public *yajña* had been established as a standard Hindu nationalist stunt. But it is clear that it staked out an ideological stance and rallied a community around that stance—a community that would eventually become the Gayatri Pariwar. A large and controversial public event—a spectacle, in Lubin's sense—the 1958 *yajña* raised a rather provocative challenge to the notion of male Brahminical priestly privilege. It was a kind of political action, only instead of holding signs and chanting in protest, they were holding *samāgrī* and chanting the Gayatri mantra.

With this historical event forming such a significant role in the Gayatri Pariwar's institutional memory, the affective resonance of that act of protest remains, even in everyday practice at Shantikunj. Each morning men and women from various castes sit around the fire as family, friends, neighbors, and even perfect strangers to perform their nearly identical roles in the *yajña*. They conjure up this affective resonance, giving it shape, and it in turn gives shape to them: they are not casteist; they are not sexist.

For upwardly mobile but disillusioned Hindus, the traditional Hindu ritual life that shaped their bodies over the course of their upbringings is brought into line with their modern universalist outlooks.

The 1958 *yajña* is not the only historical touchstone shaping the affective economies that everyday *yajña* sustains. The series of ritual-experiments that Doctor-sahib conducted in the *yajña* laboratory were not as outwardly dramatic in Gayatri Pariwar history as the 1958 *yajña*, to be sure. But the reverence with which some Gayatri parijans treated this laboratory indicated that it was quite important to the Gayatri Pariwar, so it would be a mistake to overlook it completely. As I discussed in the last chapter, the instrumentality of the *yajña* lab for establishing Doctor-sahib's authority results partly from the feelings his ritual-experiments instilled in Gayatri parijans. For many STEM-educated Shantikunj residents, ritual practice can reinforce these feelings.

Since Gayatri Pariwar discourse understands personal experience as scientific proof, *yajña* performers' bodies become the *yajña* lab. In a tiny space, the *yajña* pavilions at Shantikunj cram together dozens of bodily laboratories at a time, each one affirming the others' experiments. The affective economy is again established as these affirmations circulate among the ritual performers: they are rational; they are scientific. For upwardly mobile but disillusioned Hindus, the Hindu ritual life that shaped their bodies over the course of their upbringings is brought into line with the scientific rationality that shaped their bodies over the course of their STEM education.

## Discourse

The results of Doctor-sahib's experiments and others like them are summarized in a pamphlet called *The Integrated Science of Yagya*.[21] In this work by Rajani Joshi, the Gayatri Pariwar's ritual discourse takes a more material turn. This work focuses on what happens chemically when one performs *yajña* and on its potential environmental and medical benefits. This publication seems to reflect the Gayatri Pariwar's evolving ritual discourse after the death of Gurudev, and so it merits closer consideration.

After enumerating substances that are burned during a *yajña*, Joshi offers an analysis of the chemical composition of the resulting smoke—thymol, formaldehyde, acetic acid, methyl alcohol, etc.[22] Having established this chemical composition, Joshi goes onto situate this practice among the evils of modernity, such as "industrial wastes, rapid urbanization, deforestation, air and water pollution, disturbances in the ozone layer formation, radioactive waves, etc."[23] But *yajña* can help ameliorate some of these negative effects. Joshi argues that the formaldehyde found in *yajña* smoke has a disinfectant effect that kills bacteria. He similarly asserts that it kills or repels pests and protects crops naturally. While articulating these benefits, he references a number of studies that show that ghee burnt in a *yajña* protects a space from radiation, for example, and improves the chemical composition of nearby air while killing waterborne bacteria.[24]

Moving on to medical applications of *yajña*, Joshi asserts that "In a physical laboratory, it might not be possible to demonstrate the spiritual effects of *yagna*, but the physical and mental effects of *yagnas* can certainly be tested, and the claims to cure physical and mental diseases through *yagna* can be verified."[25] This signals a shift to the body, which is the locus of "spiritual effects," although according to Joshi these cannot be verified. Thus, he moves to the physical and mental and thereby the material. Joshi argues that inhalation is a superior vector for medication because it is faster acting than ingestion but less invasive than injection; thus, *yajña* already has an advantage over other medical treatments. He envisions "Yagnopathy" as having a place among other treatments forms of treatment—with adequate research. As in the previous section, Joshi describes a number of studies in which subjects were exposed to both a fake and real *yajña* and then their biometrics were recorded. Only the real *yajña* brought about an improvement in their conditions. Another case study presents blood sugar data from a diabetic before and after taking up regular *yajña*, again demonstrating improvements.[26]

At this point it will be helpful to draw some comparisons between *Gayatri Mahavigyan* and *The Integrated Science of Yagya*. Gurudev's approach to marshaling scientific authority involved asserting that Gayatri recitation did not work by divine intervention, showing how this practice was analogous to modern scientific ideas, and affirming that practitioners could empirically observe all of this for themselves. The representative examples I offered were almost entirely about the psychosomatic effects of Gayatri practice and generally referred to subtle physiology to make its points. In contrast, Joshi spends very little time discussing the psychosomatic and subtle physiological effects of *yajña*, bracketing it mostly in a five-page-long section at the very end of the work. Joshi instead focuses on chemistry, ecology, and medicine—all quite thoroughly in the material realm—and marshals a conception of science that is primarily laboratory based and conducted by professional researchers.

Historically speaking, the difference in the scientific rhetorics deployed by these two books may reflect changing conceptions of science, or at least what kind of science could be considered persuasive: laboratory science may seem more authoritative in post–IT-boom India than the kind of scientific rhetoric Gurudev deploys in *Gayatri Mahavigyan*. Perhaps *yajña*, with its obvious materiality, is easier than Gayatri recitation to subsume into the kind of materialist ontology laboratory science requires. On the other hand, Gayatri recitation seems rather internal and personal, thereby perhaps better suited for association with scientific rhetorics that focus on analogy and psychosomatic manipulation of subtle physiology. A move toward laboratory science may almost necessitate a shift in rhetorical focus from *yajña* to Gayatri recitation, although officially the Gayatri Pariwar still considers Gayatri recitation to be slightly more important than *yajña*. If such a shift in focus has in fact taken place, it would, finally, correlate interestingly with the leadership of Doctor-sahib, who was involved in laboratory research just like that described by Joshi.

## A Ritualized Day

The routine aspects of life at Shantikunj, well illustrated by the rigorous schedule depicted in table 4.1, were for a long time deeply frustrating to me. I worried that with things so stable, so regimented from day to day, my publications would lack the variegated and colorful anecdotes that marked the very best ethnographic writing I had read. But when I raised this concern with colleagues, they correctly pointed me toward the fact that the existence of this routine offered its own analytical possibilities that might be absent from a more chaotic environment. In hindsight, this seems like such an obvious angle to take: it suits the Gayatri Pariwar's scientific rhetoric perfectly.

The Gayatri Pariwar's scientific rhetoric emphasizes direct and natural causal links between a practice and its benefit. Rituals like *yajña* or Gayatri recitation are thus understood through a sort of functionalist logic. The ritualist performs a specific, predetermined set of actions and

Table 4.1. Shantikunj's Daily Routine[27]

| | **April–September** | **October–March** |
|---|---|---|
| Awaking Prayer | 3:30 a.m. | 4 a.m. |
| Morning *Ārati* | 4 a.m. | 4:30 a.m. |
| Guided Meditation | 4:30 a.m. | 5 a.m. |
| Darshan: Akhand Deep and Gurudev and Mataji's quarters | 5:15 a.m. | 5:45 a.m. |
| *Yajña* and *Saṃskāras* | 5:15 a.m. | 5:45 a.m. |
| Gayatri Recitation | 5:15 to 6 a.m. | 5:45 to 6:30 a.m. |
| Audience with Doctor-sahib and Jiji | 7 a.m. | 7:30 a.m. |
| Morning sermons and discourses | 8:30 a.m. | |
| First Meal | 10 a.m. | |
| Darshan: Akhand Deep and Gurudev and Mataji's quarters | 12 to 1:30 p.m. and 2 to 4:30 p.m. | |
| Jyoti Avdharan Sadhana | 1:30 to 2:30 p.m. | |
| Noon Classes | 2:30 to 4 p.m. | |
| Second Meal | 4:30 to 6 p.m. | |
| Evening *Ārati* | 5 to 5:30 p.m. | |
| *Nādyog* Meditation | 6:to 6:15 p.m. | |
| Gayatri Recitation | 6:15 to 7 p.m. | |
| Evening Discourses | 7:00 to 8:30 p.m. | |
| Night Rest | 8:30 p.m. | |

consequently receives a specific, predetermined result. Its mechanism is no less predictable than gravity causing dropped objects to fall to the earth. In this sense, ritual is absorbed into the nature-as-clockwork attitude of post-Enlightenment thought, and performing a ritual is simply a way of winding the clock. A regimented lifestyle at the ashram is nothing new, but it nonetheless ties to this aspect of the Gayatri Pariwar's worldview in an important way. Such daily routines are, themselves, rituals on a large scale. As such, the same functionalist, natural cause-and-effect logic applies to whole days at Shantikunj. To offer a less regimented day would be to offer a less scientifically formulated day with less perfectly predictable results.

Shantikunj's daily routine is thus easily rendered coherent with the particular scientific worldview espoused by the Gayatri Pariwar and emphasized in its ritual discourse. As was the case with an individual element like *yajña*, ashram residents following the daily routine are like so many researchers attempting to reproduce the results of one another's experiments as a sort of collective mutual validation. Through this process, Gayatri Pariwar rituals are rendered predictable, reliable technologies of moral self-fashioning. Here we see the beginnings of how the Gayatri Pariwar finds a place for the prestige of the STEM fields in its moral project. Gayatri Pariwar rituals are scientifically legitimated technologies for inscribing moral virtue on the body. And as I will show, Gayatri parijans understand the production of these moral bodies in sufficient numbers as the foundation for the global social transformation they aim to bring about: *satyug.*

CHAPTER 5

# Mataji and Jiji

On the exceedingly rare occasions that I left the speaker system in my room on overnight, it would come alive at about 4 a.m. An old audio recording of Mataji singing solemnly in Hindi would break the predawn silence, gently encouraging me to start my day. Night owl that I am, I generally did not appreciate this wakeup call. But for Shantikunj residents accustomed to the rigors of ashram life and personally invested in the community's familial ethos, I am sure it was refreshing to awaken to the voice of the Gayatri Pariwar's collective mother. Mataji's voice guides her children in Shantikunj through many of the community's daily ritual events, and finally, at 9 p.m., she emotively sings the day's final prayer, a sort of lullaby to conclude the day's ritual cycle.

Very early on in the course of my fieldwork at Shantikunj it became quite clear that Mataji and her daughter, Jiji, play an important role for the community. Since I have already given substantial attention to their husbands, I am overdue to consider the important contributions these women make to their community. Although it is clear enough that they lead within a structure that grants more authority to their husbands, I would suggest that much of the success of the movement rests upon these matriarchs' heads. Without their leadership, the affective bonds that give Gayatri parijans their much-celebrated sense of kinship would be far weaker.

The notion that the Gayatri Pariwar is quite literally the family of Gayatri fits a fairly widespread pattern for modern Hindu-based spiritual movements. Followers of such movements often consider one another to be collective children of their guru. Consequently, it could be easy to dismiss the kinship imagery in the Gayatri Pariwar as not pointing to anything novel or interesting. But I want to suggest, taking my cues from Shantikunj residents, that understanding this sense of kinship is crucial for understanding the Gayatri Pariwar. Considering this sense of kinship brings into focus some of the important but easily overlooked contributions the movement's female leadership makes. Their affective work in establishing this sense of kinship is an essential part of the appeal of the Gayatri Pariwar. This sense of kinship sets the Gayatri Pariwar in opposition to the alienating and morally ambiguous qualities of professional life in neoliberal India, instead framing the movement and its project with reference to the moral qualities of the family. The affective work performed by Mataji and Jiji is thus central to the Gayatri Pariwar's moral project and in turn the movement's ability to restore moral legitimacy to the knowledge and skills of the Gayatri Pariwar's disillusioned STEM professionals.

Before delving into material that mentions Mataji and Jiji specifically, I want to consider some of the sentiments Gayatri parijans expressed in interviews about the importance of the sense of kinship for their movement. While they generally do not mention Mataji or Jiji explicitly, a consideration of the movement's discourse about these women in the following section will clearly show how they shape this atmosphere of kinship. After a brief discussion of how the Gayatri Pariwar understands Mataji and Jiji in comparison to their husbands, I will make use of extant scholarly literature about Hindu women's religious lives to better understand Mataji and Jiji's roles in the Gayatri Pariwar.

## Like a Family

I asked many of the Gayatri parijans with whom I spoke what set the Gayatri Pariwar apart from other similar movements and what drew them in to this movement in particular, expecting them to say something about science. "Well, no other spiritual movement out there has such a large body of scientific data to back up their practices," they would have said. "Ah, I knew it!" I would have responded. Wouldn't that have been nice and neat for me! It also would have made for a boring argument, so thankfully things are much messier in reality: the most common sentiment was that the Gayatri Pariwar was different from other spiritual movements because it is less formal and instead feels like a family.

This attitude was well foreshadowed in Gyaneshwar's conversion narrative as I relayed in chapter 2. When he speaks of his first visit to Shantikunj, he says that Doctor-sahib and Jiji "gave me love and parental care and guidance." Soon after, when he accepted Gurudev as his guru, he decided to abandon not only his own aspirations, but also those of his family. The protestations of his birth family did little to persuade him to continue medical school until he discovered that their will was fortuitously aligned with that of his new family.

We can find a more explicit valuation of Shantikunj's familial atmosphere in the words of Ashutosh:

> There are many spiritual groups in India which are based on the philosophy of monasticism. They do not encourage marriages and they treat that having a life partner as hindering spiritual progress. . . . Gurudev has made the organization in such a way that he himself was a householder. . . . He has written so many books on marriage, on how an ideal marriage should be and how an ideal married life should be. So he always said that husband and wife can be very good supplements toward each other's spiritual progress.

Ashutosh here points to a perception shared by many of the Shantikunj residents with whom I spoke that ashrams are monastic organizations led by renunciant gurus. Indeed, many ashrams associated with reform Hindu traditions may not place restrictions on the genders of their denizens, but often expect them to be celibate and not to raise a family. While Ashutosh equates this mentality with monasticism, I would suggest that Shantikunj is still quite monastic, as indicated by the simple living conditions and intense discipline it encourages. Shantikunj thus offers a householder model for monasticism, bridging in true Gandhian populist style an emphasis on popular Indian values—in this case kinship and child-rearing—with a socially and politically engaged asceticism.

Speaking in response to the same question as Ashutosh, Dina explained how the concept of family fits in with the movement's larger social mission:

> Gurudev said that we have to build up big family. Here you can see in Shantikunj there are more than 500 families living together.

> They have one *administration*, which gives equally to everyone, so nobody quarrels, nobody feels that he is big, I am small. It is not like that. All are the same. All are equal. If these feelings will come in society, there will be no quarreling, no taking from anyone. You can say *violence, crime,* and *theft*[1] are in society, but it will all stop if we give more value to family values.

According to Dina, the movement is thus particularly appealing because of its familial approach, and more specifically its affirmation of the role of family values—that most fundamental and enduring of populist sentiments—in the reform of society. This sense of the Gayatri Pariwar as an actual family has a clear connection not only to its utopian social vision, but also to its popular appeal.

Chandrakala expressed similar sentiments while describing the Gayatri Pariwar's mission:

> *My mother and father sometimes phone, I phone them,*[2] but I don't miss them! And even they don't miss me! Because they know that I am here for my spiritual growth and also in a family. *Sādhūs and sants went here, went to the forest, left their homes and then they went for their own spiritual growth, how many can do that?*[3]

Chandrakala views the householder-ashram model as more feasible for ordinary people because they don't have to give up their family as in the more conventional renunciant model. But she also adds an important sentiment—even thought she has left her biological family, the transition is eased by the sense that she is in a new family.

## Biographical Sketches

This emphasis on family as distinguishing the Gayatri Pariwar and lending to its basic appeal connects intriguingly with the discourse about the Gayatri Pariwar's female leadership. Mataji and Jiji are praised in Gayatri Pariwar discourse for their roles in establishing a family-like atmosphere at Shantikunj—the very atmosphere Gayatri parijans emphasized in their conversations with me. Nonetheless, the official discourse about the role of Mataji and Jiji in establishing this sense of family at Shantikunj and the popular sentiment that this was what sets the Gayatri Pariwar apart were rarely connected, and certainly not in any depth. Perhaps, for most Gayatri parijans, this connection was so obvious that it should be presumed; for others, Mataji's and Jiji's contributions may have been taken for granted. Whatever the case, these women's roles in establishing a feeling of kinship among Shantikunj residents merits sustained consideration since it is demonstrably central to the ethos of the Gayatri Pariwar.

The amount of material available on the Gayatri Pariwar's female leadership is unfortunately somewhat limited. This makes it all the more important to make a concerted effort to think carefully about their roles in the community—there are important blanks that need filling in. It is clear enough that these women's authority in the movement is constrained by the hierarchical structures in which they must work.

My objective in considering the leadership of Mataji and Jiji is not to dwell on the constraining effects of the social norms in which they operate. Rather, I hope to conform to what Ann Gold has identified as a "type 2" approach to scholarship on Hindu women, one that recognizes women's marginal status but nonetheless finds meaning and hope in their personal experiences and everyday practices of empowerment. She distinguishes this approach from a "type 1" approach, which dwells endlessly on a static and inescapable patriarchal web in which women are supposedly helplessly stuck, robbed of meaningful agency.[4] In her work, Gold exemplifies this approach by showing her readers how Rajasthani village women develop "counterpoints" in their performance of yearly holiday rituals that assert women's religious authority within and against an otherwise patriarchal framework.[5] Saba Mahmood has advocated a similar interpretive practice, one that understands how women find agency within a cultural framework that differs from Western liberal norms.[6] With these frameworks in mind, how do Mataji and Jiji make their mark upon the Gayatri Pariwar by establishing a sense of kinship?

I would like to start by examining some of the scant material available on Mataji and Jiji in English—their short biographies on the Gayatri Pariwar's website. Mataji's biography dwells for some time on her maternal affect. After marrying Gurudev, the profile informs us, Mataji "took over the responsibility of looking after visitors and guests,"[7] thereby giving her an important link to hospitality—a key feminine duty in Indian culture. It goes on to characterize her in the following terms:

> Mataji considered everyone as part of her family. It was of prime importance to her, to arrange for their comfortable stay and spiritual guidance. Such was the love and affection that people come to Shantikunj for recharging themselves and to experience the peace and tranquility in their personal lives.[8]

These passages highlight a certain affective work that Mataji engaged in while married to Gurudev. She made those who came to Shantikunj feel loved and cared for, thus making them feel like they had not left home. These forms of affective work—providing hospitality, establishing a sense of kinship, making Shantikunj feel homey—are crucial contributions to the set of feelings that Gayatri parijans describe as setting the Gayatri Pariwar apart from other movements.

While I want to emphasize this affective work, and the tremendous importance it gives Mataji within her social framework, it would be a mistake to suggest that this is the only thing the movement credits her with. During the period of her co-leadership with Gurudev, Mataji led an initiative called the Mahilā Jāgraṇ Abhiyān (Women's Awakening Campaign), which involves, somewhat tellingly, encouraging women to be diligent in their domestic responsibilities. She also seems to have been active in lecturing at Shantikunj. After the death of her spouse in 1990, she briefly assumed full leadership of the Gayatri Pariwar. Much of Mataji's online biography focuses on this period, although a great deal of what is said about her leadership has to do with planning Gurudev's memorial service, serving as a medium for his messages from the subtle realms, and finally rejoining him after her death in 1994.[9] In this way, much of what Mataji accomplished as leader is tied to her relationship with her husband. This returns our attention back to the kinship structures that simultaneously constrain and empower Mataji as a leader of the Gayatri Pariwar.

Jiji's biography lacks the narrative focus of Mataji's, instead taking the form of notes on her role in the Gayatri Pariwar—an approach not terribly different from Doctor-sahib's online "CV" style profile. The sentiments included in Jiji's biography bear quite a bit of resemblance to those in Mataji's biography. For example:

> [An] embodiment of boundless love and affection for each and every one, Shraddheya Shailbala Pandya is revered as Jiji by all parijans of [the] Gayatri Pariwar. Hundreds of parijans

> come to Shantikunj, Haridwar everyday to seek blessings of Guru satta from her. . . .
>
> After the Mahaprayan of Param Vandniya Mataji in 1994, she has been looking after the whole organization with parental care and under the subtler guidance of Guru satta.[10]

Here, again, our attention is brought to the feelings she embodies, the fact that the community reveres her as a "big sister," her ability to provide maternal care, and her ability as Gurudev's daughter to serve as a conduit for Gurudev's guidance and blessings.

As with Mataji, she participated in the Women's Awakening Campaign, and sometimes lectures at Shantikunj. Her biography mentions that she has a master's degree in psychology and attributes "research-oriented thinking" to her during her university years, but does not elaborate on the significance of this training. Her biography also designates her as a "managing trustee" of the community, but does not elaborate on her achievements other than to say that she personally sees to all important correspondence. In general, then, this biography gives me the impression that while she is a modern, educated woman—qualities that align her well with her husband, Doctor-sahib—her clearest roles for the community have to do with how she makes Gayatri parijans feel: loved and cared for, whether by a mother or big sister, and connected to Gurudev, through his daughter. Like Mataji, Jiji's most valued work again seems to be the affective work of making the Gayatri Pariwar feel like a family.

In Hindi-language materials, there is a much more extensive account of Mataji's life available in the form of a text authored under the name "Brahmavarchas" called *Mahāśakti kī Lokyātrā* (*The Worldly Sojourn of the Great Goddess*). This text positions Mataji as the human incarnation of a goddess, and narrates her life in a form that seems to draw inspiration from Purāṇic sources and more recent hagiographical literature. After starting off with a meditation on "the essence of a mother" (*mātṛtattva*), the text details the wondrous visions and auspicious signs her parents experienced ahead of her birth in 1926.[11] In narrating her childhood, the author describes her preternaturally precocious and pious behavior. For example:

> *Sometimes she would quietly sit cross-legged. Seeing her in this enraptured condition, members of the household would be surprised. They were all unaware of her inner condition. None of them*

> *could fathom why this little girl was sitting in quiet solitude in this way. One day, her older brother Deendayal saw her sitting in this way and asked, "Little sister, why are you sitting quietly like this? Why not play with the other children? It looks like you bear the weight of the whole world on your head!" In response to the question, she gazed serenely toward her brother, and spoke in a serious tone, "Yes, as you say! If I did not bear the weight of the whole world, who else would?"*[12]

To further illustrate the early indicators of young Mataji's future calling, the author describes a similar encounter in which an older sibling asks why she spends so much time worshiping Shiva. "*Hey, I do a little bit of puja, and that's enough play for me. I like this way of playing more than any other.*"[13] All of this makes it quite clear that Mataji was no ordinary child, and bolsters the sense that she is in fact a divine incarnation. Her behavior is of course quite different from Krishna's famous childhood mischief in the *Bhāgavata Purāṇa*—Mataji is far better behaved—but like Krishna and a number of saintly figures in the Hindu tradition, the young Mataji shows similar signs of her divinity while those around her seem entirely unaware.

With Mataji's marriage to Gurudev in 1944 and her concurrent passage into adulthood, the story takes a familiar turn in emphasizing her motherhood (*mātṛtva*). This takes the initial form not of giving birth to her own biological children,[14] but rather of gaining the acceptance of her new stepchildren. The scope of her motherhood quickly expands to encompass the community that had formed around Gurudev's nascent periodical, *Akhand Jyoti*, where she handled correspondence and oversaw the treatment of guests.[15] To those guests, the author informs us, it felt "like they had come near their own real mother."[16] The beginnings of the sense that the Gayatri Pariwar could feel like a real family, then, began well before the founding of Shantikunj with the arrival of Mataji at *Akhand Jyoti*. In fact, it is worth noting that after *Akhand Jyoti*'s initial false start in 1938, it did not resume publication until 1946, shortly after Gurudev's marriage to Mataji. While this also corresponds neatly to the end of World War II, which was the stated reason for the initial suspension of publication, it is worth considering that Mataji's partnership and emotional labor may have been crucial in getting *Akhand Jyoti* off the ground.

Given Mataji's role at *Akhand Jyoti*, it is perhaps unsurprising that she soon felt the need to establish a space into which she and Gurudev might welcome the many visitors the publication had began to attract. *Mahāśakti kī Lokyātrā* does in fact attribute to her the founding of Gayatri Tapobhumi, Shantikunj's Mathura-based precursor.[17] Mataji continued to oversee her growing family at *Akhand Jyoti* and Gayatri Tapobhumi, keeping things in order during his lengthy Himalayan peregrinations.[18] The text shifts perspective a number of times when Gurudev makes these pilgrimages, focusing instead on these elements of his hagiography which are so central to the movement's sense of him. The text gives some importance to Mataji in the eventual move to Shantikunj, but even a great deal of this story is about Gurudev's Himalayan inspirations for taking the next step with the movement.[19]

The text continues in a more or less similar fashion, consistently emphasizing Mataji's motherly qualities as the community continues to grow under her watchful eye. After describing her period of leadership after Gurudev's death, the text closes with some discourses she delivered during this period, always addressing her listeners as children.[20] It would seem, then, that this consistently reinforced sense of Mataji's spiritual motherhood was not simply an attribution made to her by others but rather an image that she actively cultivated. This is not to say, however, that she did not also think of herself in other terms or that she was not typecast into this role to a certain extent; nor is it to say that she had complete autonomy in choosing to present herself in this way. Rather, in Mahmood's sense, it is to say that on some level, within the extant constraints, it was a meaningful expression of Mataji's agency—one that had quite an impact on the Gayatri Pariwar.

## Gendered Leadership

The ways in which the Gayatri Pariwar's leadership is gendered will become clearer by thinking briefly about how the movement understands Mataji and Jiji in comparison to their husbands. I have already done a similar analysis of Gurudev and Doctor-sahib in chapter 3, as I considered the ways in which scientific authority eased the routinization of charisma for the movement. I will build upon those comparisons here, following a similar scheme: first looking at names and titles, then at biographical styles, and finally their status in the movement more broadly.

Bhagwati Devi Sharma is *Vandanīya*, venerable, and her daughter Shailbala Pandya is *Śraddheya*, revered. Like Pandit Shriram Sharma Acharya, their titles emerge from the Sanskritic religious lexicon and do not tie them, as with Dr. Pandya, to Western-originated modes of authority. While *doctor*, *pandit*, and *ācārya* are all vocational titles that indicate certain kinds of professional achievements, *vandanīya* and *śraddheya* hold rather different resonances, describing orientations devotees might have toward them. Put slightly differently, they are not about what Mataji and Jiji have accomplished, but rather how they make people feel. Although this style of honorific is generally not applied to Gurudev or Doctor-sahib, there are of course plenty of male honorifics that have the same effect, so perhaps it is best not to read too much into this.

On the other hand, their common, informal designations in the community are perhaps more telling. *Gurudev* and *Doctor-sahib*, as with their more formal titles, speak to a kind of professional achievement, whereas *Mataji* and *Jiji*—mother and big sister, respectively—express familial relationships. It might be tempting under different circumstances to read into this the common pattern of the public, professional male and the private, domestic female. But it is clear enough from the ways in which Mataji and Jiji carry out their maternal and big-sisterly duties as leaders of the Gayatri Pariwar that their domesticity is in fact quite public in nature. Moreover, the authority carried by *Mataji* and *Jiji* is not necessarily quantitatively different from *Gurudev* and *Doctor-sahib*, but rather qualitatively different—their authority plays out through a domestic framework rather than the more vocational framework of a guru or a doctor, but is ultimately applicable to the same public.

In terms of biographical styles, things become a bit more complicated. The lives of Gurudev and Mataji are both presented quite clearly in a hagiographical style. *Mahāśakti kī Lokyātrā* and Gurudev's biographical literature paint their subjects as saintly figures who answer to a higher calling to uplift the world and possess a preternatural piety readers can admire. They nonetheless represent subtle variations on the hagiographical genre. Gurudev, with his epic Himalayan peregrinations, is perhaps closer to the norm for this genre in its modern form. He goes out into the world, experiences adversity, and carries back the authority of incorporeal yogis. While Gurudev might have been born with a special destiny, he had to go out into the world and strive to achieve his saintly guru-hood. Mataji's spiritual talents seem to be much more innate, on the other hand. Narratives about her childhood attribute to her something that goes well beyond an uncanny precocity, putting her in league not only with Rama and Krishna—befitting her own status as an avatar of Mahāśakti—but also countless other saintly figures in Hindu traditions. Mataji has no need to go off to the Himalayas to project religious authority; for her it is innate and fully developed from birth, not acquired. This manifests in her motherly treatment of Gurudev's devotees while he is off on pilgrimage. Her authority is established not through an arduous pilgrimage, but through a performance of her innate ideal femininity.

Given the relative scarcity of biographical material on Jiji, it is difficult to make such a clear analysis, so much of what I say here is tenuous. Although brief, her web biography seems to synthesize elements from Doctor-sahib's and Mataji's. It moves back and forth between points that emphasize her affective work with her Gayatri parijans as a big sister or even in a "parental" fashion and points that are somewhat more akin to Doctor-sahib's cover letter and CV-style biography—highlighting her education and some of her contributions to the movement, some of which are even listed with dates. This synthesis is itself significant: this is a new ideal woman, one who is educated and intellectually engaged like her husband but still completely committed to the cause of her family and capable of carrying out the required affective work of spreading love and compassion. Her authority would then derive from this synthesis—professional credentials are necessary, but they are not sufficient on their own like they are for Doctor-sahib. They must be backed by a suitably feminine pattern of caring for one's family. Her emotional and intellectual labor go hand in hand.

Finally, in terms of Mataji's and Jiji's status within the community, as I have already described in chapter 3, Doctor-sahib and Jiji sit next to each other to receive devotees not as a new guru his and wife, but as stewards of the late Gurudev. There is not much of a comparison to be made between them in this capacity, but the case of Mataji is perhaps more interesting. For several years after Gurudev's death, Mataji served as head of the movement before her daughter and son-in-law took over. But like her successors, she too was a steward for Gurudev, who was now understood to be guiding the movement in his incorporeal state. This is demonstrated by how *Mahāśakti kī Lokyātrā* and especially her web biography both emphasize her arrangements for Gurudev's memorial service, her capacity to channel his messages from the subtle realm, and her eventual reunion with him after death. Although she, too, persists in incorporeal form, I never encountered claims that she subtly guides the movement in the way that Gurudev does. This makes a certain kind of sense: Mataji could not continue her affective work without a body because affective work *is* embodied work.

In sum, these comparisons have demonstrated that unlike their husbands, whose religious and medical accomplishments are front and center in their biographical materials, Mataji and Jiji derive much of their status in the movement from their capacity to make Gayatri parijans feel familial love. For the younger Jiji, these emotional virtues are held in balance with her intellectual virtues. Moving forward now, I will begin to tie the picture that is emerging about Mataji and Jiji into the larger discourse about Hindu women's religious lives.

## Modern Day *Gurumātās*

Mataji and Jiji fit the bill of what has historically been called a *gurumātā*, or guru-mother, which is not to say a female guru, but rather the wife of the guru, who traditionally might act as a kind of surrogate mother to her husband's students.[21] Astonishingly little literature is available on the figure of the *gurumātā*, perhaps in part due to their limited visibility in historical and literary records as well as the modern ethnographic field. The result is that I find myself looking elsewhere for some hints on how women exercise authority in Hindu traditions: female gurus, female renunciants' (*saṃnyāsinī*), and women's participation in *yajña* and puja. Thinking about these particular *gurumātās* through these paradigms may or may not point to a deeper understanding of *gurumātās* as a class, but it will certainly clarify the significant authority Mataji and Jiji wield in the Gayatri Pariwar.

### Female Gurus and *Saṃnyāsinīs*

In her introduction to *The Graceful Guru,* Karen Pechilis calls our attention to an excellent point of departure: female gurus' disciples almost always regard them as manifestations of *śakti* (feminine energy) or perhaps a particular goddess.[22] I have encountered no such discourse about Jiji, but Mataji's hagiography, *Mahāśakti kī Lokyātrā*, reflects quite clearly that the Gayatri Pariwar presents Mataji in identical terms. The essence of an idealized and divine femininity flows through the veins of Mataji and female gurus alike, giving rise to similar hagiographical tropes and constructing authority on the basis of extant notions of feminine power.

Female gurus and *saṃnyāsinīs* are by no means mutually exclusive categories and in fact overlap a great deal, but not entirely. It is thus unsurprising that Meena Khandelwal, while thinking about Hindu women's religious authority through the lens of renunciation, also notes that *saṃnyāsinīs* emphasize their motherly qualities as an advantage their gender allows them. Khandelwal notes that this advantage is particularly pronounced with female disciples, who can develop intimate relationships with *saṃnyāsinīs* and confide in them in ways that might not seem appropriate with a *saṃnyāsin* (male renunciant).[23] Although as a male ethnographer I am limited in my ability to note if the last of these points is true of the relationships Mataji and Jiji have with the women of the Gayatri Pariwar, the rest of this is certainly consistent with the ways in which Mataji and Jiji conduct themselves as *gurumātās*.

Of course, there are also some major dissimilarities between *saṃnyāsinīs* and female gurus on the one hand and Mataji and Jiji on the other. As *Mahāśakti kī Lokyātrā* suggested, Mataji's perfect femininity involves being not only an ideal mother to Gayatri parijans, but also a perfect wife to Gurudev. *Saṃnyāsinīs*' and female gurus' femininity is typically tied to motherhood to the exclusion of any other kind of feminine gendered relationship as a way of downplaying their sexuality as women.[24] Even if this factor is partially addressed for Mataji and Jiji through their practice of marital celibacy, their femininities as *gurumātās* are not tied exclusively to motherhood—they are also tied to their roles as wives to Gurudev and Doctor-sahib.

As a way of downplaying their feminine sexuality, modern female gurus are generally unmarried or are otherwise in marriages that deviate from typical patriarchal structures, likely because such structures would introduce significant constraints on the scope of their religious authority. The well-known gurus Ammachi and Gurumayi, for example, were never married. Anandamayi Ma was married, but her marriage was unconsummated and her husband primarily related to her as a disciple.[25] Female gurus' marital status thus gives them a degree of independence from patriarchal family structures that a *gurumātā* would not generally enjoy. By remaining unmarried, female gurus function as both guru and *gurumātā* in one, reserving absolute authority to instruct and discipline students or gently nurture them as they see fit. Historically, *gurumātās* were typically not permitted such a teaching role,[26] but modern *gurumātās* like Mataji and Jiji have a kind of secondary teaching authority—they know the teachings of Gurudev better than most and are well qualified to pass them on—Mataji's mediumship for Gurudev is quite relevant here—but it would be surprising if they were to expound their own ideas without framing them quite clearly in Gurudev's teachings.[27]

## *Yajña* and Puja

While female gurus have not been a widely documented phenomenon until relatively recently, women have had important roles in a great deal of Hindu ritual life from modern times all the way back to the Vedic period. Vedic ritual—the very style of ritual that the Gayatri Pariwar is reviving—quite famously requires both a male sacrificial patron and his wife, usually referred to as *pati* and *patnī*, respectively, in ritual contexts.[28] In *Sacrificed Wife/Sacrificer's Wife*, Stephanie Jamison utilizes ancient ritual texts to reflect upon the particular role of the *patnī* during these elaborate rituals. While not as active in ritual as her male counterpart, she participates at some of the most important moments in the ritual.[29] Through her ritual participation, Jamison notes, the *patnī* introduces three interrelated elements in particular to the ritual arena: sexuality and fertility, domesticity, and hospitality and exchange.[30] While women's capacity in a Hindu cultural context to contribute sexuality and fertility to a ritual environment[31] might not be strictly relevant to understanding the importance of Mataji and Jiji for the Gayatri Pariwar given their marital celibacy, the latter two are more promising.

Jamison elaborates a great deal on hospitality in particular. Hospitality, in the sense of receiving a guest, is a domestic responsibility that generally falls primarily to women in Hindu society. It is consequently unsurprising that in the context of Vedic ritual, when it is necessary to welcome *soma* as a guest to the ritual arena, for example, the *patnī* participates in ways that parallel the ritualized hospitality she would offer any respected guest to her home.[32] Women's domestic authority over hospitality is thus one basis for her authority in ritual contexts. There is perhaps a certain disjuncture with the Gayatri Pariwar here: their daily Vedic-style rituals are not quite so elaborate, and men and women generally play identical roles. Nevertheless, Mataji's and Jiji's biographical materials have emphasized their personal attentiveness to matters of hospitality, and so this connection cannot be ignored. Just as the rituals Jamison describes hinge on the presence of the *patnī* who is willing to perform her feminine duties, so does the Gayatri Pariwar's success hinge on the affective work—hospitality or otherwise—that Mataji and Jiji contribute to the community. Given their associations with culturally situated notions about how such affective work is gendered, Gurudev and Doctor-sahib are no more able to take the place of Mataji and Jiji than a sacrificial patron is able to take his wife's in welcoming *soma* to the sacrificial arena.

Moving into the contemporary period, another helpful point of comparison to illustrate the importance of the domestic and maternal aspects of Mataji and Jiji's authority is Ashlee Andrews's " 'I am the Chief Priest of the Home.' " Andrews describes Bengali women's experiences of performing puja in domestic spaces. The women with whom Andrews speaks emphasize their intense emotional commitments to their domestic forms of ritualized worship in comparison to rule-bound male Brahmins who perform emotionless and formulaic ritualized worship professionally at public temples.[33] For these women, puja becomes a part of domestic life, an expression not only of their piety but also of their sense of familial duty. Because of their special capacity to perform ritual in this way, women gain a certain kind of ritual authority generally unavailable to men.[34]

While it may be intuitive to speak of puja, as in the case of the Bengali women Andrews studied, and *yajña*, as in the Gayatri Pariwar's case, as divergent ritual styles in Hindu traditions, one Vedic, the other Āgamic, such a distinction would be rather artificial in the modern world. In his review of Frits Staal's *Agni: the Vedic Ritual of the Fire Altar*, Brian K. Smith notes that even the intensely orthodox Nambudiri Brahmins were somewhat beholden to the Āgamic framework of modern Hindu traditions as they performed this ancient Vedic ritual. This is evident in a number of elements of the Agnicayana ritual Staal documents: the avoidance of animal sacrifice, the preliminary offerings to Shiva and Ganesha, and the presence in the ritual space of a small oil lamp, signifying Shiva's continued presence at the ritual. Smith accordingly concludes that "the Nambudiris have preserved Vedic ritual only insofar as it could be transformed into a kind of elaborate puja to Hindu gods who govern its performance and to whom it is dedicated."[35]

All of this is to suggest that it should not then be terribly far-fetched to argue that the Gayatri Pariwar's daily *yajña* is analogous in a certain sense to women's domestic puja as described by Andrews. Daily *yajña* may have a history as a domestic practice that involves the wife's participation, but like Āgamic temple ritual, it suffers from the stultifying influence of male Brahminical authority. Mataji and Jiji's influence have transformed the Gayatri Pariwar's daily *yajña* as something more akin to a domestic puja, and in so doing they have reimagined this ritual in a more affectively powerful form. This power derives in part from the ways in which Mataji and Jiji impart to Gayatri parijans a sense of kinship. It is clear enough that as *gurumātās,* these women do important work in making the Gayatri Pariwar feel like a family—the very attribute which Gayatri parijans say the Gayatri Pariwar is set apart from all other movements. By extension, Mataji and Jiji shape Shantikunj as a domestic space. In Shantikunj, *yajña* may be performed by both men and women, but the domesticity of the ritual space in which *yajña* occurs is purely the result of the affective work of Mataji, Jiji, and indubitably countless other female residents.

Much of this intersects intriguingly with a framework developed by Lindsey Harlan in "Words that Breach Walls." Using the film *Chocolat* as guiding material to interpret *ratijaga* rituals, in which Rajasthani women travel to other households to observe a nighttime vigil with other women, Harlan notes three points that are helpful in understanding how expansive Hindu women's religious authority really is, even if it seems to be confined to the domestic sphere. First, through ritual activity and everyday practice, women effect change in their environment, domestic or otherwise. Second, a woman's location in the domestic sphere should not be confused with a location in the private sphere—women's authority to carry out hospitality renders the domestic space permeable to the outside world. Third, the importance of women's everyday activities allows them to hold dramatic sway over the outside world.[36]

So, while I have argued in this chapter that Mataji's and Jiji's authority derives in great part from their capacity to make Shantikunj feel like a domestic space, Harlan's framework calls attention to how expansive this authority really is. Mataji and Jiji can and do change their space substantially: they render Shantikunj—a monastic space that might otherwise be formal and dispassionate—into an emotionally vibrant domestic space through their affective work as mother figures and hospitality providers. Through this affective work they draw an ever-widening public into their domestic space on a scale that far exceeds any *ratijaga*. This public connection allows them substantial sway over the world around them. In planning Gurudev's elaborate memorial service and channeling his posthumous messages, Mataji became the mediator of his legacy. In delivering occasional lectures at Shantikunj, which are now also posted to the web for global circulation, Mataji and Jiji project their particular understandings of Gurudev's teachings to the publics they have brought to Shantikunj.

## Conclusion

I have argued that Mataji and Jiji hold substantial authority in the Gayatri Pariwar, despite the fact that Gayatri parijans seem to view their husbands as occupying primary positions of authority within the movement. Gayatri parijans value the familial atmosphere they experience at Shantikunj and biographical materials about Mataji and Jiji seem to suggest that this atmosphere is in large part their contribution. By taking on maternal roles and making Shantikunj hospitable to guests, Mataji and Jiji project a sense of kinship that is rooted entirely in their affective work rather than in biological kinship. Creating this sense of kinship is as important if not more in making the community cohere than the priestly, pedagogic, and scientific work performed by Mataji's and Jiji's male counterparts, Gurudev and Doctor-sahib.

In their explanation of the importance of the Gayatri Pariwar's sense of kinship, Gyaneshwar, Ashutosh, Dina, and Chandrakala pointed to the family as a wholesome site that nurtures moral selves and can function as a model for a morally reformed society. This suggests that Mataji's and Jiji's affective work is integral to the Gayatri Pariwar's moral project. By creating a familial atmosphere in Shantikunj, they facilitate the moral self-cultivation of the upwardly mobile but disillusioned members of their community, providing them with an important tool for the moral project they desire as they search for a means to affirm their middle-class identity through non-consumerist means.

CHAPTER 6

# Becoming All World

An account of the Gayatri Pariwar and its use of scientific authority would not be complete without a description of the eschatological views that encapsulate its highest aspirations for humanity. This chapter explores the close links between eschatology, globalization, and scientific authority in the Gayatri Pariwar. The model of social change that makes up the core of Gayatri Pariwar eschatology focuses initially on the transformation of single persons. The positive influence of these individuals then spreads like ripples, gradually improving larger and larger segments of humanity. As my contact Dina puts it, "*Society is made of families, so if family is fixed, society will be fixed; if society is fixed, the nation will be fixed; if the nation is fixed, the world will be fixed.*"[1] The structure of my argument in this chapter follows this logic in a certain sense. Rather than encompassing progressively larger groups of people, it focuses on the progressively larger spatial scales in which the Gayatri Pariwar is situated: Shantikunj, a utopian community in miniature; Garhwal, a region which is home to Shantikunj as well as some of the most important places in Hindu sacred geography; India, where questions of religious identity continue to shape the politics of postcolonial nation-building; and finally the world, crisscrossed by seemingly space-negating communication networks.

These four spatial scales are somewhat artificial and it will very quickly become clear that the local, regional, national, and global spaces are connected to one another by flows of ideas and people. To riff on the Advaitan metaphor, each ripple spreading outward is, after all, a part of the same body of water. In my effort to understand the dynamic interconnections between the Gayatri Pariwar and the various spaces in which the movement is situated, I focus on these flows, which point to how the Gayatri Pariwar moves through space and also how space moves through it. These flows bear the presence of the global at the level of the local and vice versa.

As it spreads outwards, the ripple becomes somewhat less distinct, finally disappearing into the surface of the water around it. Likewise, as we progress toward thinking about the Gayatri Pariwar in progressively more expansive spaces, things can become quite a bit more ethereal as flows of a more material sort begin to drop away. To put it in Arjun Appadurai's terms, the ethnoscape, which appears to be quite prominent in Shantikunj and Garhwal, seems to give way to mediascapes and ideoscapes at the global level.[2] The apparent predominance of mediascapes and ideoscapes at the global level drives the Gayatri Pariwar's data-driven eschatology—the desirability of its practices must be quantified to make the best use of modern communication technology. Nonetheless, even at the global scale, the ethnoscape will turn out to be resurgent in unexpected ways.

## Shantikunj

### Bilingual Signs

The timing of my arrival at Shantikunj was not only auspicious from the perspective of the Gayatri Pariwar; it was also auspicious from my perspective as an ethnographer. The anticipation of the impending realization of the Gayatri Pariwar's "All World" aspirations was thick in the air, especially early on in my stay at Shantikunj. An event horizon had been crossed, and the movement now lurched irrevocably forward in time and outward in space toward the realization of global *satyug*. There was no turning back, and Shantikunj had its own part to play in making preparations.

When I arrived at the ashram for my brief preliminary visit and again at the beginning of my extended stay, I noticed that many of the signs that marked the space of the ashram, naming buildings and directing visitors through the unfamiliar facilities, were almost exclusively in Hindi. Facilities aimed at residents and visitors from non-Hindi-speaking regions of India would be written in regionally appropriate scripts, but signs written in non-Indic scripts were all but absent. This was, of course, in keeping with the original ethos of the Gayatri Pariwar. Gurudev had rejected the elitism of the Arya Samaj not only by embracing the Purāṇic and Āgamic streams of Hindu traditions, but also by favoring Hindi over English. But if the expected Western devotees were to feel at home in Shantikunj as the movement entered the transnational stage, Hindi signs simply would not do; a compromise had to be made.

Shantikunj rose to the challenge over the first few months of my residence there, gradually replacing Hindi-language signs with bilingual signs written in both Hindi and English.[3] These bilingual signs signify much more than where the dining hall is located or what time one can go for darshan. Their appearance struck me as a tangible manifestation of the Gayatri Pariwar's hopes that their global ambitions were coming to fruition. Moreover, their bilingualism in particular seemed to represent a tension between the Gayatri Pariwar's grassroots beginnings, with their populist orientation toward society at the most local levels and the lofty cosmopolitan telos toward which the movement aspires. The Gayatri Pariwar's success in rural India is in part due to their championing of pragmatism, vernacular language, and popular values rather than the elite English-language discourses favored by other Hindu reform movements. Their effort to reach out to global audiences brings the risk of alienating the communities that have traditionally supported the Gayatri Pariwar.

The specter of colonialism haunts the English in these bilingual signs. English was introduced to India rather forcibly, along with Western-style scientific knowledge, with Thomas Macaulay's education reforms as described in my introductory chapter. By creating a situation in which Indians who wished to advance in society were required to speak English and be versed in English-language intellectual traditions, the British created a situation in which Indian religious traditions had to justify themselves through English-language rhetorics.

This state of affairs gives rise to what Srinivas Aravamudan calls "Guru English." Guru English is a variant of English with four aspects, according to Aravamudan. As a speech register, it features a specialized vocabulary developed by gurus and Orientalist scholars that allows previously unavailable religious meanings to be communicated to Anglophone audiences. It also functions as a discourse, opening up a space for new kinds of critique from both within and without through a wide variety of wordplay. As a "transidiomatic environment," Guru English informs seemingly nonreligious linguistic activity from the background. Finally, as a "commodifiable cosmopolitanism," Guru English allows its new meanings to be packaged for consumption in the global marketplace of ideas.[4]

Before returning to the political significance of the bilingual signs, it is worth noting that my core interest in the role of science in modern Hindu traditions is deeply bound up with Guru English. Aravamudan recognizes this phenomenon as a part of Guru English in a number of places. For example, by describing how Maharishi Mahesh Yogi rebranded his Transcendental Meditation by equating Sanskrit terms of great importance in Hindu traditions with English-language scientific concepts, Aravamudan is able to suggest that TM becomes a commodified cosmopolitanism.[5] By reconciling the Hindu intellectual basis of his practices with modern, Anglocentric intellectual categories, the Maharishi makes his teachings appealing to modern Anglophone audiences worldwide.

There is of course a complication: the Gayatri Pariwar presents its scientific discourse in Hindi, not in English. Does scientific discourse look different in Hindi than it does in English? As we saw in chapter 4, *Super Science of Gayatri* freely uses Sanskrit terms like *kundalini* to describe parts of our subtle physiology that are supposed to be real in a literal sense. It is drawn into the scientific paradigm through comparison to modern scientific knowledge (in this case, nuclear physics). In *Integrated Science of Yagya*, Joshi also uses Sanskritic terminology where necessary, but brings *yajña* into the scientific paradigm by expressing the process's results in terms of a materialist ontology and our way of knowing those results in terms of falsifiable laboratory experimentation.

Sanskrit terms are of course deployed all of the time in Guru English, especially when those terms have the capacity to evoke the audiences' Orientalist fantasies. I would thus argue that the Gayatri Pariwar's invocation of science might illustrate the influence of Guru English in the movement's use of Hindi. Their Hindi may shy away from English terminology, but it bears the marks of ontological structures embedded in the English language. This influence of Guru English is also visible in certain Hindi idioms at work in the movement that are clearly back-translations of English language concepts. The most obvious of these is one that is quite central to Gayatri Pariwar discourse: *vaijñānik adhyātmavād* for scientific spirituality. While these are perfectly legitimate words in proper Hindi, they do not quite reflect everyday speech—one might communicate more clearly by simply saying "*sāyaṇṭiphik spiricūailiṭī*"—and are clearly functioning as translations of English-language concepts. Perhaps one might say, in a sort of parody of Aravamudan's Guru English, that the Gayatri Pariwar demonstrates a parallel linguistic phenomenon, a "*vaijñānik hindī*," or "Scientist Hindi."

One implication of this Scientist Hindi is that in the Gayatri Pariwar's decision to eschew English as the language of the colonization and the language of the elite, it is impossible to avoid its abiding influence. The prestige of English has remained high after the departure of the British in 1947. Globalization has only reinforced this prestige by making English the transnational lingua franca. For Indians who are politically inclined to embrace the transnational flows globalization has introduced, English may carry associations with modernity, progress, and prestige. But for others, it is a neocolonial imposition, a reminder of continued Western hegemony, an unwelcome reverberation of Macaulay's bigotry.[6]

I have been focusing my discussion up until this point on the politically fraught status of English. But in order to understand how these signs mark space at Shantikunj, it is important to consider not only the new incursion of English into the ashram, but also the continued presence of Hindi on signs that are, after all, bilingual. In "Cosmopolitan and Vernacular in History," Sheldon Pollock raises a hope for our globalizing world—that xenophobic and insular vernacularism and hegemonic, homogenizing cosmopolitanism are not the only options. For Pollock, the best future for our world is one in which we refuse to choose between the local and the global, insisting instead upon the possibility and necessity of their continued coexistence as separate entities.[7] Even with all of the postcolonial complications the reintroduction of English to Shantikunj entails, the fact that English has not displaced Hindi may confirm the possibility of Pollock's hope. On signs in Shantikunj and many other places in India, Hindi, as vernacular language, and English, as cosmopolitan language, coexist just fine. Passersby who might find the presence of one language or the other ideologically distasteful might not be the target audience for the Gayatri Pariwar's global project anyway.

What a range of meanings these bilingual signs signify! Shantikunj was once a space devoid of English and its attendant problems. Its colonial baggage and the process of jettisoning that baggage in order to indigenize English were eschewed. The absence of its elitist ethos marked the Gayatri Pariwar as distinct from other reform movements—even if it borrowed English-language categories, it did not borrow English terminology. When Gayatri parijans hang bilingual signs in Shantikunj, they are saying that the promise of globalization is worth dealing with the complications of bilingualism. The bilingualism of these signs suggests a hope that the movement can have it both ways, that it can be cosmopolitan without losing its regional populism, but only time will tell if this will be the case.

## "Spiritual Socialism" in the Dining Hall

Chinmay-bhaiya serves under his father, Doctor-sahib, as the Pro Vice-Chancellor of DSVV. As a descendant of Gurudev, he is of great importance to Gayatri parijans, who will take the dust from his feet should he happen to walk by. While meetings with Doctor-sahib and Jiji were mostly limited to formalities, Chinmay-bhaiya was much more accessible to me, and met with me regularly in his office at DSVV despite his demanding schedule. During one of my last meetings with him, I asked him why he thought the Gayatri Pariwar appealed to such a broad cross-section of Indian society. He answered,

> In Shantikunj, everything's free. You come for camps, there's no charge, no registration fee. Everything is free: lodging is free; food is free. Apart from something that you want to purchase, you can basically go without paying anything. There's no obligation for you to pay for anything. *Saṃskārs* are free. . . . Every single member of the organization gives thirty paisas a day, nine rupees a month, a negligible amount of money, but with 110 million members to give, it funds the organization. But apart from creating the financial background for the organization, what it also creates is this spiritual socialism. You know the person sitting next to you may be able to fly in a private jet and you can only afford five hundred rupees, but you both feel you equally belong to the organization. So that's why you see such a great influence in the villages of India, that you go to any village of India, and you will find at least ten to twenty families belonging to the Gayatri Pariwar.

This mention of "spiritual socialism" resonated with my own observations about Shantikunj, and I felt compelled to share my own thoughts and inquire further:

> It's interesting that you would say "spiritual socialism" because one of the first things that I noticed when I actually started living here was that in many ways in Shantikunj, it's like a classless society. You have people with different kinds of education contributing different kinds of *seva* but they all sit down at the same *bhojanālaya*;[8] they live in the same buildings. Is that a term that's commonly used in the community?

It turns out that this was a spur-of-the-moment phrase on Chinmay-bhaiya's part, and he did not seem to want me to read too much into it—perhaps he worried that I might be an old-fashioned American capitalist or perhaps this is just not the sort of image he wants to project of the Gayatri Pariwar. But it nevertheless resonates with some of his grandfather's apparent sympathies:

> Karl Marx . . . propounded an economic theory that revolutionized the whole society. The castles of capitalism were demolished and death knell of imperialism was sounded in almost two-thirds of the entire world. His book *Das Kapital* inaugurated the beginning of a new era in which the rights of the workers were recognized and a new chapter of equitable distribution of money and materials was opened. Millions of people thus got an opportunity to lead a happy life of self-reliance.[9]

Marx—like Gandhi, King, and others—utilized his talents for the good of humanity, and Gurudev understood himself as continuing in that struggle. For the Gayatri Pariwar, Shantikunj is a utopia in microcosm—a model not just for what a revitalized Indian nation-state might look like, but also for what global society might be like after the *satyug* is revived on a global scale. For Gurudev and Chinmay-bhaiya at least, this spiritual socialism is a marked part of that utopia.

One of the social spaces that is most obviously shaped by this "spiritual socialism," as I'd observed in my conversation with Chinmay-bhaiya, is the dining hall. This massive open-air pavilion was the main eating-place in Shantikunj. On the way in, diners grab a cup and stainless steel plate, then sit in rows on long strips of burlap. Typically, attendants encourage diners to sit next to whoever happened to get into the dining hall right before them. Men and women are not separated, as is often the custom in public settings in India. The taboo on members of different castes eating together and sharing utensils is ignored. Everyone eats the same food, which on most days consists of rice, *dāl*, potatoes, and *roṭī*. This lack of segregation on the basis of gender, caste, or class is implemented quite deliberately and recalls the appreciation Gurudev felt in his formative years for Ramana Maharshi's integrated dining hall.

The dining hall may seem to be an obvious place to look for spiritual socialism, but there are complications. After a few months of living in Shantikunj, I rarely ate in this dining hall. This was a habit that had begun to develop because the dining hall was an uncomfortable place for me, and persisted until the very end of my fieldwork. The dining hall was an integrated space, but it was also a space where I felt othered. Visitors to the ashram would stare, sometimes pointing, sometimes whispering, sometimes even giggling.[10] They would ask me which country I was from, a question with which foreigners who spend time in India are well acquainted. On other trips to India, such questions were normally a source of amusement, or at worst, during my more introverted moments, a minor annoyance. At first, this was also how I felt when I was asked where I was from in the dining hall, too. But once I had started to consider Shantikunj my home and I was still being asked where I was from most days, often more than once, when I sat down to eat a meal in what felt like *my* dining hall, the feeling changed. I wanted to say, "I live *here*! Where are *you* from?" but I knew that wasn't appropriate. That wasn't the spirit in which they were asking me. And it would likely only result in more staring, more whispers. Moreover, even in light of the Gayatri Pariwar's global aspirations, their impression that I was an outsider was fair, and my sense of entitlement to claim that space as my own was an unmistakable manifestation of my own white privilege.

Even if I retained control of my behavior, the underlying feeling remained. The dining hall, although intended by the Gayatri Pariwar leadership as a place of integration, became a place of alienation for me. But luckily there were alternatives. In addition to the dining hall, the ashram had a small canteen that served up snacks, sweets, and tea for a small fee. Above this canteen was an additional dining facility where flavorful, well-cooked food was served cafeteria style and eaten on at large tables and chairs, but again, for a fee. This facility seemed to cater weddings that the Gayatri Pariwar hosted, but the portion that was open to the public was generally populated by visitors to the ashram whose dress seemed to be fairly middle class. I was not completely free of probing questions in this environment either, but they came less frequently and the ability to sit at my own table rather than sitting next to a stranger on the floor made it a less stressful experience. The cafeteria became my standby for lunch, but I felt somehow guilty showing up for two meals a day there. What if the Gayatri parijans working there realized that I was so bourgeois that I was eating all of my meals in this fancy place?

All of this is not to say that Chinmay-bhaiya's characterization of Shantikunj as being spiritually socialist is off base. Even if there are alternatives to the dining hall that cost money, and even if the dining hall seems to be an uncomfortable place for non-Indians on extended stays in Shantikunj, the ideals it enshrines are noteworthy and laudable. And on a personal note, this cynical leftist author would even say that he finds it deeply inspiring. The fact that there are complications, in turn, is rather unsurprising. Other mega-ashrams, like Amritapuri in Kerala, offer simple free meals in a similar communal dining hall and tastier meals in a separate ashram facility for a fee. At Amritapuri, these facilities often serve non-Indian (or sometimes non-spicy Indian) eating options, and are consequently patronized almost exclusively by international visitors. While this seems to stray much further from Shantikunj's spiritual socialist model, these kinds of "spiritual mixed economies" are yet another of the compromises that globalization imposes upon a community that wishes to open itself to transnational flows of people.[11]

## Devatma Himalaya Mandir

Before moving on to situate Shantikunj in the religious landscape of the Garhwal Himalayas, as a sort of transition to that slightly broader spatial scale, I would like to briefly consider a small building near the dining hall called the Devatma Himalaya Mandir. Surrounded by modest but idyllic gardens, this domed structure houses a sizable diorama of the Garhwal Himalayas on which major pilgrimage places, such as the Choṭā Cār Dhām, are clearly marked. Sitting surfaces are arranged theater-style to allow devotees to have extended darshan of this important expanse of Hindu religious landscape. Regularly scheduled multimedia shows on the lives of Himalayan sages punctuate the air of quiet reverence that generally prevails in this space.

Figure 6.1. Devatma Himalaya Mandir, Shantikunj.

Although, as we are about to see, Shantikunj is very much a part of the religious landscape of the Garhwal Himalayas, Devatma Himalaya Mandir is provocative because it suggests that Shantikunj contains and encompasses one of the most important places in Hindu geography. It offers these pilgrims a message: "You don't have to go any further along the pilgrimage trail. You can stop here. Everything that you can find there is contained within Shantikunj."[12] Whereas the dining hall brought together Indians from various walks of society and thus represented a sort of pan-Indianism and the bilingual signs mark Shantikunj as ready for flows of people on a transnational scale, the Devatma Himalaya Mandir is suggestive of Shantikunj's relationship to regional flows of pilgrims.

## Garhwal

Haridwar has an important place in the sacred geography of Hindu traditions. Like Mathura, the original home of Akhand Jyoti, Haridwar is one of the Sapta Purī, the seven most sacred cities for Hindus. Set on the banks of the Ganges, it is an important site for Hindu death rituals. Every twelve years, it hosts the massive Kumbh Mela, drawing millions of pilgrims. It also has a place on the yearly Hindu pilgrimage calendar, as it is the gateway to the Garhwal Himalayas' important pilgrimage centers, the Choṭā Cār Dhām.

In this section, I expand the scope of my analysis of the spatial situation of the Gayatri Pariwar by considering flows of people not in and around Shantikunj, as in the foregoing material, but through Haridwar and Garhwal more generally. This includes pilgrims heading up the pilgrimage trail to the Choṭā Cār Dhām and the transnational flow of non-Indian travelers to Rishikesh, and a flow of Hindu nationalist ideology and institutions as shown by the case of the Bharat Mata Temple.

In the case of Shantikunj, we gained a sense of how regional, national, and global networks were intensely felt even in the highly localized space of a single community. This theme will repeat in the case of Garhwal, perhaps even more starkly. The Garhwal region, especially those parts of it that are situated along tourist and pilgrimage circuits, is home to a cluster of important nodes in vast networks through which bodies and meaning flow. These nodes reflect the transplantation of interests that are often times quite external to Garhwal. Moreover, these networks and their flows are not distributed evenly throughout the region, and it will become clear that Shantikunj's location in Haridwar does not confer equal access.

## The Choṭā Cār Dhām

Every year during the summer and monsoon, countless pilgrims pass through Haridwar and Rishikesh on their way to the Choṭā Cār Dhām. In contrast to the Cār Dhām of Badrinath, Puri, Rameswaram, and Dwaraka, which sit near the four cardinal corners of the subcontinent, the Choṭā Cār Dhām of Badrinath, Kedarnath, Gangotri, and Yamunotri[13] are relatively close together and constitute a single pilgrimage circuit. As a preliminary step to visiting these four shrines, pilgrims will stop in Haridwar, and more specifically Har Ki Pauri. Har Ki Pauri is traditionally understood as the very spot where the Ganges leaves the Himalayas and enters the densely populated North Indian plains. In this sense, although Haridwar does not quite have Varanasi's religious clout, it occupies a strategic point in Hindus' sacred geography. It straddles the mundane, everyday life of the

Gangetic Plain and the lofty, inaccessible transcendence of the Himalayan peaks: bathe in the waters at Har Ki Pauri and you will be ready to move on through the land of sages that lies beyond.[14]

Gurudev's decision to move the center of his mission from Mathura to Haridwar thus brought the Gayatri Pariwar important strategic advantages. Haridwar is an important conduit for two kinds of flows: people, flowing upstream as pilgrims, and religious authority, flowing downstream from the mountains and into the plains. Shantikunj's location in Haridwar allows it to mediate both of these flows. Pilgrims flow through the ashram on their way to the Choṭā Cār Dhām or back, gaining exposure to the Gayatri Pariwar, associating the movement with whatever meaningful experiences their Himalayan sojourn brings. And just as the Ganges brings the Hindu populations of the plains purifying water from Shiva's matted locks, the Gayatri Pariwar brings the wisdom of the Himalayan sages at Nandanvan down to the masses of ordinary people with their populist sensibilities.

Choṭā Cār Dhām season is the busiest time of year at Shantikunj, when the ashram bursts at the seams with pilgrims heading to and returning from these shrines. It is so busy that I was moved out of my three-bed room in Gargi Bhavan, which was built to house visitors from abroad and was thus outfitted with a shower, hot water heater, and Western-style toilet. My new residence in Patanjali Bhavan, with its more standard Indian bathroom, had only two beds and the move thus opened up an extra bed for the incoming pilgrims.

I am ashamed to say that I made this move with some grumbling. I had long ago decided that I was not a hardy enough ethnographer to tolerate an Indian-style bathroom and selfishly wondered what a difference a single bed would make. In hindsight, I was clearly in the wrong on all accounts, and, as Somnath had repeatedly assured me, the more central location of Patanjali Bhavan proved advantageous for my work. In any event, I do not just present this vignette to send myself up for the soft, uptight, demanding white middle-class American that I am, but also to illustrate a point about the Gayatri Pariwar's priorities. I have no doubt that the Gayatri Pariwar considered my work important and wanted to offer me the best hospitality possible for reasons described at the outset of this book. But the pilgrims who pass through Shantikunj during Choṭā Cār Dhām season? They are the real focus of the movement, in keeping with the movement's populist roots. The Gayatri Pariwar's willingness to displace me to spare a single bed for incoming pilgrims demonstrates an impressive commitment to remaining consistent with their guiding principles even when doing so complicates the global connections the movement is trying to forge. As a critic of colonialisms both old and new, I laud their refusal to compromise even as I lament my own grumbling. But I wonder, neither for the first time nor for the last, if this incident points to an intractable tension between the Gayatri Pariwar's populist principles and its global aspirations.

The pilgrims whose large numbers resulted in my move to Patanjali Bhavan are not the only ones whose journeys bear mentioning. Gurudev's auto-hagiographies deal quite extensively with pilgrimage, setting them up as a major source of his religious authority. These pilgrimages wind up the Ganges to Gangotri and beyond, to Nandanvan, which sits above the Ganges' glacial source. These journeys, too difficult for all but the most pious pilgrims and the most ardent trekkers, associate Gurudev with a place of tremendous symbolic import. He has gone to a point in Hindu geography that is beyond the source of the Ganges, the very lifeline of Hindu traditions. If Haridwar, as the city in which the Ganges leaves the mountains and enters the plains, is the gateway to a supramundane world of the Himalayan Ganges, Gurudev, in his pilgrimages to Nandanvan, could be said to have passed through a second gateway to a world still less mundane, where it is possible to dwell among bodiless sages.

The journey upstream may be the pilgrimage proper, and for the ordinary pilgrim, the journey downstream is simply a trip home, but Gurudev's downstream journey is of crucial importance for the Gayatri Pariwar. His entering the Himalayan Ganges at Haridwar and coming out the other side at Gangotri matters because he then returns to Haridwar, bringing the beyond-Gangotri ethos with him. Haridwar may mediate between the Himalayan Ganges and the Gangetic plain, but Gurudev offers a form of mediation that goes one step further.

Just as the Devatma Himalaya Mandir suggests that Shantikunj encompasses the Garhwal Himalayan pilgrimage sites to or from which many visitors of Shantikunj are traveling, Gurudev himself embodies the Himalayas as a result of his intensive pilgrimages. The result is that there are multiple equivalences at play here, a situation that is quite common in considerations of Hindu deities, holy people, pilgrimage places, and *mūrtis*:[15] Gurudev embodies the Himalayas and represents their sages; Shantikunj reflects the will of Gurudev and these sages, and is a slice of Himalayan culture in a place accessible to all. These equivalences offer a message to the pilgrims who flow through Shantikunj: you don't need to go any further than here!

To Rishikesh

Every Saturday morning, I would walk out of the main gate of Shantikunj, cross Haridwar-Rishikesh road, and flag down an auto heading northeast, up the Ganges. Just barely squeezing in, typically with a limb or two sticking out, I would ignore both the obvious danger and the curiosity of my fellow passengers as I donned headphones in the hopes of drowning out the endless drone of honking horns. About an hour later, I would toss the driver a few rupees as his vehicle disgorged its passengers near Sivananda's ashram, ever popular with Westerners, in Rishikesh.

Although I had gone deeper into the Himalayas, this was my weekly break from the feeling, almost inescapable at Shantikunj, that I did not fit in, that I was an outsider. Few Westerners pause in Shantikunj, or for that matter in Haridwar. Most of them pass straight through to Rishikesh, whether they are visiting Himalayan shrines with the Hindu pilgrims, using the city as a base for outdoor sports like trekking or rafting, or availing themselves of the city's world-famous yoga ashrams. I was pursuing simpler pleasures: lunch at Green Italian restaurant; some time to read a novel and drink some sort of sweet, icy concoction at the Cafe Coffee Day in Ram Jhula; a nice, quiet sit down with my feet dangling into the river at a mostly empty expanse of the riverbank; some more time with the same novel and a different sweet, icy concoction at the Cafe Coffee Day in Laxman Jhula; and finally a good people-watching table at Devraj Coffee Corner, accompanied by fresh fruit juice and pizza done the Tibetan way.

Readers who pine for Rishikesh as it once was, before it got the tourist treatment, may scoff at the notion that I found some respite in these trips. Admittedly, Rishikesh is full of dreadlocked hippies stoned out of their minds, wide-eyed wannabe yogis unironically underlining passages in books on Tantric sex, and trekkers strutting around with their outdoorsy hubris too big even for their oversized backpacks. The musical stylings of Krishna Das, with his horribly mispronounced sterile kirtans, pipe through storefronts offering harem pants, "handmade" religious paraphernalia, and Hindi lessons while almost every restaurant—café, rather—offers up not-too-spicy versions of at least three of the following cuisines: North Indian, South Indian, Chinese, Italian, Mexican, Continental, and Israeli.

But all of that is the point. In Rishikesh, I was just as out of place as everything else.

Even if it was only true in the most banal sense, Rishikesh seemed more cosmopolitan than Haridwar. Perhaps this cosmopolitanism is of the kind that worried Pollock—the homogenizing force coming from a hegemonic place that does not coexist with the vernacular, with the local. Rishikesh is not a bilingual sign, it is a sign written only in English. This may account for what a guilty pleasure these weekly trips were for me. But if Rishikesh was an English-only sign, certainly Haridwar could have been Hindi-only. I took weekly trips into town in Haridwar as well for sitar lessons near what seemed to be the young, hip part of town. There was even a Domino's Pizza, and I ate there after almost every lesson, affront to my New Jersey heritage though it was. But even in the Domino's my presence was still received as something of an anomaly. None of this is to say that there are no places that can live up to the model of the bilingual signs in Shantikunj. Neither Haridwar nor Rishikesh seems to do it on its own, but rather they seem to work in tandem as a pair, like two sides of a twelve-mile-thick coin.

Given all that I have said here about my own experiences, it is perhaps not surprising that relatively few Westerners came to Shantikunj to visit. In the rare event that they did—it was, after all, listed in *The Rough Guide to India*—Somnath would call my cell and ask me if I could come to Abroad Cell to speak with them and help them get oriented. The first few times, I jumped at the opportunity, excited at the prospect of not being the sole Westerner in the ashram. "How did you wind up living here?" they would often ask me. "Well, I'm doing field research for my study of modern Hindu traditions and science," I'd answer. Perhaps they would proceed to make some small talk about my research for a minute or two. Their tone then often changed as they asked, "Do you think you would live here if it weren't for your research?" I would reply, "Well, the people here are really great, and I think this is a wonderful place to experience a side of Hindu traditions that you might not see in some of the places that are more popular with Westerners." Typically I would never see them again, but sometimes I would bump into them at most two days later. "It just isn't my thing. I'm moving on to Rishikesh," they would tell me.

Whereas Shantikunj's location in Haridwar is of great strategic importance for those who understand and care about the sacred geography in which it is situated, it does not have this same effect for the average casual international visitor. It is possible that it even confers a disadvantage with this crowd. Rishikesh, with its profound significance in the geography of contemporary romantic Orientalists, is nearby, its siren call audible in the distance. For international visitors looking to fulfill their Orientalist fantasies, the fact that Haridwar holds very deep significance for Hindus holds little sway. Even though they generally have to connect through Haridwar on their way to Rishikesh, they seldom stop and when they do, it is typically not for long. Shantikunj's location in Haridwar, not in a place that international visitors stop but near one, may reduce the Gayatri Pariwar's access to the flow of the transnational ethnoscape and hamper its All World ambitions.

## Bharat Mata's Shadow

"You should go to the Bharat Mata temple," Somnath told me. "It is a good place." I knew that I would indeed have to pay a visit to Bharat Mata (Mother India) during my stay in Haridwar, but had been putting it off. In contrast to the older Bharat Mata temple in Varanasi, with its Gandhian tone, Haridwar's Bharat Mata temple was built in the 1980s and has strong Hindu nationalist associations. Bharat Mata was popularized in the 1882 anti-colonial novel *Ānandamaṭh*, and was adopted by the growing Indian independence movement to signify an Indian nation unified in its resistance to British imperialism.[16] In this sense, she was part of a precolonial nation-building project—one that seemed uniquely Hindu.[17] If India could be personified as a distinct, coherent, idealized entity like Bharat Mata, surely the nation, too, could be united. It is important to recognize that despite her essentialist implications, for some Hindus Bharat Mata simply represents their own reverence for India and is not intended to represent a vision of the Indian nation-state that excludes non-Hindus. Nonetheless, she remains a powerful and pervasive image in the rhetoric of Hindu nationalists because in their discourse, Muslims and Christians are viewed as suspect for their orientation toward sacred geographies outside of India. The result is a perception of disloyalty to Bharat Mata as the divine manifestation of the Indian subcontinent.[18]

Given these associations, it took some time to work up the nerve to visit the Bharat Mata temple. When I thought about going there, I worried that the experience would fill me with anger or sadness at the injustices that have been inflicted upon India's religious minorities in

Bharat Mata's name. By the end of June, I had put off this visit for nearly six full months when a friend and colleague from the United States, Samantha (a pseudonym), told me she was in the area. After doing some research work in Delhi, she had decided to stay for some time at a hotel in Rishikesh for a "writing retreat" before treating herself to a week or so of intensive yoga training in one of Rishikesh's major ashrams. Since I had already met up with her during one of my weekly trips to Rishikesh, she decided to return the favor by visiting me in Haridwar, where she wanted to visit the Bharat Mata temple. Her sense that the visit would be good fun quickly displaced my anxieties, and I found myself looking forward to the excursion.

Construction on the Bharat Mata temple started in 1978, just seven years after Shantikunj was founded. The Bharat Mata temple of Haridwar represents the vision of Swami Satyamitranand, a major leader of the VHP. He selected Haridwar as the location for this temple because of its popularity with pilgrims and its associations with ancient sages[19]—a rationale similar to the one I have attributed to the Gayatri Pariwar in founding Shantikunj nearby. Satyamitranand intended the Bharat Mata temple to serve as a center for Hindu piety, a political symbol of India's national unity, and a tool for educating visitors about the traditions that contribute to that unity.[20]

The Bharat Mata temple is a thoroughly modern eight-story tower, with each floor dedicated to a different theme. Entering on the first floor, the eye is drawn to a massive diorama of India, with important locations marked off, located near the center of the floor and occupying a great deal of space. The ritual importance of this image is made apparent by the marigold petals worshipers have strewn across it. Just behind this diorama, the white marble *mūrti* of Bharat Mata herself gazes impassively over the land she embodies from the north. The walls of the next floor up are lined with over a dozen figures, most of whom were leaders of the struggle against the British spanning from the Sepoy Rebellion up to independence. Although major Indian nationalist figures from a variety of backgrounds and espousing a variety of ideologies are represented on this floor—including a single Muslim, Ashfaqulla Khan—a significant number are unsurprisingly forebears of the Hindu nationalist movement. Three heroes in the Hindu and Sikh struggles against the Mughal Empire join their ranks. The third floor is similarly laid out, but turns visitors' attention to a variety of ideal Hindu women, mostly taken from religious literature with two early modern queens serving as exceptions. The fourth floor, dedicated to India's holy people, is easily the most crowded with statuary. Devotional poets and key figures of the Vedānta school of thought account for the majority of these figures, but they are joined by Gautama Buddha, Mahavira, and Guru Gobind Singh, founders of traditions that Hindu nationalists generally consider Hindu. The only nods to Islam are through certain figures that are of importance to both Hindus and Muslims, like Kabir, Sai Baba, and Jhulelal.

The fifth floor offers a sort of break by taking on a different format from the previous three. The walls of this room are decorated by a number of paintings, each depicting scenes associated with different states in India in the form of landscapes, architecture, and cultural practices. Also on display are passages from the texts of a wide variety of religious traditions present in India, including Islam and Christianity. In a certain sense, although the presentation style of this room is less temple-like, this floor recapitulates and reframes the message of the first floor, where Bharat Mata overlooks the diorama of India. Rather than a seemingly monolithic representation of the physical land of India and its personified essence, the fifth floor starts to acknowledge the multiple contexts and regional specificity of Indianness to a certain extent. But given the larger context of the Bharat Mata temple as a whole, it is clear enough that this diversity must be subsumed in the larger normative-essentialist framework of a Hindu nation.

The final three floors, dedicated to Śākta, Vaiṣṇava, and Śaiva deities respectively, do not differ terribly from modern multi-deity temples. But since these sets of Hindu deities are arranged vertically in the Bharat Mata temple, their order is worth noting. It is clear enough from its position on the top floor that the Shiva temple is intended to be the climax of these religious encounters. As was the case with the fifth floor, there is a message of unity in including Śākta, Vaiṣṇava, and Śaiva deities under one roof, but the larger context or in this case the physical structure in which this message of unity is communicated makes a normative statement of hierarchy. In the Bharat Mata temple's attempt to build a unified nation bound by an essentialized, singular Hindu tradition, even deities must be drawn into a set hierarchical framework.

At the top of the temple, visitors are situated spatially a third time as they gaze out upon the landscape of Haridwar from their elevated vantage point. Lise McKean, in an account of her visit to the Bharat Mata temple in the mid-'90s, quotes a guidebook she received as extolling this view: "The view of the Himalayas: of the Sapta Dhara [seven streams, said to have been formed so that, during its descent, the Ganges would bypass the ashrams of the seven ancient sages]; of the scenic view of entire campus of the Sapta Sarowar area from the balconies of this floor, is breath-taking and transquilizing [*sic*] to the eye."[21] This focus on the meaningful status of the environs of Haridwar is not surprising given Satyamitranand's rationale for situating the temple here. As was the case with the Himalayan diorama at Devatma Himalaya Mandir in Shantikunj, visitors are to draw inspiration from and feel connected to the region to which Haridwar stands as a gate and to the ancient sages who have inhabited it—or perhaps still do. But just as the meaning of that Himalayan diorama is conditioned in part by its location in Shantikunj, the meaning of the view from the top of the Bharat Mata temple is conditioned by everything that visitors have encountered during their journey through the temple's eight stories: this specific expanse of land, the darshan that visitors are experiencing from this balcony, is inextricably tied to the story the Bharat Mata temple has presented, together with all of its ideological content; the essence of the Hindu nation is what you are seeing right here: Haridwar.

Samantha and I had been situated in space three times. First, the whole massive expanse of India appeared before us, seemingly monolithic, its essence manifest nearby as Bharat Mata. Second, the diversity of India's many regions and religious traditions played out before us, not to illustrate meaningful differences we must live with but to demonstrate Bharat Mata's capacity to encompass and contain all in her homogenizing body. Third, the essence of India, the very heart of Bharat Mata is right here in the Garhwal Himalayas. After this experience, Samantha did not care to stay in Haridwar much longer. She haggled with an auto-rickshaw driver just outside the gate of the Bharat Mata temple, then returned to her hotel in Rishikesh. Envious, I began the short walk home, never straying far from the shadow of the Bharat Mata temple.

This experience had reaffirmed my personal sense of a dichotomy between Haridwar and Rishikesh. This is because my sense of Haridwar's vernacularism—its anti-cosmopolitanism, perhaps—was reinforced by its Hindu nationalist associations. Granted, both cities had a common regional network running through them—the Choṭā Cār Dhām pilgrimage trail, giving them a common flow of people. But in each of these cities is also associated with distinct networks. Whereas Rishikesh occupies a major node for the global networks of yoga practitioners and outdoors sports enthusiasts, Haridwar occupies a major node for the national network of right-wing Hindu identity politics. As a consequence, Shantikunj's location in Haridwar does not simply raise questions about the Gayatri Pariwar's ability to tap into the flow of pilgrims or inability to tap into the flow of international visitors who skip Haridwar in favor of nearby Rishikesh. It raises an additional question of if and how Shantikunj might be entangled in the national political networks that converge nearby. As Somnath's recommendation that I visit the Bharat Mata temple suggests, this spatial convergence is no mere coincidence, but as I will argue in the coming section, the connections are quite complex.

## India

### The Gayatri Pariwar and the Sangh Parivar

According to Lise McKean, author of *Divine Enterprise: Gurus and the Hindu Nationalist Movement*, the question of the Gayatri Pariwar's Hindu nationalism is a straightforward one. McKean's objective in this monograph is to show how contemporary gurus' activities coincide meaningfully with the advance of Hindu nationalism and economic liberalization in India. Gurus' spiritual teachings and the inherent hierarchical structure of their institutions have functioned as a sort of opium not only of the people but also of the bourgeoisie by deemphasizing the material world, naturalizing inequality, and prioritizing a pan-Hindu solidarity that overrides class struggle.[22]

McKean's work is set in Haridwar and Rishikesh because she sees both cities, and particularly Haridwar, as having particularly strong connections to Hindu nationalist spiritualities. Before providing more in-depth analyses of other institutions from this region, she gives an overview of the religious and political landscape of this region. This is the context for her brief discussion of the Gayatri Pariwar. I have already covered much of what she covers in her short summary of the movement, although her commitment to exposing gurus as charlatans shilling for capitalist and Hindu nationalist ideology results in a tone somewhat different from mine. After raising some admittedly troubling points about how the movement might naturalize poverty as emerging from a lack of industriousness rather than a lack of socioeconomic justice,[23] she dismisses the scientific instruments at Brahmavarchas Research Center as cultic props[24] before closing with the following attempt to tie the Gayatri Pariwar to Hindu nationalism:

> The Indian Government issued a postage stamp to honor Acharya Sharma, and high-ranking officials—including Indian president Shankar Dayal Sharma—attend Parivar yajnas. This suggests that the Parivar has well-placed allies. Perhaps these influential allies find in the Parivar a large and populist front organization for the Hindu nationalist movement: Sharma's teachings resonate with the tenets of Hindu nationalism, and the Gayatri Parivar has had a long association with the VHP. Acharya Sharma had been a member of the VHP's Central Margdarshak Mandal, an advisory body of religious leaders.[25]

I am willing to charitably interpret the conspiratorial tone of McKean's suspicion that powerful, shadowy Hindu nationalists are using the Gayatri Pariwar as a populist front as merely an element of her polemical style. But nonetheless it seems to me that the significance of a popular religious leader gracing a one-rupee postage stamp on the occasion of his death and the presence of a leading INC politician[26] at Gayatri Pariwar *yajña* is overstated in her argument. Of greater interest are the closing points of this paragraph. As for Gurudev's involvement in the VHP, while it certainly seems like a reasonable possibility, it is difficult to draw any rigorous conclusions without a more precise account of his activities. Unfortunately, I have not found any other source to confirm or elaborate upon McKean's assertion. Perhaps since McKean visited Shantikunj in the early '90s in the immediate aftermath of the violence of Hindu nationalists' Ram Janmabhoomi movement and before Doctor-sahib rose to power, the Gayatri Pariwar has distanced itself slightly from the VHP. In any event, I must agree with McKean's assertion that Gayatri Pariwar teachings resonate with certain aspects of Hindu nationalist ideology. Questions about these resonances have frequently arisen in conversations I have had with colleagues about this movement. Anticipating that many readers will have similar questions, I turn now to an explicit consideration of the nature and extent of the interplay between the Gayatri Pariwar and well-known Hindu nationalist movements, if only for the sake of revealing the complexity and ambiguity of this interplay.

Although available Gayatri Pariwar materials make no noteworthy reference to the VHP or the Sangh Parivar more generally, the movement's accounts of Gurudev's life do make an effort to tie him to Madan Mohan Malaviya, one of the progenitors of the Hindu nationalist movement. Doctor-sahib offers the most extensive account of their relationship in *Odyssey of the Enlightened*. Gurudev's father, Pandit Roop Kishore Sharma, had an abiding friendship with Malaviya because they studied at the same *gurukl* as children. When Malaviya inaugurated Banaras Hindu University in February 1916, Gurudev and his father participated in the ceremony. Young Gurudev participated in a *Sarasvatī pūjā* that was led by Malaviya. Impressed by Gurudev's performance, Malaviya offered to conduct his *upanayana*, a rite of passage into the religious life of a high-caste Hindu male. Gurudev was too young at the time, but a few years later, at the age of eight, he and his father returned to Varanasi, where Malaviya introduced Gurudev to the practice that became so central to his life: Gayatri recitation.[27]

Pandya and Jyotirmay's characterization of Malaviya and his legacy focuses on his central role in founding Banaras Hindu University. No mention is made of his leadership in the Hindu Mahasabha, an organization he helped to found in 1914. Headquartered in Haridwar, the Hindu Mahasabha advocated for Hindus and fought against what they perceived as preferential treatment for Muslims and the lower castes. Although it was comparatively less powerful than the RSS, which was founded eleven years later,[28] it constituted a distinct bloc in the Indian National Congress and thus marked a turning point in the development of a Hindu nationalism.

I have already described Gurudev's association with the Arya Samaj and mentioned their proto–Hindu-nationalist sensibilities in chapter 1, but it bears considering again in this new context. Not only did the Arya Samaj prefigure Hindu nationalists' militant attitudes toward their perceived opponents and the practice of "reconverting" Muslims and Christians, but some of their members were involved in the Hindu Mahasabha, most prominently Lajpat Rai and Swami Shraddhanand.[29] The Hindu Mahasabha and the Arya Samaj were thus bound up in the same proto–Hindu-nationalist networks, and it is clear enough that Gurudev was situated in these networks from quite an early age—before Savarkar published *Hindutva*, arguably the foundational work of Hindu nationalist ideology, and before Hedgewar founded the RSS, the oldest organization in the Sangh Parivar.

Gurudev's intellectual formation clearly began in a proto–Hindu-nationalist milieu. Hedgewar, Savarkar, and their ilk drew upon this same milieu to give form to an orthodox model of Hindu nationalism, which was institutionalized in the RSS. Being formed in the same milieu, Gurudev may well have had certain affinities with the Sangh Parivar, and perhaps even viewed his aims as being aligned with theirs at certain times. But it would be an oversimplification to place the Gayatri Pariwar within that orthodox Hedgewar-Sarvarkar model of Hindu nationalism—the Sangh Parivar and the Gayatri Pariwar spring from common ancestors, but have branched off in slightly different directions.

If the proto–Hindu-nationalist milieu accounts for one parent lineage for the Gayatri Pariwar, a Gandhian lineage would be the other parent, and as I have already argued in chapter 1, the resemblance to the Gandhian side of the family is stronger. Although Gandhi has as of late been incorporated into Hindu nationalist ideology, for much of the twentieth century the relationship between the Gandhian and Hindu nationalist political streams was one of deep antipathy. Thus Gurudev's efforts to synthesize these two seemingly disparate political streams from a relatively early point in Indian history accounts for the Gayatri Pariwar's subtle points of deviation from orthodox Hindu nationalism.

Moving on from questions of intellectual genealogy to what the Gayatri Pariwar actually says and does, the question of the extent of the movement's affinity to Hindu nationalism remains murky. I will start with what I consider the Gayatri Pariwar's most important point of disjuncture from the much of the Sangh Parivar—the Gayatri Pariwar does not seem to have any propensity to violence. Not only have they not advocated violence toward India's religious minorities through their discourse, but they also seem to eschew the paramilitary drills for which the Sangh Parivar is famous (although the Gayatri Pariwar's Republic Day program did include a rather innocuous Tae Kwon Do demonstration by some teenagers).

Whether or not the Gayatri Pariwar's lack of interest in violence and paramilitary activity stems from a Gandhian nonviolence I cannot say, but it would be quite out of sync with their professed attitude toward India's religious diversity. Unlike orthodox Hindu nationalists, the Gayatri Pariwar does not take a militant stance toward Muslims and Christians, does not question their patriotism, and is not interested in "reconverting" them to Hindu traditions. In fact, the Gayatri Pariwar generally does not even claim a Hindu identity for itself.

But this is where things become more complicated. Despite this lack of interest in articulating a Hindu identity and reconverting Muslims and Christians to it, the Gayatri Pariwar *does* espouse the notion that everyone should practice *yajña* and Gayatri recitation. It is not necessary to change one's religion to do this because, according to the Gayatri Pariwar, these practices have nothing to do with one's religious identity, or for that matter, one's caste, gender, or nationality. In Gayatri Pariwar thought, it is not "Hindu-ness," but rather Gayatri recitation and *yajña* that express the essential values of India and ought to bind the nation together. Clearly, despite the Gayatri Pariwar's willingness to allow for religious difference and despite the relatively non-aggressive means through which the Gayatri Pariwar spreads, there are familiar echoes of a homogenizing essentialism here.

The affinities between the Gayatri Pariwar and orthodox forms of Hindu nationalism should be clear enough. The Gayatri Pariwar envisions practices as non-Hindu that in many circles would be considered quite clearly Hindu, and it puts them forth as building blocks for the nation. Some might cynically conclude from this description that the Gayatri Pariwar is playing disingenuously with semantics in order to push for "reconversion" without admitting it.

But whatever we think of the notion that *yajña* and the Gayatri mantra are not really Hindu, there is a subtle distinction here that is very meaningful when imagining the Gayatri Pariwar's nation-building endgame: Muslims and Christians can keep their identities and still be Indian. In fact, in a certain sense, they are no less Indian than people who identify as Hindu but do not practice Gayatri recitation and *yajña*. The fact that Gayatri parijans do not express distaste for non-Hindus leads me to believe that the Gayatri Pariwar is actually quite earnest in the distinction they are attempting to make. Thus, when scholars wish to think critically about the Gayatri Pariwar and movements like it that bear certain affinities to Hindu nationalism, we must be rigorous in determining the exact extent and nature of those affinities before imposing the category upon them.

## One Nation, Under Gayatri

With the messy work of considering the overarching relationship between the Gayatri Pariwar and Hindu nationalist ideologies and institutions out of the way (but with some questions of praxis admittedly still looming), I want to consider how the Gayatri Pariwar understands its nation-building project in its own terms. Because the process of nation-building is intimately linked with ritual practice understood through scientific discourse for the Gayatri Pariwar, parts of this discussion will echo my more extensive discussion of ritual and science in chapter 4. That discussion was generated by my questions about the formation of identities and moral selves, especially in relation to Shantikunj's upwardly mobile but disillusioned residents, and was thus rather etic in nature. While I covered the scientific rationale behind Gayatri Pariwar ritual practice, I connected it most clearly to personal morality rather than to a wider public moral project. The Gayatri Pariwar understands personal morality as the foundation of its social reform project and eschatology, and it is to that project that I now turn. As I think through this material, I will be drawing on the work of Joseph Alter, whose analyses of the many entanglements of health, morality, politics, and nationalism in India are a great help in teasing out the threads of the Gayatri Pariwar's eschatological praxis.

The motto of the Gayatri Pariwar is a good place to start thinking about the movement's approach to nation-building: "*Ham badaleṁge, yug badalegā, ham sudhareṁge, yug sudharegā*"—"We will change, the era will change; we will be reformed, the era will be reformed." At the conclusion of a variety of ritual functions, Gayatri parijans chant this affirmation together in unison. It reflects the inextricable connection in Gayatri Pariwar thought between personal betterment, collective betterment, and eschatological hope. Granted, Gurudev may be continuously intervening in history to facilitate the revival of *satyug* on a national and, ultimately, global scale, but Gayatri parijans ultimately regard the revival of *satyug* as contingent on concrete social change facilitated by their own individual efforts to better themselves.

This eschatological vision is called the Yug Nirmāṇ Yojnā or "Plan for the Transformation of the Era" in Gayatri Pariwar discourse. Perhaps the most comprehensive and systematic articulation of what Gayatri parijans must do in order to bring about this new era takes the form of Gurudev's " '100 Point Program' for the Transformation of the Era." These points, which call for personal, familial, and institutional observances, are arranged into ten sections. A brief account of these sections and some of their more notable subordinate points will provide an excellent window on the Gayatri Pariwar's nation-building project.

The first two sections cover personal and public health, respectively. Of the nineteen points Gurudev offers on health, eleven have to do with the preparation and consumption of food—the best ingredients, how they should be prepared, how much and how often we should eat, the importance of avoiding waste, and the necessity of a weekly fast. Gurudev further encourages Gayatri parijans to be hygienic, avail themselves of natural medicine, and take up yoga and other forms of exercise. Intoxicants are to be avoided and sexual activity, even in the context of marriage, is to be minimized both for the sake of our personal health and for reducing the burden of overpopulation.[30]

This focus on diet, fasting, celibacy, and Nature Cure suggests a strong connection to Gandhi, especially when they are articulated at the outset of a practical program for social change and nation-building. As Joseph Alter argues at length in *Gandhi's Body: Sex, Diet, and the Politics of Nationalism*, for Gandhi, physical health and personal morality were inextricably linked and together formed the foundation of a free India.[31] This connection is clearest in Gurudev's rationale for advocating that his followers strive to be celibate: "The stricter a person is in this regard, the healthier he will be. This is even more essential for intellectuals and students because the unrestrained use of the senses produces mental weakness and creates hurdles in achieving their goals." In *Moral Materialism: Sex and Masculinity in Modern India*, Alter, building upon insights from Romila Thapar, helpfully points to how exactly this becomes bound up with social change and nation-building. Historically, celibate world-renouncers have been able to utilize their position outside of society to present their critiques of social institutions as disinterested and therefore more authoritative. In being celibate and taking on other quasi-ascetic practices like fasting, Gandhi and any of his followers who took up similar practices were marshaling that same kind of ascetic moral authority in their nation-building efforts.[32]

A number of sections deal with the reform of various social institutions and the roles individuals have in making all of this happen. Section 3, for example, deals with making education more accessible and more in tune with Gayatri Pariwar morality. Sections 6 and 7 call for Gayatri parijans in the publishing industry and the arts to use their talents to promote good values rather than to provide mere entertainment. Section 9 focuses on the political system, describing the importance of responsible voting for Gayatri parijans before calling for a more streamlined justice system, less corruption, and greater economic equity.[33]

Sections 4, 5, and 8 deal with religious, familial, and civic activities. Gurudev describes the importance of believing in a deity for his followers, and the necessity of scriptural study and a complete ritual life as part of a broader program of self-discipline. For the most part, the language here seems to refer to a general conception of religion, but Hindu traditions come up specifically, especially in the context of ritual activity. Community members should be charitable with one another, sharing resources and time as needed. They should collaborate on civic projects and even undertake pilgrimages together. As for family, this becomes another site for the exchange of Gayatri Pariwar values through structured interactions like study, prayer, and meditation. Gurudev's comments on parenting are particularly of note here: having children is not about our own selfish desires, but to serve the nation. Consequently parents must undertake child-rearing with such ends in mind.[34] "During pregnancy," Gurudev says, "the emotional state of the mother is transferred to the child."[35]

Although there is not much surprising about the Yug Nirmāṇ Yojnā's recommendations for better institutional and social praxis, this last point is particularly intriguing. An echo of Gurudev's interest in the body, which was so central in the first two sections, makes another appearance here. The biological process of forming a child's body during pregnancy is inextricable from the formation that child's moral self. This is a good example of what Alter would call "biomorality," in which bodily state and moral being are one and the same.[36] Much of Alter's discourse on biomorality deals with diet and especially sex—the morality or immorality of our practices in these regards have distinct manifestations in our body, and thus bodily integrity signifies moral integrity.[37] This seems to be an even deeper biomorality, one in which our moral selves are written into our bodies at a moment when we could not possibly have any kind of moral consciousness ourselves. Rather, our biomoral predispositions are shaped by our mother's biomorality—a heavy burden for mothers indeed.

This brings us at last to section 10 in Gurudev's "100 Point Program," "The Spiritual Foundation of the New Era." Here, bundled together with points about self-analysis and selfless action, we find the Gayatri mantra and *yajña*:

> 70. Gayatri Worship
>
> The Gayatri *Mahamantra* is the primordial source of culture and civilization. It contains all great teachings in a seed form that can elevate or advance life. The main purpose of

> performing worship is to seek inspiration to be able to steer our feelings and tendencies on the righteous path. . . . Gayatri can be considered a complete and universal mode of worship for humankind. . . . Those who practice other types of worship should continue doing so, but should add Gayatri Mantra to their routine as well.
>
> 71. The Necessity of Yagya
>
> Gayatri is the symbol of righteous feelings. Likewise, *Yagya* is the symbol of righteous actions. The inspiration to continuously offer those things we like best for the good of society represents the divine inspiration of *Yagya*. . . . We should include Yagya observance in our daily routine in order to continually remind ourselves of this spirit.[38]

There can be no doubt that the Gayatri Pariwar advocated the kinds of personal and social reforms I have described in the previous paragraphs, but it is clear enough that Gayatri recitation and *yajña* sit at the core of the movement, or as the heading of section 10 would suggest, they are the foundation of its eschatological praxis.

One noteworthy aspect of these practices is their apparent universalism in Gayatri Pariwar discourse. Although this claim is made most explicitly about the Gayatri mantra above in point 70, Gayatri parijans make similar claims about *yajña* as well. Point 70 suggests that the Gayatri mantra's universalism stems from the fact that it is pre-cultural and encapsulates everything that is good about humanity. While I did encounter some rhetoric of this sort during my stay at Shantikunj, a more common claim, which was extended to both Gayatri recitation and *yajña*, was that these practices were universal because they had been scientifically validated. Since these practices were scientific in this sense, they had nothing to do with religious identity because scientific claims are universal. Through this rhetoric, scientific authority becomes a way of disconnecting practices we might conventionally understand as Hindu from any such religious identity and presenting them as universal.

This is furthermore closely connected with the ways in which the Gayatri Pariwar uses the term "spiritual"—including in the heading of section 10. Sources routinely described spirituality (or *adhyātmavād*) as being something that was universal and not done merely because of tradition but as a result of a deliberate personal choice for known ends. In this sense, scientific rhetoric is what allows the Gayatri Pariwar to convert practices that might be conventionally understood as particularistic religious practices into universal spiritual practices. The modernists' perception of science as a universal method for knowing the world has made it possible for scientific authority to be deployed in situations like this to generate new universalisms.

Of course, the Gayatri Pariwar's discourse about what these practices do to the body is very closely connected with these ideas. The Gayatri Pariwar understands Gayatri recitation and *yajña* as having tangible effects on the physical and subtle body that are predictable, repeatable, and observable. This includes better physical and psychological health both directly and indirectly, through the stimulation of energy centers in the subtle body. It also purifies the environment, leading to greater public health. These fundamental elements of section 10 of this Yug Nirmāṇ Yojnā circle right back around to sections 1 and 2, on personal and public health. Gayatri recitation and *yajña* fit right in with diet and celibacy in possessing a certain biomoral resonance. But there is something different about Gayatri recitation and *yajña*. Whereas diet and celibacy involve disciplining innate bodily predispositions to foster biomorality, Gayatri recitation and *yajña* are disciplines that operate outside of the field of such bodily predispositions. The Gayatri Pariwar thus presents these practices as biomoral technologies, fostering a tangible biomorality in a manner that can be understood within a biomoral framework.

Such an understanding of Gayatri recitation and *yajña* suggests that they have been absorbed into a yogic framework. In *Yoga in Modern India*, Joseph Alter traces a trajectory for yoga that bears a marked resemblance to the Gayatri Pariwar's understanding of its own central practices. The history Alter traces for yoga involves a shift from the magic and mysticism that fascinated Orientalist scholars and the figures like Vivekananda and Aurobindo, Hindu reformers who would become major proponents of Hindu traditions in the West. This resulted in a conception of the yogic body that focused on "physical fitness, applied medical research, and pragmatic populism rather than arcane philosophy and spiritualism."[39]

We clearly see in the Gayatri Pariwar's conception of Gayatri recitation and *yajña* a parallel project, but the connections go even deeper. In the early twentieth century, Gandhi popularized a system of alternative medicine called Nature Cure in India. Although it originated in Europe some decades earlier, it seems that Nature Cure's ontological and physiological assumptions match up surprisingly well with those of yoga. The result is that yoga and Nature Cure are both almost inextricably intertwined as medical practices in India.[40] Since Gandhi was also one of Gurudev's forebears, it is only natural that elements of Nature Cure appear among the systems of alternative medicine that Gurudev advocates in his "100 Point Program." I would not go so far as to say that the Gayatri recitation and *yajña* are integrated with Nature Cure in the same sense that yoga is. Rather, I would argue that the presence of Nature Cure in the constellation of ideas that Gurudev advocates signifies that the Gayatri Pariwar's reconceptualization of Gayatri recitation and *yajña* through populist and medical discourses implies a very close link to what has happened with yoga. The intellectual processes that brought yoga into line with modernity and the colonial and postcolonial circumstances that made those intellectual processes both necessary and possible are quite akin to what has happened with Gayatri recitation and *yajña* in the Gayatri Pariwar.

Nature Cure fed into Gandhi's biomoral obsessions, structuring life at his ashrams and shaping his vision for India's future.[41] Gayatri recitation, *yajña*, and a host of other practices bound up with biomorality similarly structure life at Shantikunj and represent the Gayatri Pariwar's aspirations for the nation—one in which good health and morality, inextricably linked, characterize all social relations. Persons with biomoral integrity can go on to serve the nation, building it up, making it strong and unified, and preparing it to realize its full potential. Such a nation, a compound body in a certain sense, must realize its own biomoral integrity before it can truly take its place on the global stage.

## A Gathering of Elders

From March 4 through 7, 2012, the World Council of Elders of Ancient Traditions and Cultures and International Center for Cultural Studies held the Fourth International Conference and Gathering of the Elders on the campus of DSVV. On Somnath's recommendation, I attended this event, and it was one of the most ethnographically rich periods of my fieldwork. In some sense, it was an ethnographer's dream: in a span of four days I conversed with a Nepali folklorist about how his research was changing under the Maoist regime, listened to a live recitation of the Kyrgyz national epic, discussed with a Maori woman how anthropology strives to atone for its colonial complicity, saw slides from a massive gathering of Hungarians who were trying to revive their pre-Christian religious and cultural traditions, and finally listened to a Mayan elder speak out against the New Age appropriation of the Mayan calendar. But through all of this I was plagued by a difficult question of ethnographic ethics: should I parse for my new acquaintances from around the world the Hindu nationalist subtexts that ran throughout the conference?

The International Center for Cultural Studies, it turns out, is an offshoot of the RSS.[42] Perhaps it is unsurprising, then, that during this orthodox Hindu nationalist perspectives had generally been absent from the Shantikunj community were evident in some of the conference's guests. Just after the opening keynote in DSVV's large auditorium, I was approached by a software engineer who was attending the event as a member of the RSS. He told me that the RSS helps to organize this conference because only Indian culture can bring people from so many different cultures together. After the following session an older man with the Aurangabad branch of the VHP[43] struck up a conversation with me, and informed me that this conference was for cultures that have been victims of "aggressive cultures" who destroy others' ways of life. The following day, while relaxing with a cup of tea in the outdoor dining tent, a third Sangh parijan approached me. A medical doctor from the UK, he told me that he worked for a "missionary charity" called the HSS.[44] This description of the HSS intrigued me, so I asked, "Do you mostly do missionary outreach to the Indian community in the UK?" His response surprised me. The HSS in the UK was working to instill Indian values like respect for parents, tolerance, and "non-conversion" in the general British population.

Diverse as the event's delegates were, many of the conference's panelists were Indian and quite a few had elements of Hindu nationalist ideology in their presentations. Their discourse filled in the gaps left by these private conversations with members of the RSS, VHP, and HSS. These panelists suggested that all human civilizations derive from Indian civilization, and so, when Maori people, Hungarian Neopagans, and Mayan elders come to India, it is like a return to their roots, to their mother, to a place where the original traditions of humanity have been preserved. No other culture has this motherly status, nor has any resisted the aggression

Figure 6.2. DSVV's competitive yoga team demonstration at the International Conference and Gathering of the Elders.

of Christianity and Islam so effectively. Hindus must consequently be a leader for indigenous peoples, and must restore humanity to its original Hindu values.

This is what Hindu nationalism looks like when it goes global. It is a project that is full of inversions. The quest for humanity's origins and the project of pushing humanity to its modernist *telos* become one and the same: our future *telos* is our origin in the ancient Hindu golden age. The result is that colonialism and the neocolonial dimensions of globalization no longer look like projects of dispersal, of cultural flows moving from centers of power to the periphery, but a drawing in, a folding of the degenerate periphery back into a monolithic pristine center. This discourse about the role that Hindu nationalism sees itself playing as India emerges as a key player on the global stage is a chilling reverberation from the impact of European fascism on orthodox forms of Hindu nationalism.

For all of the reasons I have given above, I am in retrospect quite confident that the Gayatri Pariwar could not be accurately described as a Hindu nationalist organization. But being party to so much Hindu nationalist rhetoric on the premises of DSVV so early during my fieldwork, I worried about the extent of the Gayatri Pariwar's affinity—they must have known they were hosting a conference that was run by the Sangh Parivar, right? But it would be a mistake to read into that too much, I reasoned. After all, it could be the case that the Gayatri Pariwar just liked the idea of this specific conference without necessarily agreeing with the Hindu nationalist ideologies that led the International Center for Cultural Studies to organize it. With this hope tenuous in my heart, I went forward.

After the Conference and Gathering of the Elders ended on Holi Puja, the Gayatri Pariwar invited the delegates to stay and celebrate. After a small group of us who remained ate dinner together, we were escorted to the site where the Holi bonfire was being set up. We sat together on plastic chairs while a large crowd of Shantikunj residents gathered nearby. Before the bonfire was lit, Doctor-sahib addressed the crowd at length in Hindi. In the course of his lecture, Doctor-sahib touched upon a theme that had become rather familiar over the course of the conference. He told the crowd that there was no such thing as "America Mata," only Bharat Mata. This was the source of India's unique appeal. This was why India had to reach out to the rest of the world.

The Gayatri Pariwar continues onwards, a stream that does not run in parallel with its Hindu nationalist cousins, but that crisscrosses it, exchanging ideas as India's social circumstances change. I have not heard Gayatri parijans condemn Islam and Christianity with the same venomous rhetoric as orthodox Hindu nationalists, and that is important. But embedded in Doctor-sahib's sentiments about Bharat Mata's role in the world is a certain sense of global "spiritual" (if not explicitly religious) hierarchy—an old theme that reflects Vivekananda's appropriation of the dichotomy of the "spiritual India" and "material West" in service of nationalism as he prepared to embark on his famous journey to the United States.

Things have gotten quite a bit messier in thinking about the Gayatri Pariwar at the national scale, and they are about to get messier still. Whereas within Shantikunj and at the regional level, space seemed to be constructed in a manner that was coherent and intuitive despite many interconnecting flows, at the national level, the intensity of circulation is such that it becomes rather difficult to follow and tends to abstraction. The significance of Haridwar in Hindu nationalist networks has recurred, most notably in conjunction with Madan Mohan Malaviya, who established the proto–Hindu-nationalist Hindu Mahasabha there. Thus we have seen that even prior to its inception and its move to Haridwar, the Gayatri Pariwar has been entangled in Hindu nationalist networks. We have seen how Shantikunj becomes a microcosm for a nation-building project that deploys Gayatri recitation and *yajña* as biomoral technologies that are closely tied to a Gandhian framework. The healthy, moral, coherent, nation the Gayatri Pariwar is trying to build will be ready to work on a global scale to bring about the Gayatri Pariwar's eschatological vision: the revival of *satyug*.

Early on in this chapter, I introduced the image of Shantikunj's bilingual signs as emblematic of the problems the Gayatri Pariwar faces in realizing this aspiration. Much of what I have outlined so far about the way the Gayatri Pariwar situates itself in the space of the Indian nation points to monolingualism. I would not consider this problematic, to be clear, nor do I consider it particularly surprising considering the Gayatri Pariwar's deep populist and anti-colonial commitments. Particularly telling in this regard is the parallel trajectory the Gayatri Pariwar's conception of Gayatri recitation and *yajña* has taken with India's yoga–Nature Cure complex. This trajectory, as Alter suggests, runs quite counter to the Orientalisms that bolstered the popularity of Hindu traditions in the West. Even the rhetoric I encountered during Holi puja, while quite explicitly about globalization, was aimed not at persuading outsiders to be receptive to elements of Hindu traditions but rather at inspiring a predominately Hindu audience to take up the banner. How, in the absence of these Orientalisms and with such populist nationalist sentiments at the movement's core, might the Gayatri Pariwar develop a Guru English to suit its own bilingualism?

## The World

### Data-Driven Eschatology

My question finds the beginnings of an answer in a call for papers for the International Vedic Conference on "Veda and Thought Revolution," hosted at DSVV just one week after the Gathering of the Elders. It begins thus:

> Scientific progress of last 200 years has brought total change in the scope, form and dimensions of the modern problems

> swarming over humanity's present and future. Now, various cultures of the world and diverse schools of thought are mutually interacting and affecting each other at a frenzied speed. In this era of globalization, thoughts do wield greater power than the biggest weapons in the arsenals of superpowers. The tide of collective-mind (*Jan-manas*) creates the circumstances in its favor. Not weapons, but the force of thoughts alone can counter this tide of collective-mind. Sharpness and strength of thoughts are the foundation of the real power in this 'flat-world.' This is the age in which thoughts are at war with thoughts. Whatever school of thought will have strong sway over collective-mind, that will create favorable circumstances in the society. Only the strong and beneficent thoughts will create the circumstances in favor of humanity's bright future.

What this passage suggests is that one of the central concepts in the Gayatri Pariwar's eschatology, Vicār Krāṃti (or Thought Revolution), has taken on a different shape in the information age. The nature of this change in shape is worth exploring in some depth, especially because it sheds light on the complex relationships between religion, science, and technology in our world.

In a certain sense Vicār Krāṃti has always been network-dependent. According to this concept, when a single person's thoughts change, it is reflected in that person's actions. Those actions have an impact on the person's immediate family, changing their thoughts and in turn their actions. This revolution continues to spread, through each person's networks, to the community, the nation, and eventually, the world. Vicār Krāṃti has historically been quite contingent upon networks in one of the word's older senses: a group of people connected by a web of relationships based in conventional, face-to-face social interactions. This model of social change might make a certain amount of sense when dealing with smaller groups of people and in the context of the Gayatri Pariwar's grassroots organizing. It reflects the logic of Gurudev's nation-building project, with its Gandhian roots. At larger scales, as cultural and linguistic differences become more dominant and face-to-face networks offer interconnections that are fewer and increasingly tenuous, the situation changes. Thus as the Gayatri Pariwar shifts its attention beyond the confines of India, new strategies are required.

The rise of global communication technology and its pervasive status in our everyday life allows for the exchange of information "at a frenzied speed," to borrow the CFP's phrase. It has created new networks—networks that are not constrained by the limits of bodily interaction upon which Vicār Krāṃti can capitalize. But the lack of materiality in these interactions necessitates a substantial change in how this process will have to work for the Gayatri Pariwar. A conventional model of Vicār Krāṃti demands that once a person's thoughts have been transformed, they must perform these transformed thoughts corporeally in order to influence those nearby. But there can be no question of such a corporeal performance of that sort through the virtual, immaterial networks of contemporary communication technology.

Nigel Thrift's notion of "qualculation" is a great help in understanding how the Gayatri Pariwar solves this problem—or perhaps, does not even see it as a problem at all. In *Non-Representational Theories*, Thrift articulates a paradigm shift we are currently undergoing as a result of a massive spike in our computers' calculative capacity. While humans have continued to assign numbers to things in the world as our mathematical thinking has grown in sophistication—street addresses, geographic distances, and population statistics to name a few—contemporary information technology has rendered calculation applicable to virtually everything, signaling a shift to qualculation. Qualculation allows us to address not only quantitative questions but also qualitative ones through the use of sophisticated programs that are capable of increasingly accurate models of reality and that are increasingly readily available to the general populace. The normalization of qualculation brings with it the possibility of the extension of the body and its senses into new, virtual spaces.[45]

The Gayatri Pariwar's efforts to actualize Vicār Krāṃti are informed by such a qualculative framework. Faced with an inability to offer its intended audience, well beyond the physical confines of India but connected by the same digital communications networks, the Gayatri Pariwar qualculates the bodies of its members by studying them in laboratories, hooking them up to instruments, recording their biometrics as data, and making that data available online. While the ability to collect biometrics is not new, the ubiquity of qualculation in our world creates a social context in which a body should be no better or different than a suitably comprehensive set of data describing its qualities. This qualculation does not simply allow for a transfiguration of the body to the digital landscape, but also mimics its performative capacities. Bodies perform their biomorality just as easily when they have taken the form of data as they do in their material forms. When our health and our morality are conflated, the same data set can perform both.

My description here reflects a position outside of the qualculative framework, and thus relies on distinctions between the materiality of bodies and the immateriality of their data or between performed biomorality and its representation. I instinctively cling to the notion that these distinctions matter, but at the same time I harbor a certain skepticism that I am merely deceiving myself as to the nature of the social reality I inhabit and, for that matter, the one in which the Gayatri Pariwar is attempting to globalize. Perhaps in some phenomenological sense, contemporary information technology has not changed the way in which Vicār Krāṃti works, but rather in the context of its qualculative framework has allowed it to be extended unaltered through radically contracted space.

Science does not merely allow for the transfiguration of biomoral bodies into data that may be circulated through global communication technology. According to a number of Gayatri parijans, science provides a universal, culturally neutral means to justify their practices for those who do not come from a Hindu background. Consider, for example, the following sentiment in *Thought Revolution*: "To the Western ear, the practice of infusing higher vibrations into the subtle atmosphere may sound superstitious or at least unscientific, however, laboratory studies have recently begun to verify its claims of healing and environmental purification."[46] Due to the epistemic power of science, what seems like a culturally situated practice that would not make sense to Westerners is assumed to take on a different character.

One thing that intrigued me about this discourse at the earliest stages of my research project is how it seems to displace any sense of wonderment or sublime experience with a seemingly disenchanted view of their practices. During my time at Shantikunj, I certainly observed that Gayatri parijans experience no shortage of powerful emotion as a result of their involvement in the Gayatri Pariwar. Why not build a globalizing strategy around the intense experiences to which their spiritual lives have given them access?

Sianne Ngai's *Our Aesthetic Categories* articulates an aesthetic theory that illuminates how the zany, the cute, and the interesting—categories that are associated with production, consumption, and circulation respectively—

have become central to postmodern aesthetic experience. Ngai's analysis of the interesting offers substantial insight into this problem. Drawing on a variety of scholars writing in or about a number of disciplines, Ngai notes that the interesting is consistently noted for its capacity to align its subjects into a network. It has this effect because of its ambiguous position between affect and cognition: it is an indeterminate feeling that something is noteworthy because it deviates somehow from established norms and thus merits deeper consideration. When a group of people in a network perceive something as merely interesting, that thing becomes marked as worth discussing but no final, discussion-stopping judgment is applied to it, so the group can have an ongoing discussion about it circulating it through their network all the way.[47] On account of its indeterminacy and incompleteness, the interesting persists through time, whereas the sublime is a "sudden blazing, and without future."[48]

Science becomes a mechanism to present the benefits of practices like Gayatri recitation and *yajña* as merely interesting in this sense. This aesthetic quality allows these practices to be broken down and circulated through global information networks in ways that Gayatri parijans' sublime experiences never could be. How, indeed, would such experiences be possible to circulate between parties? A sublime experience is had by a person, but once put into words and posted online ceases to be sublime in the same sense. But by expressing what Gayatri parijans get out of their practices in scientific terms, as data, it becomes eminently suitable to share, comment on, and otherwise circulate. If the Gayatri Pariwar and its practices were to be the subject of a listicle with a click-bait title and well-produced info-graphics, the interesting scientific data it has propagated about its practices would doubtlessly garner more circulation and discussion than a collection of anecdotes about sublime personal experiences (albeit perhaps not in the religious studies contingents of social networking sites).

None of this speculation about qualculation and the circulation of merely interesting data is intended to state definitively that the Gayatri Pariwar has hit on a winning strategy for globalization. It has rather been an attempt to tease out how the movement is attempting, whether successfully or not, to utilize available technologies to achieve its goal of globalizing its practices. In general, it points to a fascinating alternative to the problem of developing enough fluency in Guru English to become a bilingual movement. Science has been a part of Guru English more or less since the beginning, but the particular intensity with which the Gayatri Pariwar deploys science to generate data will make it possible for the movement to leave language behind almost entirely. With enough data to back up its practices, the question of bilingualism and language in general could become moot in the face of an endless array of numbers.

## A *Yajña* in Upstate New York

In the summer of 2013, the Gayatri Chetna Centre in Piscataway, NJ, arranged a series of *yajña*s to be conducted in the northeastern United States. One of these was held in Manlius, NY, a well-to-do town near my home in Syracuse. I attended this event along with my PhD Advisor, Joanne Waghorne, on a hot July afternoon, eager to see how the Gayatri Pariwar functions in a diasporic context.

The quiet suburban cul-de-sac was lined with cars from various states in the eastern US, some surprisingly distant. When we arrived at the address listed on our flier, it was clear enough that we were in the right place. A large crowd of Hindu Americans bustled back and forth between an impressive house and its spacious back yard, where a large canopy had been erected for the event. Many in the crowd were wearing *kurtā*-pajamas and saris that were reminiscent not so much of the simple saffron of Shantikunj as they were of a Hindu wedding or similar formal social function. Our presence seemed to be a bit of a surprise to our hosts, who inquired with polite interest about our work and expressed his concern over our comfort at the event. We were the only guests at this event who were not South Asian, a familiar experience for us as ethnographers of Hindu traditions, but perhaps his worries were understandable.

Once the makeshift *yajñaśāla* was prepared, the afternoon's program began, and the community that had gathered began trickling into the shade under the canopy, although some families and especially young people continued to socialize nearby for the duration of the event. Senior Shantikunj residents presided over the program, delivering lectures, singing songs, and leading and commenting on the *yajña*. Joanne and I were originally seated with other guests, but somewhat inexplicably, they were asked to separate from us and from that point on we were isolated from the rest of the group. Much of the program was conducted in Hindi and sometimes Gujarati, even for this multigenerational group of Hindu Americans gathering in Upstate New York.

In a certain respect, the goings on at this *yajña* resemble a dichotomy that Joanne Waghorne herself described in "The Hindu Gods in a Split-Level World." At the Sri Siva Vishnu Temple in Maryland, Waghorne noticed that the upper floor was reserved for conventional ritual activities that appealed to predominately immigrant-generation adults, whereas the lower floor, where classes and cultural events took place, better served the needs of younger second-generation Hindu Americans.[49] Much of the discourse on Asian American immigrant religion across the generations notes how religious institutions allow the immigrant generation to reconstruct in microcosm the world they have left behind. The second generation, having less intense attachments to their parent's homeland, look instead for a space to form and express their unique identities as Asian Americans, or in this case more specifically Hindu Americans.[50] In this sense, the split-level setup that Waghorne describes ensures that the needs of both generations are thoroughly met.

A similar dichotomy appeared at this *yajña*, but with a twist. Here, it was not so much that the adults were conducting *yajña* upstairs while the children took a class downstairs, but rather the adult ritual activity took place inside the *yajña* pavilion while the youth were left outside, with no particular structured cultural activity other than informal socialization. The activities inside the pavilion may well have fulfilled the older generation of Hindus' desires to replicate a piece of their homeland. The lecturing style and ritual activities were indeed quite similar to those I witnessed at Shantikunj. The only noticeable differences were that the languages used were Hindi and Gujarati in New York State instead of exclusively Hindi at Shantikunj, and the *yajña* was explained in greater detail for the diaspora crowd.

But it is unclear how any of this would have appealed to most of the second-generation youth. Some of them may have been competent in Hindi or Gujarati and some may have even known a bit of both. Those who did not know one or both of these languages may very well have appreciated an opportunity to better their language skills. Other less linguistically inclined young people may have been more enthusiastic about participating in the ritual if they had had an alternate way of understanding its rationale. Indeed, as Eleanor Nesbitt and others have shown, providing younger Hindu Americans with structured environments in which they can study their tradition through English-language materials seems to foster more consistent participation across generations in Hindu-based movements like the Gayatri Pariwar.[51]

Figure 6.3. The author, inside the *Yajña* Pavilion, Manlius, NY (photo by Joanne Waghorne).

Joanne and I may have been inside the pavilion as we participated in the *yajña*, but perhaps in reality we should have occupied the outside space as well. It was a curious echo of my experience in the dining hall: Shantikunj visitors treated me like an outsider despite the fact that I was a resident; at this *yajña* in a northeastern United States suburb not unlike the one in which I grew up, I felt like an outsider despite my long stay at Shantikunj. But in reality the alienation Joanne and I experienced should not have surprised us at all. The space inside the pavilion was intended to be a reconstruction of immigrant-generation Indian Americans' old homeland, and our presence was genuinely disruptive to that reconstruction. It was not for us.

It is hard to avoid acknowledging that the kind of bilingualism that prevailed at the Upstate New York *yajña*—Hindi-Gujarati rather than Hindi-English—has implications for the Gayatri Pariwar's global aspirations. Yes, this type of bilingualism serves the social needs of immigrant-generation Hindu Americans quite well. But it leaves their children outside of the pavilion for the most part, and has a similar effect on the non-Hindus who the Gayatri Pariwar also wants to reach. Nor does it seem that the mathematical data generated by the Gayatri Pariwar's research is sufficient to bridge the gap, at least absent a bilingualism of the right sort.

Since I know the Gayatri Pariwar has understood my presence as another step toward its impending global success, I feel somewhat guilty in taking such a negative angle on this event. It does not do justice to the community that hosted me during my research in Shantikunj. So I want to shift to a slightly different tone here as I conclude this vignette. At the time of the Upstate New York *yajña*, it had barely been over a year since Shantikunj's bilingual signs went up. It is clear enough that the Gayatri Pariwar has a substantial network in the diaspora and that it fulfills important needs for immigrant-generation Hindu Americans. Doubtless many of their children will follow, even if, at times, they are left outside of the pavilion.

## International Yoga Day

On June 21, 2015, International Yoga Day was observed for the first time, and the Gayatri Pariwar was eager to participate. Several weeks later, I received an email from a Gayatri parijan with an attached slideshow that highlighted events that the Gayatri Pariwar had organized either independently or in collaboration with others in locations such as Atlanta, Sydney, Dar-es-Salaam, and Kuala Lumpur. The slideshow also depicted apparently unaffiliated International Yoga Day events such as the massive gathering in Times Square. These proceedings are framed by quotes from Gurudev, Doctor-sahib, and, perhaps most intriguingly, Indian Prime Minister Narendra Modi, all emphasizing the importance of a practice that, like yoga, integrates and renders whole a human being by operating on both physiological and psychological levels.

One of the distinctive aspects of Modi's administration has been his emphasis on yoga. This has included not only efforts directed toward the Indian population through the development of a ministry to promote and regulate yoga and other indigenous and alternative health practices, but also a transnational effort to emphasize the Indian roots of the global phenomenon into which yoga has evolved. A member of the Hindu nationalist Bharatiya Janata Party, Narendra Modi became Prime Minister of India about two years after the conclusion of my field research. Modi is the face of a new Hindu nationalism, one that has thoroughly integrated

Gandhi into its lineage and is conscious, more than ever, of India's place on the global stage. Through the success of International Yoga Day, Modi has pointed the way toward a cosmopolitan biomorality that represents the new opportunities available to the Gayatri Pariwar in the Modi era. Perhaps in that context, the Gayatri Pariwar's International Yoga Day slideshow is photographic evidence that *satyug* is just around the corner.

# Conclusion

## Enchanted Science

On July 4, 2012, scientists working at CERN announced that they had observed a particle that was consistent with the long-theorized Higgs boson. The scientific community by and large kept its claims understated, emphasizing the need for further observation. Journalists and popular science enthusiasts were generally less sober in their reception of the "discovery" of the so-called "God particle."[1] This was, admittedly, exciting stuff—who could blame them for reacting with such fervor? The Higgs boson had been the last gap in the Standard Model of particle physics, after all. And that would make it the God particle of the gaps.

This preliminary observation meant different things to different people, even as it seemed to elicit similarly intense affective responses. I conducted my interview with Gyaneshwar just after the announcement, and he told me that CERN had discovered empirical proof of the existence of God. One more specific claim that I heard at the time was that this observation gave empirical proof to Advaita Vedānta, since this God particle was to be found in all matter. And in the midst of all of this excitement in India, social media brought me into contact with an American New Atheist who triumphantly declared that this was another nail in the coffin for religion. Angered by the lack of nuance in his claim and larger conception of religion, I wasted hours on that argument and things got pretty heated. The next day, ashamed of our aggressive rhetoric, we apologized to one another. We realized we had both been under a lot of stress lately and our moods had shaped our discourse.

When I was in the field participating in and observing situations like this and the others I have described in this book, I must admit that I had failed to note the intensity of the emotions attached to science. Looking back at myself, I wonder how I could have been so dense. The questions that generated this project are reflective of my earlier understanding of how people experience science: "Didn't the appeal of believing in miraculous happenings lie in an escape from the humdrum mundanity of modern disenchantment? Weren't scientific explanations completely antithetical to that appeal?" The assumptions in these questions line up somewhat with Lawrence Babb's famous account of Sai Baba's popularity among middle-class Hindus—their seemingly superstitious belief in Sai Baba's magic suggests a kind of re-enchantment.[2] But my perspective at the other end of this project is similar to one put forward by Michael Saler: moderns are not disenchanted; rather, we are enchanted with science.[3] To the New Atheist and Gyaneshwar alike, scientific explanations are anything but disenchanting. They are bound up with hope and excitement and laden with culturally situated meanings that extend well beyond understanding why certain particles have mass. The idea of performing *yajña* as part of a laboratory experiment becomes much less counterintuitive if we work from the supposition that science itself is enchanted, and that, to riff on Latour, we have never been disenchanted.[4]

Critics of science studies might declare, in their best "gotcha" tone, that what I have described in this book is enchantment not with science, but rather with pseudoscience. Meera Nanda would surely be among their ranks. In *Prophets Facing Backward: Postmodern Critiques of Science and Hindu Nationalism in India*, Nanda asserts that science studies scholars are responsible for delegitimizing "real" science and encouraging postcolonial peoples to develop their own alternative sciences. But these sciences have no legitimacy, according to her. She describes them as being merely designed to reaffirm extant tradition, and ultimately points to the way they service fascistic Hindu nationalist ideology.[5] So for her, the enchantment comes into the picture from the extant traditions that are being fused with scientific institutions. And this can happen partly because of a sort of scientific illiteracy that science studies has bred.

The margins of my copy of Nanda are crammed with frustrated scrawlings from before my fieldwork. While I retain many of the questions I had at that time, my own research has left me with a new question about her work. The historical and social contexts for Nanda's work are rather similar to my own—she speaks of upward mobility, technological change, and economic liberalization since 1991, for example. The middle classes who benefit from these trends also benefit from the alternative sciences, what she calls "anti-modernist ideas,"[6] because it allows them to keep others in their place while their own quality of life improves.

What puzzles me is that Nanda is not so keen to track the rise of these so-called anti-modernist ideas against the rapidly growing numbers of STEM-educated professionals in the historical period that she seems to be concerned with. The picture that has emerged over the course of my own research is that these STEM-educated professionals are the very people who have embraced these "anti-modernist" alternative sciences. How can we not locate a meaningful correlation between the rapidly growing numbers of scientists and engineers in India and the contemporary proliferation of alternative sciences?

What we see happening in India cannot be attributed exclusively to the delegitimizing consequences of critiques of science, much less to a lack of scientific literacy among STEM-educated Hindus. Rather, as I have shown in this book, the rise of "alternative sciences" in India has to do at least in part with the effects of neoliberalism on science and technology. In the context of contemporary India's political economy, we see the ever-increasing ubiquity of scientific authority, with the ways in which scientific institutions have become bound up with the hopes and dreams of a new middle class, with the expansion in scope of the scientific method to explore fields of inquiry that are less and less tangible, with the deepening divides between highly specialized bodies of scientific knowledge, and with scientific institutions' links to the prestigious transnational (and often neocolonial) networks that have emerged in the age of globalization. This is what it looks like when science is the way of knowing things and technology is the way to advance in society; this is what it looks like when science and technology have won decisive intellectual and economic victories. Moreover, science and technology work in India have a deep history of association with Nehruvian middle-class moral projects. Given this state of affairs, it is entirely understandable that so many Gayatri parijans turned to STEM fields for their education and careers.

But for the disillusioned STEM professionals I met at Shantikunj, there was no sense of joyous moral fulfillment that affirms middle-class identity to be found in available STEM jobs. The Nehruvian promise of a role in India's development had dried up with liberalization. The prime beneficiaries of STEM work in India's new political economy were not society at large, but a handful of individuals pursuing their own personal gain. Where was the middle-class moral respectability in that? The result is a subset of the Indian population with an intense emotional investment in science and technology that was, in this capitalist context, not yielding the desired return.

This state of affairs creates a moral crisis for some Indian STEM professionals—science and technology have lost their moral legitimacy because they seem to be mere instruments of self-enrichment. For these disillusioned STEM professionals, the Gayatri Pariwar represents a much-needed intervention in this crisis because it envisions a role for science and technology in their moral project. Through its use of scientific authority, the Gayatri Pariwar is able to claim universal intellectual legitimacy for ritual practices that refine one's moral character in ways that send ripples of reform out through society. Through communication technology, it is also able to project the intellectual legitimacy of these character-refining rituals out to the world, giving Shantikunj's STEM professionals an opportunity to communicate their middle-class morality to a global public.

# Notes

## Introduction

1. It is a common belief among Hindus that the universe progresses cyclically through four *yugas* (eras) that become progressively worse—Satya, Treta, Dwāpara, and Kali. Hindus also generally agree that we are currently in the Kali Yuga.

2. "Members of the Gayatri family"; in other words, a Gayatri Pariwar member.

3. Republic Day is a patriotic holiday in India observered on the anniversary of its constitution coming into effect. Basant Panchami is a Hindu holiday celebrating the imminent arrival of spring. It has strong associations with education via its focus on the goddess Saraswati.

4. Brahmavarchas, ed., *Thought Revolution: A Western Introduction to the Work of Acharya Shriram Sharma* (Haridwar, India: Yugantar Chetna Publications, 2011), 2.

5. Hereafter I will generally write "Gayatri Pariwar." This is not only for brevity's sake, but is also in keeping with an earlier naming convention in the movement that still seems to hold in conversation with members.

6. Science, technology, engineering, and mathematics.

7. Lise McKean, *Divine Enterprise: Gurus and the Hindu Nationalist Movement* (Chicago: University of Chicago Press, 1996), 45–53.

8. Meera Nanda, *Prophets Facing Backward: Postmodern Critiques of Science and Hindu Nationalism in India* (New Brunswick, NJ: Rutgers University Press, 2003), 80–82.

9. In general, I will follow community conventions in referring to the Gayatri Pariwar's leadership for two main reasons. First, these titles give readers a sense of how the community understands these leaders—indeed, the significance of these titles becomes an important component of my argument in subsequent chapters of this book. And second, because the Gayatri Pariwar is led by a single

family, using titles tends to be less ambiguous than simply referring to leaders by their last name and less cumbersome than using both first and last name.

10. The Gayatri mantra is a Vedic hymn that has remained quite important in contemporary Hindu traditions. *Yajña* is a ritual of offering that also derives from Vedic texts.

11. Cf. Christophe Jaffrelot, *The Hindu Nationalist Movement in India* (New York: Columbia University Press, 1998).

12. This set of four shrines in the Garhwal Himalayas, Badrinath, Kedarnath, Ganagotri, and Yamunotri, are quite important in the North Indian Hindu religious landscape.

13. Jonathan Z. Smith, *Relating Religion: Essays in the Study of Religion* (Chicago: University of Chicago Press, 2004), 194.

14. On the problems of using a socially constructed category with culturally specific meanings like science while thinking about intellectual exchange between India and the West, see Peter Gottschalk, *Religion, Science, and Empire: Classifying Hinduism and Islam in British India* (New York: Oxford University Press, 2012), 21, and Joseph S. Alter, *Yoga in Modern India: The Body Between Science and Philosophy* (Princeton: Princeton University Press, 2010), 28–9.

15. Michael Shermer, *Why People Believe Weird Things: Pseudoscience, Superstition, and Other Confusions of Our Time* (New York: W.H. Freeman, 1997), 167, quoted in Nanda, *Prophets Facing Backward*, 68.

16. Karl R. Popper, *Conjectures and Refutations: The Growth of Scientific Knowledge* (New York: Routledge, 2002), 310.

17. Sandra Harding, *Sciences from Below: Feminisms, Postcolonialities, and Modernities* (Durham, NC: Duke University Press, 2008), 6.

18. Thomas S. Kuhn, *The Structure of Scientific Revolutions* (Chicago: University of Chicago Press, 1996).

19. Gyan Prakash, *Another Reason* (Princeton University Press, 1999).

20. Gottschalk (*Religion, Science, and Empire*, 33) similarly distances himself from the troublesome term *science*, focusing instead on *scientism* for the purposes of his project. I propose my own schema here because it allows for a kind of flexibility that is helpful for my project without sacrificing precision.

21. Jonathan B. Edelmann, "Hindu Theology as Churning the Latent," *Journal of the American Academy of Religion* 81, no. 2 (2013): 429–30; for examples of how the term "theology" might be used in relation to scientific discourse, see Jonathan B. Edelmann, *Hindu Theology and Biology: The Bhāgavata Purāṇa and Contemporary Theory* (New York: Oxford University Press, 2012) and Jonathan B. Edelmann, "Hinduism and Science: Contemporary Considerations," *Zygon* 47, no. 3 (2012): 624–42.

22. Melissa Gregg and Gregory J. Seigworth, eds., *The Affect Theory Reader* (Durham, NC: Duke University Press, 2010), 7–8; Ann Cvetkovich, *Depression:*

*A Public Feeling* (Durham, NC: Duke University Press, 2012), 4–5, differentiates between a Deleuzian approach to doing affect theory, which utilizes the terms *affect*, *emotion*, and *feeling* in distinct, clearly defined ways, and a Public Feelings approach, in which the meanings of these terms overlap and they serve as "points of departure for discussion rather than definition." It is this latter tradition that I draw upon most closely when I talk about affect and emotion.

23. Donovan O. Schaefer, *Religious Affects: Animality, Evolution, and Power* (Durham, NC: Duke University Press, 2015), 7.

24. Cvetkovich, *Depression*; Gregg and Seigworth, *The Affect Theory Reader*; Kathleen Stewart, *Ordinary Affects* (Durham, NC: Duke University Press, 2007).

25. Sara Ahmed, "Affective Economies," *Social Text* 22, no. 2 (79) (2004): 119–20; Sara Ahmed, *The Cultural Politics of Emotion* (New York: Routledge, 2013), 1.

26. Gregg and Seigworth, *The Affect Theory Reader*, 5.

27. Ruth Behar, *The Vulnerable Observer: Anthropology that Breaks Your Heart* (Boston: Beacon Press, 1997), 9–16.

28. Wendy Doniger O'Flaherty, *Women, Androgynes, and Other Mythical Beasts* (Chicago: University of Chicago Press, 1982), 9–10; Wendy Doniger O'Flaherty, *The Origins of Evil in Hindu Mythology* (Delhi: Motilal Banarsidass, 1988), 5–7.

29. The formal transliteration is *Gāyatrī*, but as the diacritical marks are left off in many English-context presentations of the name, for consistency it will be rendered as *Gayatri* throughout, except in quoted excerpts.

30. Doris Srinivasan, "Saṃdhyā: Myth and Ritual," *Indo-Iranian Journal* 15 no. 3 (1973): 161–69.

31. Krishna Lal, "Sāvitrī: From Saṃhitas to Gṛhyasūtras," *Annals of the Bhandarkar Oriental Research Institute* 52, no. 1 (1971): 226–8.

32. C. Mackenzie Brown, *The Triumph of the Goddess: The Canonical Models and Theological Visions of the* Devī-Bhāgavata Purāṇa (Albany: State University of New York Press, 1990), 164; *Devī Bhāgavata Purāṇa* 12.9.

33. Tracy Pintchman, *The Rise of the Goddess in the Hindu Tradition* (Albany: State University of New York Press, 1994), 118.

34. Dayananda, *The Light of Truth: The Satyartha Prakasha*. trans. Chiranjiva Gharadwaya, www.aryasamajjamnagar.org/download/satyarth_prakash_eng.pdf, 31–3.

35. One of a number of elaborate precolonial observatories designed to accurately measure the positions of celestial bodies; see Barry Perlus, "Architecture in the Service of Science: The Astronomical Observatories of Jai Singh II," www.jantarmantar.org/Architecture_Science_web.pdf. For a fascinating discussion of the relations between religion, science, and sovereignty in the building of the Jantar Mantars, see also Bonnie G. MacDougall, "Jantar Mantar: Architecture,

Astronomy, and Solar Kingship in Princely India," *Cornell Journal of Architecture*, 1996, http://ecommons.cornell.edu/handle/1813/2977.

36. Nanda, *Prophets Facing Backward*.

37. Sheldon Pollock, "Forms of Knowledge in Early Modern South Asia: Introduction," *Comparative Studies of South Asia, Africa and the Middle East* 24, no. 2 (2004): 19.

38. Sheldon Pollock, "Introduction: Working Papers on Sanskrit Knowledge-Systems on the Eve of Colonialism," *Journal of Indian Philosophy* 30, no. 5 (2002): 433–7.

39. Dominick Wujastyk, "Indian Medical Thought on the Eve of Colonialism," *International Institute for Asian Studies Newsletter* 31 (July 2003): 21.

40. Lawrence McCrea, "Novelty of Form and Novelty of Substance in Seventeenth Century Mīmāmsā," *Journal of Indian Philosophy* 30, no. 5 (2002): 481.

41. Pollock, "Introduction," 431.

42. Prakash, *Another Reason*; Zaheer Baber, *The Science of Empire: Scientific Knowledge, Civilization, and Colonial Rule in India* (Albany: State University of New York Press, 1996).

43. Gottschalk, *Religion, Science, and Empire*; Ronald Inden, *Imagining India* (Bloomington: Indiana University Press, 2001); Prakash, *Another Reason*.

44. Kapil Raj, *Relocating Modern Science: Circulation and the Construction of Knowledge in South Asia and Europe, 1650–1900* (New York: Palgrave Macmillan, 2010).

45. Srinivas Aravamudan, *Guru English: South Asian Religion in a Cosmopolitan Language* (Princeton, NJ: Princeton University Press, 2005); C. Mackenzie Brown, *Hindu Perspectives on Evolution: Darwin, Dharma, and Design* (New York: Routledge, 2012); Pratik Chakrabarti, *Western Science in Modern India: Metropolitan Methods, Colonial Practices* (Hyderabad, India: Orient Blackswan, 2004); Harding, *Sciences from Below*; Nanda, *Prophets Facing Backward*; Prakash, *Another Reason*.

46. Nanda, *Prophets Facing Backward*.

47. Lola Williamson, *Transcendent in America: Hindu-Inspired Meditation Movements as New Religion* (New York: NYU Press, 2010), 100–3.

48. Aravamudan, *Guru English*, 243–245.

49. Brown, *Hindu Perspectives on Evolution*, 173–227.

50. Corinne G. Dempsey, *The Goddess Lives in Upstate New York: Breaking Convention and Making Home at a North American Hindu Temple* (New York: Oxford University Press, 2005); Corinne G. Dempsey and Selva J. Raj, *Miracle As Modern Conundrum in South Asian Religious Traditions* (Albany: State University of New York Press, 2009).

51. Alter, *Yoga in Modern India*, 30–1.

# Chapter 1

1. Pranav Pandya and Jyotirmay, *Odyssey of the Enlightened*, vol. 1, ed. Shambhudas, trans. R.P. Khare and Madhuri Nadig (Haridwar, India: Shri Vedmata Gayatri Trust, 2009), 17.

2. Ibid., 27–8.

3. Ibid., 31–3.

4. Ibid., 38, 112.

5. Ibid., 115–33; Shriram Sharma, *My Life: its Legacy and Message*, trans. Satya Narayan Pandya and Shambhudas (Haridwar, India: Shri Vedmata Gayatri Trust, 2011), 20.

6. Sharma, *My Life*, 23–4, 31.

7. Pandya and Jyotirmay, *Odyssey of the Enlightened*, 107.

8. Pandya and Jyotirmay, *Odyssey of the Enlightened*, 161–2, 260.

9. Ibid., 342; *maiṃ āpkī tarah bannā cāhtā hūṃ*; Pranav Pandya and Jyotirmay, *Cetnā kī Śikhar Yātrā*, vol. 1 (Haridwar, India: Shri Vedmata Gayatri Trust, 2001), 293.

10. Pandya and Jyotirmay, *Odyssey of the Enlightened*, 315–16.

11. Ibid., 331.

12. Ibid., 344.

13. Ibid., 333; *Rāṣṭra aur saṃskṛti ke prati samāj meṃ gaurav jagātā hūṃ. . . . Apnī ātmā meṃ bal jagāo. Ātmatej kī upāsnā karo*; Pandya and Jyotirmay, *Cetnā kī Śikhar Yātrā*, 285.

14. Pandya and Jyotirmay, *Odyssey of the Enlightened*, 335; *Lekin [svataṃtratā] kī icchā karnā aur apne āpko usmeṃ lagā denā bhī sādhanā hai;* Pandya and Jyotirmay, *Cetnā kī Śikhar Yātrā*, 287.

15. A Gandhian term for "untouchables," sometimes also called Dalits.

16. Pandya and Jyotirmay, *Odyssey of the Enlightened*, 348.

17. Ibid., 376–83.

18. Pandya and Jyotirmay (*Odyssey of the Enlightened*, 367) assert that he agreed with the philosophy of the Theosophical Society but preferred the Arya Samaj on a more practical level.

19. Ibid., 366.

20. Pandya and Jyotirmay, *Odyssey of the Enlightened*.

21. Ibid., 374.

22. Ibid., 436; Gurudev's tenure as head of the Arya Samaj in Mathura is further corroborated through communication with a scholar named Om Prakash Juneja. Juneja is unaffiliated with the Gayatri Pariwar, but was associated with the Arya Samaj through his father during his childhood. Juneja recalls hearing Gurudev lecture under the auspices of the Arya Samaj during this period (personal communication, May 24, 2010).

23. Pandya and Jyotirmay, *Odyssey of the Enlightened*, 464–8.

24. J.E. Llewellyn, *The Arya Samaj as a Fundamentalist Movement: A Study In Comparative Fundamentalism* (New Delhi: South Asia Books, 1993), 8–9, 87–8.

25. Pandya and Jyotirmay, *Odyssey of the Enlightened*, 92.

26. It is worth being clear here that there have been other Hindu movements that have tended toward monotheism, the notion of a formless deity, or both, notably the Hindi *nirguṇ sānt* tradition including such as the followers of Kabir and Raidas.

27. A kind of ritual worship involving the waving of a lamp.

28. Pandya and Jyotirmay (*Odyssey of the Enlightened*, 15) claim that Gurudev wrote "simple commentaries and translation [sic] in Hindi of all the four *Vedas*, eighteen *Puranas*, one hundred and eight *Upanishads*, twenty *Smritis*, twenty four *Gitas*, etc. [to make] them readily available to the masses."

29. Llewellyn, *The Arya Samaj*, 92.

30. Ibid.

31. Ibid., 128; Dayananda, quoted in Kripal Chandra Yadav and K.S. Arya, *Arya Samaj and the Freedom Movement* (New Delhi: Manohar, 1988), 9.

32. Llewellyn, *The Arya Samaj*, 128; Yadav and Arya (*Arya Samaj and the Freedom Movement*) give a far more extensive account of the role of Arya Samajists in the independence movement, albeit with a clear Arya Samaj agenda.

33. Llewellyn, *The Arya Samaj*, 92.

34. Ibid., 128.

35. Ibid., 9.

36. Ibid., 121.

37. Shriram Sharma, *Super Science of Gayatri*, trans. Satyanarayan Pandya and Shambhudas (Haridwar, India: Shri Vedmata Gayatri Trust, 2010), 163.

38. Llewellyn, *The Arya Samaj*, 102.

39. Dayananda, *The Light of Truth*, 55.

40. Ibid., 206.

41. Llewellyn, *Arya Samaj*, 88.

42. Cf. Shriram Sharma, *Revival of Satyug* (Haridwar, India: Shri Vedmata Gayatri Trust, 2011).

43. Llewellyn, *The Arya Samaj*, 125–6.

44. Jaffrelot, *The Hindu Nationalist Movement*, 14.

45. Llewelyn, *The Arya Samaj*, 99; Jaffrelot, *The Hindu Nationalist Movement*, 16.

46. Jaffrelot, *The Hindu Nationalist Movement*, 16.

47. Prakash, *Another Reason*, 107.

48. Ibid., 92–3.

49. Ibid., 76, 94–5.

50. Ibid., 80, 86–8.

51. Sharma, *Super Science of Gayatri*, 154.

52. David Arnold, *Gandhi* (New York: Routledge, 2001), 15, 44.

53. Ibid., 186–87.

54. Ibid., 169, 175–76.

55. Ibid., 172–73.

56. Ibid., 216–18; Mohandas K. Gandhi, *'Hind Swaraj' and other Writings*, ed. Anthony J. Parel (New York: Cambridge University Press, 2009), 52–3.

57. Arnold, *Gandhi*, 225; Jaffrelot, *The Hindu Nationalist Movement*, 71, 86–7.

58. Pandya and Jyotirmay, *Odyssey of the Enlightened*, 341; edited to conform to standard American English punctuation; *Bāpū ne kahā, "Āśram meṃ prātaḥkālīn kāryakramoṃ kī taiyāriyāṃ cal rahī hoṃgī. Tumne yahāṃ kī prārthnā meṃ bhāg liyā." Śrīrām ne svīkṛti meṃ sir hilāyā. Bāpū ne pūchā, "Kyā acchā lagā?"*

*"Sabhī kuch acchā lagā," Śrīrām ne kahā, "lekin Īśavāsya Upaniṣad ke maṃtroṃ ne bahut taraṃgit kiyā. Vh prārthnā pratidin doharāūṃga."*

*"Prārthnā doharāne se kyā hogā?" bāpū ne praśn kiyā. Turaṃt iskā koī uttar nahīṃ diyā ja sakā"*; Pandya and Jyotirmay, *Cetnā kī Śikhar Yātrā*, 292.

59. Pandya and Jyotirmay, *Odyssey of the Enlightened*, 1:341–2.

60. Arnold, *Gandhi*, 165–6.

61. Joseph S. Alter, *Gandhi's Body: Sex, Diet, and the Politics of Nationalism* (Philadelphia: University of Pennsylvania Press, 2000), 138.

62. My intention here is not to imply that Dayananda did not advocate practices like celibacy and fasting, although he only permitted the latter for its supposed health benefits and not for religious merit. But it was not a central motif for him as it was for Gandhi and Gurudev, and he did not articulate any kind of link between moral bodies, healthy bodies, and an ideal, independent nation.

63. Prakash, *Another Reason*, 184–6.

64. Nanda, *Prophets Facing Backward*, 26.

65. Arnold, *Gandhi*, 74–5, 87.

66. Alter, *Gandhi's Body*, 22–3.

## Chapter 2

1. Pandya and Jyotirmay, *Odyssey of the Enlightened*, 424; respectively meaning "self-rule" and "Rām's rule." *Rāmrājya* suggests a golden age of peace, prosperity, and happiness brought on by the rule of a *dharmic* king, Like Rāma of the *Rāmāyaṇa*. The concept played a major role in Gandhi's rhetoric about post-independence India; cf. Gandhi, *Hind Swaraj*.

2. Brahmavarchas, *Thought Revolution*, 146.

3. Pandya and Jyotirmay, *Odyssey of the Enlightened*, 464.

4. Brahmavarchas, *Thought Revolution*, 147.

5. Ibid., 148–51.

6. Ibid., 152–3.

7. Ibid., 153.

8. This terminology no doubt calls to mind the RSS, a movement that in a certain sense could be described as a cousin to the pacifist Gayatri Pariwar (see chapter 6).

9. Sanjay Joshi, *Fractured Modernity: Making of a Middle Class in Colonial North India* (New York: Oxford University Press, 2001), 2, 7–10.

10. Sanjay Srivastava, "National Identity, Bedrooms, and Kitchens: Gated Communities and New Narratives of Space in India," in *The Global Middle Classes: Theorizing through Ethnography*, ed. Rachel Heiman, Carla Freeman, and Mark Liechty (Santa Fe, NM: School for Advanced Research Press, 2015), 82–3.

11. Leela Fernandes, *India's New Middle Class: Democratic Politics in an Era of Economic Reform* (Minneapolis: University of Minnesota Press, 2006), 20–1; Ritty A. Lukose, *Liberalization's Children: Gender, Youth, and Consumer Citizenship in Globalizing India* (Durham NC: Duke University Press, 2009), 4–5.

12. Srivastava, "National Identity, Bedrooms, and Kitchens," 82–3.

13. Ruchira Ganguly-Scrase and Timothy J. Scrase, *Globalisation and the Middle Classes in India: The Social and Cultural Impact of Neoliberal Reforms* (Routledge, 2008), 41–2; Mark Liechty, "Middle Class Deja Vu: Conditions of Possibility, from Victorian England to Kathmandu," in *The Global Middle Classes: Theorizing through Ethnography*, ed. Rachel Heiman, Carla Freeman, and Mark Liechty (Santa Fe, NM: School for Advanced Research Press, 2015), 278–9; Lukose, *Liberalization's Children*, 4–8.

14. Craig Jeffrey, *Timepass: Youth, Class, and the Politics of Waiting in India* (Stanford, CA: Stanford University Press, 2010), 2.

15. Ibid., 5–6.

16. *Maiṇ soctī thī kī jab maiṇ* job *kar rahī hūṇ*

17. These are basic Hindu lifecycle rituals marking a child's first solid food and beginning of education, respectively.

18. *unhone hamāre ghar meṇ*

19. Jarrett Zigon, "Moral Breakdown and the Ethical Demand: A Theoretical Framework for an Anthropology of Moralities," *Anthropological Theory* 7, no. 2 (2007): 133–4.

20. This observation is shaped in part by Gareth Fisher's *From Comrades to Bodhisattvas: Moral Dimensions of Lay Buddhist Practice in Contemporary China* (Honolulu: University of Hawaii Press, 2014). Fisher makes similar use of the concept of moral breakdown to analyze the creative ways in which certain Beijing residents draw on Buddhism in their efforts to deal with problems associated with post-Maoist China's developing market economy (3–5).

21. Ganguly-Scrase and Scrase, *Globalisation and the Middle Classes in India*, 41–2; Liechty, "Middle Class Deja Vu," 278–9; Lukose, *Liberalization's Children*, 4–8.

22. Joanne Waghorne, "The Gentrification of the Goddess," *International Journal of Hindu Studies* 5, no. 3 (2001): 227–67.

23. A bamboo flute.

24. Prema Kurien, *A Place at the Multicultural Table: The Development of an American Hinduism* (New Brunswick, NJ: Rutgers University Press, 2007), 58–85.

25. "Pilgrimage site."

## Chapter 3

1. "Uninterrupted lamp," in this case referring to an oil lamp that Gurudev and his successors are said to have kept burning continuously since 1926.

2. Pandya, *The Pioneers of Scientific Spirituality*, 174–7.

3. Sharma, *My Life*, back cover.

4. All World Gayatri Pariwar. "Dr. Pranav Pandya," accessed February 3, 2018, www.awgp.org/about_us/present_mantor/dr_pranav_pandy.

5. All World Gayatri Pariwar. "Mata Bhagwati Devi Sharma," accessed February 3, 2018, www.awgp.org/about_us/patron_founder/mata_bhagwati_devi_sharm.

6. Dev Sanskriti Vishwavidyalaya, *Dev Sanskriti Vishwavidyalaya: A Unique University* (Haridwar: Dev Sanskriti Vishwavidyalaya). Pamphlet.

7. Ibid.

8. Max Weber, *The Theory of Social and Economic Organization*, ed. Talcott Parsons, trans. A.M. Henderson (New York: Free Press, 1964), 328.

9. Ibid., 333–5.

10. Ibid., 341.

11. Ibid., 358.

12. Ibid., 329.

13. Ibid., 359–62.

14. Charles Lindholm, "Introduction: Charisma in Theory and Practice," in *The Anthropology of Religious Charisma: Ecstasies and Institutions*, ed. Charles Lindholm (Palgrave Macmillan, 2013), 10; Max Weber, *From Max Weber: Essays in Sociology*, ed. H.H. Gerth and C. Wright Mills (New York: Oxford University Press, 1958), 357.

15. Clifford Geertz, "Centers, Kings, and Charisma: Reflections on the Symbolics of Power," in *Rites of Power: Symbolism, Ritual, and Politics since the Middle Ages*, ed. Sean Wilentz (Philadelphia: University of Pennsylvania Press, 1999), 14.

16. Ibid., 15–16.

17. Charles Lindholm, *Charisma* (Oxford: Wiley-Blackwell, 1994), 4, 8.

18. Ibid., 175.

19. C. Julia Huang, *Charisma and Compassion: Cheng Yen and the Buddhist Tzu Chi Movement* (Cambridge, MA: Harvard University Press, 2009), 4–5.

20. Lindholm, *Charisma*, 11; C. Julia Huang-Lemmon, "The Gender of Charisma: Notes from a Taiwanese Buddhist Transnational NGO," in *The Anthropology of Religious Charisma: Ecstasies and Institutions*, ed. Charles Lindholm (London: Palgrave Macmillan, 2013), 103.

21. Ahmed, "Affective Economies," 119–20; Ahmed, *The Cultural Politics of Emotion*, 1.

22. Cvetkovich, *Depression*, 2–12; Gregg and Seigworth, *The Affect Theory Reader*, 7; Stewart, *Ordinary Affects*, 2.

23. Leela Prasad, *Poetics of Conduct: Oral Narrative and Moral Being in a South Indian Town* (New York: Columbia University Press, 2006), 174–5.

24. Ibid., 178–80.

25. In a broader discussion of social authority in *Authority: Construction and Corrosion* (Chicago: University of Chicago Press, 1994), Bruce Lincoln similarly notes a role for a "theatrical array" of material objects that form an important basis for the otherwise mostly discursive phenomena of authority and persuasion (5–9).

26. Weber, *The Theory of Social and Economic Organization*, 363–6.

27. Tamal Krishna Goswami and Ravi M. Gupta, "Krishna and Culture: What Happens When the Lord of Vrindavana Moves to New York City," in *Gurus in America*, ed. Thomas A. Forsthoefel and Cynthia Ann Humes (Albany, NY: State University of New York Press, 2005), 88–9.

28. Edwin Bryant and Maria Ekstrand, eds., *The Hare Krishna Movement: The Postcharismatic Fate of a Religious Transplant* (New York: Columbia University Press, 2004), 4–6.

29. Cf. Goswami and Gupta, "Krishna and Culture."

30. Karen Pechilis, "Gurumayi, the Play of Shakti and Guru," in *The Graceful Guru: Hindu Female Gurus in India and the United States*, ed. Karen Pechilis (New York: Oxford University Press, 2004), 225–8.

31. Lola Williamson, "The Perfectibility of Perfection: Siddha Yoga as a Global Movement," in *Gurus in America*, ed. Thomas A. Forsthoefel and Cynthia Ann Humes (Albany: State University of New York Press, 2005), 150.

32. Charles Lindholm, ed., *The Anthropology of Religious Charisma: Ecstasies and Institutions* (Palgrave Macmillan, 2013), 10.

33. Hugh Urban, "Osho, from Sex Guru to Guru of the Rich: The Spiritual Logic of Late Capitalism," in *Gurus in America*, ed. Thomas A. Forsthoefel and Cynthia Ann Humes (Albany, NY: State University of New York Press, 2005).

34. Paramahansa Yogananda, *Autobiography of a Yogi* (Los Angeles: Self-Realization Fellowship, 1998), 3, 11, 343–4.

35. Shriram Sharma, *Companions in Solitude*, translated by V.A. Shivashankaran (Haridwar, India: Shri Vedmata Gayatri Trust, 2011), 9; Sharma, *My Life*, 19–20.

36. Sharma, *My Life*, 31–2.

37. I have also been able to find a small bi-fold pamphlet, *Dr. Pranav Pandya, MD (Medicine)*. In comparison with the web version, its format is largely the same and the material overlaps significantly. Nevertheless, the pamphlet is older and less extensive, so I will focus on the web version.

38. All World Gayatri Pariwar, "Dr. Pranav Pandya."

39. Ibid.

40. Ibid.

41. The fact that she and her mother are addressed by kinship terms in a movement called the Gayatri "Family" is also relevant here, and the gendered aspects of the movement's authority structure warrants extended consideration. My focus in this article has been Gurudev and Doctor-sahib due to the patriarchal nature of this *pariwar*, but I discuss the important role Mataji and Jiji play for the movement in my larger project.

42. McKean, *Divine Enterprise*, 51–2.

## Chapter 4

1. We can see fine examples of this trend in Rammohan Roy's Brahmo Samaj and in Vivekananda's tendency to distance himself from the ritualism of his forebear, Ramakrishna.

2. On the capacity of ritual practice to construct and structure identities and communities, cf. Catherine Bell, *Ritual Theory, Ritual Practice* (New York: Oxford University Press, 2009), and Roy A. Rappaport, *Ritual and Religion in the Making of Humanity* (Cambridge: Cambridge University Press, 1999).

3. Ahmed, *The Cultural Politics of Emotion*, 1, 9–10.

4. Ahmed, "Affective Economies," 119–20.

5. Llewellyn, *The Arya Samaj*, 99; Jaffrelot, *The Hindu Nationalist Movement*, 16.

6. Yajñavālkya is the philosophical protagonist of the *Bṛhadārāṇyaka Upaniṣad.*

7. Cf. *Bṛhadārāṇyaka Upaniṣad* 3.1.2.

8. Sharma, *Super Science of Gayatri*, 18; *Yadi ve samajh pāveṃ ki unkī sādhanā se kyā-kyā sūkṣma prakriyāyeṃ ho rahī haiṃ, to yah samajhne meṃ der na*

*lagegī ki yah sab kuch kahīṃ se anāyās dān nahīṃ mil rahā hai daran ātma-vidyā kī suvyavasthit vaijñānik prakriyā kā hī yah pariṇām hai. Gāyatrī sādhanā koī andha-viśvās nahīṃ, ek ṭhos vaijñānik kṛty hai aur uske dvārā lābh bhī suniścit hī hote hai*; Shriram Sharma, *Gāyatri Mahāvijñān* (Mathura, India: Yug Nirman Yojana, 2010), 27.

9. Sharma, *Super Science of Gayatri*, 16; *śraddhāmay viśvās. Viśvās se sabhī manovijñānavettā paricit haiṇ. Ham apnī pustakoṃ aur lekhoṃ meṃ aise asaṃkhya udāharaṇ anekoṃ bār de cuke haiṃ, jinse siddh hotā hai ki keval viśvās ke ādhār par log bhay kī vajah se akāraṇ kāl ke mukh meṃ cale gaye aur viśvās ke kāraṇ mṛtaprāy logoṃ ne navajīvan prāpt kiyā*; Sharma, *Gāyatri Mahāvijñān*, 25.

10. Sharma, *Super Science of Gayatri*, 25–26; *Ve is sūkṣm vivecan meṃ jane kī icchā nahīṃ karte ki kis prakār kuch vaijñānik niyamoṃ ke ādhār par sādhanā śram kā dīdhā-sādā phal unheṃ milā. Is vivecanā se unheṃ prāyaḥ aruci hotī hai. Unkā kahnā hai ki Bhagavatī Gāyatrī kī kṛpā ke prati kṛtajñatā hī hamārī bhakti-bhāvnā ko babaṛhāyegī aur usī se hameṃ adhik lābh hogā, unkā yah mantavya bahut had tak ṭhīk hī hai. . . . Gāyatrī sādhanā dvārā ek sūkṣma vijñān sammat praṇālī se lābh hote haiṃ, yah jānkar bhī is mahāttva se ātm sambandh kī dṛṛhtā karne ke liye kṛtajñatā aur bhakti bhāvnā kā pūṭ adhikādhik rakhnā āvaśyak hai*; Sharma, *Gāyatri Mahāvijñān*, 39.

11. In Yogic physiology, the *brahmanāḍī* is an energy conduit that runs up the base of the spine.

12. In Yogic physiology, *kundalini* is a pool of energy that rests at the base of the spine.

13. Sharma, *Super Science of Gayatri*, 120–121; *Do paramāṇuoṃ ko toṛne, milāne yā sthānāṃtarit karne kā sarvottam sthān kuṇḍalinī kendra meṃ hotā hai, kyoṃki anya sab jagah ke caitanya paramāṇu gol aur cikne hote haiṃ par kuṇḍalinī meṃ yah mithun liptā huā hai. Jaise yūreniyam aur pleṭoniyyam dhātu meṃ paramāṇuoṃ kā gunthan kuch aise ṭeṛh-tirache ḍhaṃg se hotā hai ki unkā toṛā jāna anya padārthoṃ ke paramāṇuoṃ kī apekṣā adhik saral hai, usī parkar kuṇḍalinī sthit sphulliṃg paramāṇuoṃ kī gatividhi ko icchānukūl saṃcalit karnā adhik sugam hai*; Sharma, *Gāyatri Mahāvijñān*, 244–5.

14. Sharma, *Super Science of Gayatri*, 121; *Jis prakār āj parmāṇu kī śodh meṃ pratyek deś ke vaijñānik vyast haiṃ, usī prakār pūrvakāl meṃ ādhyātmik vijñānvettāoṃ ne, tatvadarśī ṛṣiyoṃ ne mānav-śarīr ke antargat ek bīj parmāṇu kī atyadhik śodh kī thī. . . . Isliye prācīnakāl meṃ kuṇḍalinī jāgaraṇ kī utnī hī tatpartā se śodh huī thī, jitnī ki ājkal parmāṇu vijñān ke bare meṃ ho rahī hai*; Sharma, *Gāyatri Mahāvijñān*, 244–5.

15. Sharma, *Super Science of Gayatri*, 124; *Śabd kī tarageṃ vāyu ke paramāṇu tathā rogoṃ ke kīṭāṇu hameṃ āṃkhoṃ se dikhāī nahiṃ paṛte to bhī unke astitva se inkār nahiṃ kiyā jā saktā. In cakroṃ ko yogiyoṃ ne apnī yog dṛṣṭi se dekhā hai aur unkā vaijñānik parīkṣaṇ karke mahatvapūrṇ lābh uṭhāyā hai*; Sharma, *Gāyatri Mahāvijñān*, 248.

16. "This is for Gayatri, this is not mine."

17. In Shriram Sharma, *Procedure of Yagya*, ed. Shambu Dass, trans. K. Poddar (Mathura, India: Yug Nirman Yojana, 2009), the Gayatri Pariwar's ritual manual, the number of repetitions is specified at 24, but the manual allows for a reduction in this number if time constraints do not allow it. Given the large number of people who needed to do *yajña* every morning, it should not be surprising that typically each group did fewer than 24 repetitions—typically more like 12 or 18, although I never could get an accurate count.

18. Peter van der Veer, *Religious Nationalism: Hindus and Muslims in India* (Berkeley: University of California Press, 1994), 166–7.

19. Timothy Lubin, "Veda on Parade: Revivalist Ritual as Civic Spectacle," *Journal of the American Academy of Religion* 69, no. 2 (2001): 379, 387–8.

20. Kalyani Devaki Menon, *Everyday Nationalism: Women of the Hindu Right in India* (Philadelphia: University of Pennsylvania Press, 2012), 124–5.

21. Rajani Joshi, *The Integrated Science of Yagya* (Mathura, India: Yug Nirman Yojana, 2010); *Yagya* is a variant transliteration of *yajña*.

22. Ibid., 5–10.

23. Ibid., 13.

24. Ibid., 14–19.

25. Ibid., 20; *yagna* is a variant transliteration of *yajña*.

26. Ibid., 21–6.

27. All World Gayatri Pariwar. "Daily Routine at Shantikunj," *All World Gayatri Pariwar*, accessed February 3, 2018. www.awgp.org/about_us/shantikunj/daily_routine_at_shantikunj.

## Chapter 5

1. *Hiṃsā, aparādh, lūṭ*

2. *Mere māmī pāpā kabhi* phone *karte haiṃ, maiṃ unko* phone *kartī hūṃ*

3. *Sādhū-saṃt yahāṃ cale gaye, van meṃ cale gaye, ghar se choṛ diya aur phir vahaṃ pe ve apne* spiritual growth *ke liye jāte haiṃ yā . . . kitna kar sakte haiṃ?*

4. Ann Gold, "Counterpoint Authority in Women's Ritual Expressions: A View from the Village," in *Jewels of Authority: Women and Textual Tradition in Hindu India*, ed. Laurie L. Patton (New York: Oxford University Press, 2002), 178–9.

5. Ibid.

6. Saba Mahmood, *Politics of Piety: The Islamic Revival and the Feminist Subject* (Princeton: Princeton University Press, 2011), 10–15.

7. All World Gayatri Pariwar, "Mata Bhagwati Devi Sharma."

8. Ibid.

9. Ibid.

10. All World Gayatri Pariwar, "Shraddheya Shailbala Pandya," accessed February 3, 2018, www.awgp.org/about_us/present_mantor/shraddheya_shailbala_pandy.

11. Brahmavarchas, *Mahāśakti kī Lokyātrā* (Mathura, India: Yug Nirman Yojana), 11–13.

12. *Kabhī-kabhī vah gumsum-sī cupcāp pālthī mārkār baiṭh jātī. Unheṃ is bhāvmagna daśā meṃ baiṭhe dekhkar ghar ke sadashyoṃ ko acaraj hotā. Ve sab unkī* aṃtardaśā *se aparicit the. Unmeṃ se koī soc nahīṃ pātā thā ki yah choṭī-sī baccī ākhir is tarah kyoṃ ekāṃt meṃ śāṃt hokar baiṭhī hai. Ek din baṛe bhāī Dīndayāl ne unheṃ is tarah baiṭhe dekhkar pūch liyā, "Lālī, tū is tarah cupcāp śāṃt kyoṃ baiṭhī hai, baccoṃ ke sāth kheltī-kūdtī kyoṃ nahīṃ? Tujhe dekhkar to aisā lagtā hai kit ere sir par sari duniyā kā bhār hai!" Praśna ke uttar meṃ unhoṇe baṛe hī śāṃt netroṃ se baṛe bhāī kī or dekhā, phir baḍe hī gaṃbhīr svaroṃ meṃ bolim,"Hāṃ, so to hai. Sari duniyā kā bhār mujhe par nahīṃ, to aur kis par hogā"*; ibid., 17.

13. *Āre maiṃ koī puja thoṛe hī kartī hūṃ, yah to bas khel hai. Mujhe sab kheloṃ meṃ yah khel sabse jyādā pasaṃd hai*; ibid., 19.

14. The text does not describe the birth of Mataji's biological children for several chapters, perhaps to establish her in a seemingly even more selfless role as mother to those who are not her own flesh and blood.

15. Brahmavarchas, *Mahāśakti kī Lokyātrā*, 28–34.

16. *Jaise ve apnī sagī māṃ ke pās āe haiṃ*; ibid., 35.

17. Ibid., 38.

18. Ibid., 52.

19. Ibid., 54–6.

20. *beṭe, bacce*; ibid., 102 ff.

21. Catherine Clementin-Ojha, "The Tradition of Female Gurus," *Manushi* 31 (1985): 2, quoted in Karen Pechilis, "Introduction: Hindu Female Gurus in Historical and Philosophical Context," in *The Graceful Guru: Hindu Female Gurus in India and the United States*, ed. Karen Pechilis (New York: Oxford University Press, 2004), 6; strictly speaking, Jiji would not be a *gurumātā* by this definition since her husband is not technically a guru. Nevertheless, it is clear enough that she has inherited a status quite similar to Mataji's for the community, and so *gurumātā* is a sufficiently accurate term for her position.

22. Pechilis, "Introduction," 8–9.

23. Meena Khandelwal, *Women in Ochre Robes: Gendering Hindu Renunciation* (Albany: State University of New York Press, 2003), 184–5.

24. Ibid.

25. Pechilis, "Introduction," 7.

26. Clementin-Ojha, "The Tradition of Female Gurus," 2; Pechilis, "Introduction," 6.

27. It is noteworthy here that this is not necessarily entirely gendered—the same would hold true for the Gayatri Pariwar's post-charismatic patriarch, Doctor-sahib, as I have argued in chapter 3.

28. Mary McGee, "Ritual Rights: The Gender Implications of Adhikāra," in *Jewels of Authority: Women and Textual Tradition in Hindu India*, ed. Laurie L. Patton (New York: Oxford University Press, 2002), notes that from certain perspectives in the Mīmāṃsā school of thought, women could perform these kinds of rituals themselves. Nonetheless, this was not common practice for much of history.

29. Stephanie Jamison, *Sacrificed Wife/Sacrificer's Wife: Women, Ritual, and Hospitality in Ancient India* (New York: Oxford University Press, 1996), 38.

30. Ibid., 39.

31. Ibid., 53.

32. Ibid., 115–16; see also Ellison Findly, "The Housemistress at the Door: Vedic and Buddhist Perspectives on the Mendicant Encounter," in *Jewels of Authority: Women and Textual Tradition in Hindu India*, ed. Laurie L. Patton (New York: Oxford University Press, 2002).

33. Ashlee Andrews, " 'Gopāl is my Baby': Vulnerable Deities and Maternal Love at Bengali Home Shrines." *Journal of Hindu Studies* 12, no. 2 (2019), 231–2.

34. Ibid., 236–7.

35. Brian K. Smith, "Vedic Fieldwork,' Review of Frits Staal, Agni," *Religious Studies Review* 11 (1985): 142–4.

36. Lindsey Harlan, "Words That Breach Walls: Women's Rituals in Rajasthan," in *Women's Lives, Women's Rituals in the Hindu Tradition*, ed. Tracy Pintchman (New York: Oxford University Press, 2007), 72–3.

## Chapter 6

1. *Parivār se samāj bantā hai, to parivār ṭhīk hogā, to samāj ṭhīk hogā, aur samāj ṭhīk hogā, to rashtra ṭhīk hogā, or rāṣṭra hogā to vishva hogā.*

2. Cf. Arjun Appadurai, "Disjuncture and Difference in the Global Cultural Economy," *Theory, Culture & Society* 7 (1990): 295–310.

3. Multilingual signs are of course extremely commonplace in India, but since they are new to Shantikunj, and reflect a departure from the movement's earlier vernacularism, I see great significance in the Gayatri Pariwar's move toward a bilingualism that is well established elsewhere in the Indian public sphere.

4. Aravamudan, *Guru English*, 6–7.

5. Ibid., 243.

6. Ibid., 1–2, 4–5.

7. Sheldon Pollock, "Cosmopolitan and Vernacular in History," in *Cosmopolitanism*, ed. Carol A. Breckenridge et al. (Durham, NC: Duke University Press, 2002), 46–8.

8. Dining hall.

9. Sharma, *My Life*, 166; *Kārl Mārks ne . . . arthśāstra rūpī aise darśan ko janm diyā jisne samāj meṃ krāṃti lā dī. Pūṃjīvādī kile ḍhahate cale gae evaṃ sāmrājyavād do tihāī dharatī se samāpt ho gayā.* Dās Kaipīṭal *rūpī is racnā ne ek navyug kā śubhāraṃbh kyā jismeṃ śramikoṃ ko apne adhikār mile evaṃ pūṃjī ke samān vitaraṇ kā yah adhyāy khulā jismeṃ karoṛdoṃ vyaktiyoṃ ko sukh-cain kī, svāvalamban pradhān jiṃdagī jī sakne kī svataṃtratā milī*; Sharma, *Hamārī Vasīyat Aur Virāsat* (Mathura, India: Yug Chetna Press 2011), 170.

10. I want to be very clear here that permanent ashram residents by and large did not treat me this way—they were excellent hosts who made me feel like part of the community and had no particular power to prevent this from happening.

11. See also Laurah Klepinger, "Flexible Labor in a Spiritual Economy: Peace, Work, and Inequality in Globalized Yoga" (PhD diss., Syracuse University, 2015).

12. This is of course not a unique claim; cf. Anne Feldhaus, *Connected Places: Region, Pilgrimage, and Geographical Imagination in India* (New York: Palgrave Macmillan, 2003).

13. Badrinath and Kedarnath are dedicated to Vishnu and Shiva, respectively, while Gangotri and Yamunotri are dedicated to the goddesses Ganga and Yamuna, and are situated at the sources of their associated rivers.

14. For an extended discussion of Haridwar's place in India's religious landscape, cf. James Lochtefeld, *God's Gateway: Identity and Meaning in a Hindu Pilgrimage Place* (New York: Oxford University Press, 2010).

15. Cf. Feldhaus, *Connected Places*, 157 ff.

16. Lise McKean, "Bhārat Mātā: Mother India and Her Militant Matriots," in *Devi: Goddesses of India*, ed. John Stratton Hawley and Donna Marie Wulff (Berkeley: University of California Press, 1996), 253–5.

17. Personifying the nation as a goddess may seem like quite a Hindu move, or at the very least may seem to be far removed from the approach to nation-building taken by the secular liberal democracies of the West. Nonetheless, Liberty, perhaps deriving from the Roman goddess Libertas, appears in the iconography of both France, as Marianne, and the United States, as Columbia. While not objects of worship like Bharat Mata, they did similarly enshrine the ideals of the nation and serve to evoke fervent patriotism. These similarities are worth exploring thoroughly but such an exploration is outside the scope of this project.

18. Cf. Sumathi Ramaswamy, *The Goddess and the Nation: Mapping Mother India* (Durham, NC: Duke University Press, 2010).

19. McKean, "Bhārat Mātā," 263.

20. Ibid., 264–5.

21. Samanvaya Sewa Trust, quoted in McKean, "Bhārat Mātā," 264.

22. McKean, *Divine Enterprise*, 1, 9, 12.

23. McKean, *Divine Enterprise*, 47; While the material McKean presents in support of her thesis here is compelling, my research about the Gayatri Pariwar leads me to believe that a more extensive examination of the Gayatri Pariwar would lead to a more complex picture of the movement's socioeconomic ideology than McKean is able to provide. Their critique of the welfare state and championing of hard work seem to be counterbalanced to a certain extent by their own rather extensive charitable activities and their rejection of contemporary middle-class lifestyles in favor of the lifestyles of ordinary Indians. One possible factor leading to my different perception is that the much more advanced state of economic liberalism in India at the time of my visit to Shantikunj and the ascent of the new generation of leadership has led to a shift in the Gayatri Pariwar's socioeconomic vision.

24. McKean, *Divine Enterprise*, 51–2.

25. Ibid., 53.

26. The Indian National Congress party, or INC, has generally been the leading political party of India's central government; its main challenger starting in the '90s was the Hindu nationalist Bharatiya Janata Party, or BJP.

27. Pandya and Jyotirmay, *Odyssey of the Enlightened*, 34–8, 54–5.

28. Jaffrelot, *The Hindu Nationalist Movement*, 33.

29. Llewellyn, *The Arya Samaj*, 129–31.

30. Brahmavarchas, *Thought Revolution*, 112–18.

31. Alter, *Gandhi's Body*, 138.

32. Joseph S. Alter, *Moral Materialism: Sex and Masculinity in Modern India* (New Delhi: Penguin, 2012), 26–27.

33. Brahmavarchas, *Thought Revolution*, 118–20, 127–32, 136–7.

34. Ibid., 120–7, 132–5.

35. Ibid., 125.

36. In developing the concept of biomorality, Alter synthesizes Inden and Marriott's notion of "biomoral substance-code" with Foucault's biopolitics; McKim Marriott and Ronald Inden, "Caste Systems," *Encyclopedia Britannica*, 1976; Michel Foucault, *"Society Must Be Defended": Lectures at the Collège de France, 1975–1976* (New York: Picador, 2003).

37. Alter, *Moral Materialism*, 72–3; Joseph S. Alter, "Gandhi's Body, Gandhi's Truth: Nonviolence and the Biomoral Imperative of Public Health," *The Journal of Asian Studies* 55, no. 2 (1996): 7.

38. Brahmavarchas, *Thought Revolution*, 138–9.

39. Alter, *Yoga in Modern India*, 7–8.

40. Ibid., 109–10.

41. Ibid., 140.

42. Or Rashtriya Swayamsevak Sangh, a Hindu nationalist organization that has served as progenitor of several other organizations with the same ideology, collectively known as the Sangh Parivar.

43. Or Vishwa Hindu Parishad, an offshoot of the RSS.

44. Or Hindu Swayamsevak Sangh, the international wing of the RSS.

45. Nigel Thrift, *Non-Representational Theory: Space, Politics, Affect* (New York: Routledge, 2007), 89–95, 98–9, 102–3.

46. Brahmavarchas, *Thought Revolution*, 148.

47. Sianne Ngai, *Our Aesthetic Categories: Zany, Cute, Interesting* (Cambridge, MA: Harvard University Press, 2012), 113–16, 132, 170.

48. Tomkins, quoted in Ngai, *Our Aesthetic Categories*, 134.

49. Joanne P. Waghorne, "The Hindu Gods in a Split Level World: The Sri Siva-Vishnu Temple in Suburban Washington, D.C.," in *Gods of the City: Religion and the American Urban Landscape*, ed. Robert A. Orsi (Bloomington: Indiana University Press, 1999), 121–3.

50. Cf. Tony Carnes and Fenggang Yang, eds., *Asian American Religions: The Making and Remaking of Borders and Boundaries* (New York: NYU Press, 2004); Kurien, *A Place at the Multicultural Table*; Waghorne, "The Hindu Gods in a Split Level World."

51. Eleanor Nesbitt, "The Contribution of Nurture in a Sampradaya to Young British Hindus' Understanding of Their Tradition," in *Religious Reconstruction in the South Asian Diasporas: From One Generation to Another*, ed. John R. Hinnells (New York: Palgrave Macmillan, 2007), 68.

## Conclusion

1. This nickname, which some scientists find grating but has nonetheless gained currency in the media, seems to derive from Leon Lederman, *The God Particle: If the Universe Is the Answer, What Is the Question?* (Boston: Mariner Books, 2006).

2. Lawrence A. Babb, *Redemptive Encounters: Three Modern Styles in the Hindu Tradition* (Berkeley: University of California Press, 1986), 200.

3. Michael Saler, "Modernity and Enchantment: A Historiographic Review," *The American Historical Review* 111, no. 3 (2006): 692–716.

4. Bruno Latour, *We Have Never Been Modern*, trans. Catherine Porter (Cambridge, MA: Harvard University Press, 1993).

5. Nanda, *Prophets Facing Backward*, 2–3, 18–30.

6. Ibid., 31.

# Glossary

**_Akhand Jyoti_** A periodical started by Gurudev around the time of World War II that served as an important institutional precursor to the Gayatri Pariwar.

**ārati** A form of ritualistic worship involving singing and waving a lamp in front of an image of a deity.

**Arya Samaj** A reform movement founded by Swami Dayananda Saraswati noted, like the Gayatri Pariwar, for its focus on Vedic-style ritual.

**aucitya** In traditional Indian poetics, the concept of dramaturgical propriety that demands all elements of a scene evoke the same *rasa*.

**bansuri** A bamboo flute.

**BJP** The Bharatiya Janata (Indian People's) Party; a political party affiliated to the RSS, espousing a Hindu nationalist ideology.

**Chinmay-bhaiya** Chinmay Pandya, a prominent Gayatri parijan; the grandson of Gurudev and Mataji, son of Jiji and Doctor-sahib.

**Choṭā Cār Dhāma** set of four pilgrimage places in the Garhwal Himalayas: Badrinath, a temple to Vishnu; Kedarnath, a temple to Shiva; and Gangotri and Yamunotri, which mark the origins of the Ganges and Yamuna Rivers, respectively.

**Doctor-sahib** Pranav Pandya, who presently leads the Gayatri Pariwar with his wife, Jiji; son-in-law of Gurudev and Mataji.

**DSVV** Dev Sanskriti Vishwavidyalaya (University of Divine Culture), the university of the Gayatri Pariwar.

**Gayatri mantra** An early Vedic hymn that forms the core of Gayatri Pariwar practice.

**Gayatri Tapobhumi** The previous headquarters of the Gayatri Pariwar, located in Mathura.

**Gurudev** Shriram Sharma, who founded the Gayatri Pariwar along with his wife Mataji.

**HSS** The Hindu Swayamsevak Sangh (Hindu Volunteer Organization), the international branch of the RSS.

**Jiji** Shailbala Pandya, the daughter of Gurudev and Mataji, who leads the movement together with her husband, Doctor-sahib.

**Mataji** Bhagwati Devi Sharma, Gurudev's wife and partner in founding the Gayatri Pariwar.

**puja (pūjā)** The popular form of Hindu ritualistic worship.

**rasa theory** A traditional theory of aesthetics focused on the ability of creative works to elicit *rasas*, or aestheticized moods, in their audience.

**RSS** The Rashtriya Swayamsevak Sangh (National Volunteer Organization), an influential Hindu nationalist organization from which the BJP and VHP derive.

**saṃnyāsa/saṃnyāsī/saṃnyāsinī** Renunciation/male renunciant/female renunciant; the last of the four traditional stages of life for Hindu men.

***satyug*** In Hindu cosmology, a bygone golden age; the Gayatri Pariwar aims to revive it.

**Shantikunj** The headquarters and main ashram of the Gayatri Pariwar.

**STEM** Science, technology, engineering, and mathematics.

**vaijñānik adhyātmavād** "Scientific spirituality."

**Vedas** An ancient corpus of Hindu texts from which the Gayatri Pariwar's practice of Gayatri recitation and *yajña* derive.

**VHP** Vishwa Hindu Parishad (Hindu World Council); A Hindu nationalist organization related to the RSS that engages in cultural activities and political activism.

**vijñān** Science.

***yajña*** A form of Vedic-style ritualistic offering; a central practice of the Gayatri Pariwar.

# Bibliography


Ahmed, Sara. "Affective Economies." *Social Text* 22, no. 2 (79) (2004): 117–39.

———. *The Cultural Politics of Emotion*. New York: Routledge, 2013.

All World Gayatri Pariwar. "Daily Routine at Shantikunj." Accessed February 3, 2018. www.awgp.org/about_us/shantikunj/daily_routine_at_shantikunj.

———. "Dr. Pranav Pandya." Accessed February 3, 2017. www.awgp.org/about_us/present_mantor/dr_pranav_pandy.

———. "Mata Bhagwati Devi Sharma." Accessed February 3, 2018. www.awgp.org/about_us/patron_founder/mata_bhagwati_devi_sharm.

———. "Shraddheya Shailbala Pandya." Accessed February 3, 2018. www.awgp.org/about_us/present_mantor/shraddheya_shailbala_pandy.

Alter, Joseph S. "Gandhi's Body, Gandhi's Truth: Nonviolence and the Biomoral Imperative of Public Health." *The Journal of Asian Studies* 55, no. 2 (1996): 301–22.

———. *Gandhi's Body: Sex, Diet, and the Politics of Nationalism*. Philadelphia: University of Pennsylvania Press, 2000.

———. *Moral Materialism: Sex and Masculinity in Modern India*. New Delhi: Penguin, 2012.

———. *Yoga in Modern India: The Body Between Science and Philosophy*. Princeton, NJ: Princeton University Press, 2010.

Andrews, Ashlee. "'Gopāl is my Baby': Vulnerable Deities and Maternal Love at Bengali Home Shrines." *Journal of Hindu Studies* 12, no. 2 (2019): 224–41.

Appadurai, Arjun. "Disjuncture and Difference in the Global Cultural Economy." *Theory, Culture & Society* 7 (1990): 295–310.

Aravamudan, Srinivas. *Guru English: South Asian Religion in a Cosmopolitan Language*. Princeton, NJ: Princeton University Press, 2005.

Arnold, David. *Gandhi*. New York: Routledge, 2001.

Babb, Lawrence. *Redemptive Encounters: Three Modern Styles in the Hindu Tradition*. Berkeley: University of California Press, 1986.

Baber, Zaheer. *The Science of Empire: Scientific Knowledge, Civilization, and Colonial Rule in India.* Albany: State University of New York Press, 1996.

Behar, Ruth. *The Vulnerable Observer: Anthropology that Breaks Your Heart.* Boston: Beacon Press, 1997.

Bell, Catherine. *Ritual Theory, Ritual Practice.* New York: Oxford University Press, 2009.

Brahmavarchas. *Mahāśakti kī Lokyātrā.* Mathura, India: Yug Nirman Yojana, n.d.

———, ed. *Thought Revolution: A Western Introduction to the Work of Acharya Shriram Sharma.* Haridwar, India: Yugantar Chetna Publications, 2011.

Brown, C. Mackenzie. *Hindu Perspectives on Evolution: Darwin, Dharma, and Design.* New York: Routledge, 2012.

———. *The Triumph of the Goddess: The Canonical Models and Theological Visions of the* Devī-Bhāgavata Purāṇa. Albany: State University of New York Press, 1990.

Bryant, Edwin, and Maria Ekstrand, eds. *The Hare Krishna Movement: The Post-charismatic Fate of a Religious Transplant.* New York: Columbia University Press, 2004.

Carnes, Tony, and Fenggang Yang, eds. *Asian American Religions: The Making and Remaking of Borders and Boundaries.* New York: NYU Press, 2004.

Chakrabarti, Pratik. *Western Science in Modern India: Metropolitan Methods, Colonial Practices.* Hyderabad, India: Orient Blackswan, 2004.

Clementin-Ojha, Catherine. "The Tradition of Female Gurus." *Manushi* 31 (1985): 2–8.

Cvetkovich, Ann. *Depression: A Public Feeling.* Durham, NC: Duke University Press, 2012.

Dayananda. *The Light of Truth: The Satyartha Prakasha.* Translated by Chiranjiva Gharadwaya. Accessed July 26, 2020. www.aryasamajjamnagar.org/download/satyarth_prakash_eng.pdf.

Dempsey, Corinne G. *The Goddess Lives in Upstate New York: Breaking Convention and Making Home at a North American Hindu Temple.* New York: Oxford University Press, 2005.

Dempsey, Corinne G., and Selva J. Raj. *Miracle As Modern Conundrum in South Asian Religious Traditions.* State University of New York Press, 2009.

Denton, Lynn. *Female Ascetics in Hinduism.* Albany: State University of New York Press, 2004.

Dev Sanskriti Vishwavidyalaya. *Dev Sanskriti Vishwavidyalaya: A Unique University.* Dev Sanskriti Vishwavidyalaya, n.d.

Edelmann, Jonathan B. "Hinduism and Science: Contemporary Considerations." *Zygon* 47, no. 3 (2012): 624–42.

———. *Hindu Theology and Biology: The Bhāgavata Purāṇa and Contemporary Theory.* New York: Oxford University Press, 2012.

———. "Hindu Theology as Churning the Latent." *Journal of the American Academy of Religion* 81, no. 2 (2013): 427–66.

Feldhaus, Anne. *Connected Places: Region, Pilgrimage, and Geographical Imagination in India*. New York: Palgrave Macmillan, 2003.

Fernandes, Leela. *India's New Middle Class: Democratic Politics in an Era of Economic Reform*. Minneapolis: University of Minnesota Press, 2006.

Findly, Ellison. "The Housemistress at the Door: Vedic and Buddhist Perspectives on the Mendicant Encounter." In *Jewels of Authority: Women and Textual Tradition in Hindu India*, edited by Laurie L. Patton, 32–50. New York: Oxford University Press, 2002.

Fisher, Gareth. *From Comrades to Bodhisattvas: Moral Dimensions of Lay Buddhist Practice in Contemporary China*. Honolulu: University of Hawaii Press, 2014.

Foucault, Michel. *"Society Must Be Defended": Lectures at the Collège de France, 1975–1976*. New York: Picador, 2003.

Gandhi, Mohandas K. *'Hind Swaraj' and Other Writings*. Edited by Anthony J. Parel. Cambridge: Cambridge University Press, 2010.

Ganguly-Scrase, Ruchira, and Timothy J. Scrase. *Globalisation and the Middle Classes in India: The Social and Cultural Impact of Neoliberal Reforms*. New York: Routledge, 2008.

Geertz, Clifford. "Centers, Kings, and Charisma: Reflections on the Symbolics of Power." In *Rites of Power: Symbolism, Ritual, and Politics since the Middle Ages*, edited by Sean Wilentz. Philadelphia: University of Pennsylvania Press, 1999.

Gold, Ann. "Counterpoint Authority in Women's Ritual Expressions: A View from the Village." In *Jewels of Authority: Women and Textual Tradition in Hindu India*, edited by Laurie L. Patton, 177–202. New York: Oxford University Press, 2002.

Goswami, Tamal Krishna, and Ravi M. Gupta. "Krishna and Culture: What Happens When the Lord of Vrindavana Moves to New York City." In *Gurus in America*, edited by Thomas A. Forsthoefel and Cynthia Ann Humes. Albany: State University of New York Press, 2005.

Gottschalk, Peter. *Religion, Science, and Empire: Classifying Hinduism and Islam in British India*. New York: Oxford University Press, 2012.

Gregg, Melissa, and Gregory J. Seigworth, eds. *The Affect Theory Reader*. Durham, NC: Duke University Press, 2010.

Harding, Sandra. *Sciences from Below: Feminisms, Postcolonialities, and Modernities*. Durham, NC: Duke University Press, 2008.

Harlan, Lindsey. "Words that Breach Walls: Women's Rituals in Rajasthan." In *Women's Lives, Women's Rituals in the Hindu Tradition*, edited by Tracy Pintchman, 65–84. New York: Oxford University Press, 2007.

Heifetz, Daniel. "From Gurudev to Doctor-sahib: Religion, Science, and Charisma in the All World Gayatri Pariwar." *Method & Theory in the Study of Religion* 30, no. 3 (2018): 252–78.

———. "Religion, Science, and the Middle Class in the All World Gayatri Pariwar." *International Journal of Hindu Studies* 23, no. 1 (2019): 27–42.

———. "Yajña without Dharma? Ritual and Morality in the All World Gayatri Pariwar." *Nidān: International Journal for Indian Studies* 1, no. 2 (2016): 14–31.

Huang, C. Julia. *Charisma and Compassion: Cheng Yen and the Buddhist Tzu Chi Movement.* Cambridge, MA: Harvard University Press, 2009.

Huang-Lemmon, C. Julia. "The Gender of Charisma: Notes from a Taiwanese Buddhist Transnational NGO." In *The Anthropology of Religious Charisma: Ecstasies and Institutions*, edited by Charles Lindholm. London: Palgrave Macmillan, 2013.

Inden, Ronald. *Imagining India.* Bloomington: Indiana University Press, 2001.

Jaffrelot, Christophe. *The Hindu Nationalist Movement in India.* New York: Columbia University Press, 1998.

Jamison, Stephanie. *Sacrificed Wife/Sacrificer's Wife: Women, Ritual, and Hospitality in Ancient India.* New York: Oxford University Press, 1996.

Jeffrey, Craig. *Timepass: Youth, Class, and the Politics of Waiting in India.* Stanford, CA: Stanford University Press, 2010.

Joshi, Rajani. *The Integrated Science of Yagya.* Mathura, India: Yug Nirman Yojana, 2010.

Joshi, Sanjay. *Fractured Modernity: Making of a Middle Class in Colonial North India.* New York: Oxford University Press, 2001.

Khandelwal, Meena. *Women in Ochre Robes: Gendering Hindu Renunciation.* Albany: State University of New York Press, 2003.

Klepinger, Laurah. "Flexible Labor in a Spiritual Economy: Peace, Work, and Inequality in Globalized Yoga." PhD diss., Syracuse University, 2015.

Kuhn, Thomas S. *The Structure of Scientific Revolutions.* Chicago: University of Chicago Press, 1996.

Kurien, Prema. *A Place at the Multicultural Table: The Development of an American Hinduism.* New Brunswick, NJ: Rutgers University Press, 2007.

Lal, Krishna. "Sāvitrī: From Saṃhitas to Gṛhyasūtras." *Annals of the Bhandarkar Oriental Research Institute* 52, no. 1 (1971): 225–9.

Latour, Bruno. *We Have Never Been Modern.* Translated by Catherine Porter. Cambridge, MA: Harvard University Press, 1993.

Lederman, Leon. *The God Particle: If the Universe Is the Answer, What Is the Question?* Boston: Mariner Books, 2006.

Liechty, Mark. "Middle Class Deja Vu: Conditions of Possibility, from Victorian England to Kathmandu." In *The Global Middle Classes: Theorizing through*

*Ethnography*, edited by Rachel Heiman, Carla Freeman, and Mark Liechty. Santa Fe, NM: School for Advanced Research Press, 2015.

Lincoln, Bruce. *Authority: Construction and Corrosion*. Chicago: University of Chicago Press, 1994.

Lindholm, Charles. *Charisma*. Oxford: Wiley-Blackwell, 1994.

———. "Introduction: Charisma in Theory and Practice." In *The Anthropology of Religious Charisma: Ecstasies and Institutions*, ed. Charles Lindholm, 1–30. London: Palgrave Macmillan, 2013.

———, ed. *The Anthropology of Religious Charisma: Ecstasies and Institutions*. London: Palgrave Macmillan, 2013.

Llewellyn, J.E. *The Arya Samaj as a Fundamentalist Movement: A Study in Comparative Fundamentalism*. New Delhi: South Asia Books, 1993.

Lochtefeld, James. *God's Gateway: Identity and Meaning in a Hindu Pilgrimage Place*. New York: Oxford University Press, 2010.

Lubin, Timothy. "Veda on Parade: Revivalist Ritual as Civic Spectacle." *Journal of the American Academy of Religion* 69, no. 2 (2001): 377–408.

Lukose, Ritty A. *Liberalization's Children: Gender, Youth, and Consumer Citizenship in Globalizing India*. Durham, NC: Duke University Press, 2009.

MacDougall, Bonnie G. "Jantar Mantar: Architecture, Astronomy, and Solar Kingship in Princely India." *Cornell Journal of Architecture*, 1996. http://ecommons.cornell.edu/handle/1813/2977.

Mahmood, Saba. *Politics of Piety: The Islamic Revival and the Feminist Subject*. Princeton, NJ: Princeton University Press, 2011.

Marriott, McKim, and Ronald Inden. "Caste Systems." *Encyclopedia Britannica*, 1976.

McCrea, Lawrence. "Novelty of Form and Novelty of Substance in Seventeenth Century Mīmāmsā." *Journal of Indian Philosophy* 30, no. 5 (2002): 481–94.

McGee, Mary. "Ritual Rights: The Gender Implications of Adhikāra." In *Jewels of Authority: Women and Textual Tradition in Hindu India*, edited by Laurie L. Patton, 32–50. New York: Oxford University Press, 2002.

McKean, Lise. "Bhārat Mātā: Mother India and Her Militant Matriots." In *Devi: Goddesses of India*, edited by John Stratton Hawley and Donna Marie Wulff, 250–80. Berkeley: University of California Press, 1996.

———. *Divine Enterprise: Gurus and the Hindu Nationalist Movement*. Chicago: University of Chicago Press, 1996.

Menon, Kalyani Devaki. *Everyday Nationalism: Women of the Hindu Right in India*. Philadelphia: University of Pennsylvania Press, 2012.

Nanda, Meera. *Prophets Facing Backward: Postmodern Critiques of Science and Hindu Nationalism in India*. New Brunswick, NJ: Rutgers University Press, 2003.

Nesbitt, Eleanor. "The Contribution of Nurture in a Sampradaya to Young British Hindus' Understanding of Their Tradition." In *Religious Reconstruction in the South Asian Diasporas: From One Generation to Another*, edited by John R. Hinnells, 51–72. New York: Palgrave Macmillan, 2007.

Ngai, Sianne. *Our Aesthetic Categories: Zany, Cute, Interesting*. Cambridge, MA: Harvard University Press, 2012.

O'Flaherty, Wendy Doniger. *The Origins of Evil in Hindu Mythology*. Delhi: Motilal Banarsidass, 1988.

———. *Women, Androgynes, and Other Mythical Beasts*. Chicago: University of Chicago Press, 1982.

Pandya, Pranav. *The Pioneers of Scientific Spirituality*. Translated by Rajani Joshi et al. Haridwar, India: Shri Vedmata Gayatri Trust, 2009.

Pandya, Pranav, and Jyotirmay. *Cetnā kī Śikhar Yātrā*, vol. 1. Haridwar, India: Shri Vedmata Gayatri Trust, 2001.

———. *Odyssey of the Enlightened*, vol. 1. Edited by Shambhudas. Translated by R.P. Khare and Madhuri Nadig. Haridwar, India: Shri Vedmata Gayatri Trust, 2009.

Patton, Laurie L., ed. *Jewels of Authority: Women and Textual Tradition in Hindu India*. New York: Oxford University Press, 2002.

Pechilis, Karen. "Gurumayi, the Play of Shakti and Guru." In *The Graceful Guru: Hindu Female Gurus in India and the United States*, edited by Karen Pechilis, 219–44. New York: Oxford University Press, 2004.

———. "Introduction: Hindu Female Gurus in Historical and Philosophical Context." In *The Graceful Guru: Hindu Female Gurus in India and the United States*, edited by Karen Pechilis, 3–50. New York: Oxford University Press, 2004.

Perlus, Barry. *Architecture in the Service of Science: The Astronomical Observatories of Jai Singh II*. n.d. www.jantarmantar.org/Architecture_Science_web.pdf.

Pintchman, Tracy. *The Rise of the Goddess in the Hindu Tradition*. Albany: State University of New York Press, 1994.

———, ed. *Women's Lives, Women's Rituals in the Hindu Tradition*. New York: Oxford University Press, 2007.

Pollock, Sheldon. "Cosmopolitan and Vernacular in History." In *Cosmopolitanism*, edited by Carol A. Breckenridge, Sheldon Pollock, Homi K. Bhabha, and Dipesh Chakrabarty. Duke University Press, 2002.

———. "Forms of Knowledge in Early Modern South Asia: Introduction." *Comparative Studies of South Asia, Africa and the Middle East* 24, no. 2 (2004): 19–21.

———. "Introduction: Working Papers on Sanskrit Knowledge-Systems on the Eve of Colonialism." *Journal of Indian Philosophy* 30, no. 5 (2002): 431–39.

Popper, Karl R. *Conjectures and Refutations: The Growth of Scientific Knowledge*. New York: Routledge, 2002.

Prakash, Gyan. *Another Reason*. Princeton, NJ: Princeton University Press, 1999.

Prasad, Leela. *Poetics of Conduct: Oral Narrative and Moral Being in a South Indian Town*. New York: Columbia University Press, 2006.

Raj, Kapil. *Relocating Modern Science: Circulation and the Construction of Knowledge in South Asia and Europe, 1650–1900*. New York: Palgrave Macmillan, 2010.

Ramaswamy, Sumathi. *The Goddess and the Nation: Mapping Mother India*. Durham, NC: Duke University Press, 2010.

Rappaport, Roy A. *Ritual and Religion in the Making of Humanity*. Cambridge: Cambridge University Press, 1999.

Saler, Michael. "Modernity and Enchantment: A Historiographic Review." *The American Historical Review* 111, no. 3 (2006): 692–716.

Schaefer, Donovan O. *Religious Affects: Animality, Evolution, and Power*. Durham, NC: Duke University Press, 2015.

Sharma, Shriram. *Companions in Solitude*. Translated by V.A. Shivashankaran. Haridwar, India: Shri Vedmata Gayatri Trust, 2011.

———. *Gāyatrī Mahāvijñān*. Mathura, India: Yug Nirman Yojana, 2010.

———. *Hamārī Vasīyat Aur Virāsat*. Mathura, India: Yug Nirman Yojana, 2011.

———. *My Life: Its Legacy and Message*. Translated by Satya Narayan Pandya and Shambhudas. Haridwar, India: Shri Vedmata Gayatri Trust, 2011.

———. *Procedure of Yagya*. Edited by Shambu Dass. Translated by K. Poddar. Mathura, India: Yug Nirman Yojana, 2009.

———. *The Revival of Satyug*. Haridwar, India: Shri Vedmata Gayatri Trust, 2011.

———. *Super Science of Gayatri*. Translated by Satya Narayan Pandya and Shambhudas. Haridwar, India: Shri Vedmata Gayatri Trust, 2010.

Shermer, Michael. *Why People Believe Weird Things: Pseudoscience, Superstition, and Other Confusions of Our Time*. New York: W.H. Freeman, 1997.

Smith, Brian K. " 'Vedic Fieldwork.' Review of Frits Staal, Agni." *Religious Studies Review* 11 (1985): 136–45.

Smith, Jonathan Z. *Relating Religion: Essays in the Study of Religion*. Chicago: University of Chicago Press, 2004.

Srinivasan, Doris. "Saṃdhyā: Myth and Ritual." *Indo-Iranian Journal* 15, no. 3 (1973): 161–78.

Srivastava, Sanjay. "National Identity, Bedrooms, and Kitchens: Gated Communities and New Narratives of Space in India." In *The Global Middle Classes: Theorizing through Ethnography*, edited by Rachel Heiman, Carla Freeman, and Mark Liechty. Santa Fe, NM: School for Advanced Research Press, 2015.

Stewart, Kathleen. *Ordinary Affects*. Durham, NC: Duke University Press, 2007.

Thrift, Nigel. *Non-Representational Theory: Space, Politics, Affect*. New York: Routledge, 2007.

Urban, Hugh. "Osho, from Sex Guru to Guru of the Rich: The Spiritual Logic of Late Capitalism." In *Gurus in America*, edited by Thomas A. Forsthoefel and Cynthia Ann Humes. Albany: State University of New York Press, 2005.

van der Veer, Peter. *Religious Nationalism: Hindus and Muslims in India*. Berkeley: University of California Press, 1994.

Waghorne, Joanne. "The Gentrification of the Goddess." *International Journal of Hindu Studies* 5, no. 3 (2001): 227–67.

———. "The Hindu Gods in a Split Level World: The Sri Siva-Vishnu Temple in Suburban Washington, D.C." In *Gods of the City: Religion and the American Urban Landscape*, edited by Robert A. Orsi, 105–30. Bloomington: Indiana University Press, 1999.

Weber, Max. *From Max Weber: Essays in Sociology*. Edited by H.H. Gerth and C. Wright Mills. New York: Oxford University Press, 1958.

———. *The Theory of Social and Economic Organization*. Edited by Talcott Parsons. Translated by A.M. Henderson. New York: Free Press, 1964.

Williamson, Lola. "The Perfectibility of Perfection: Siddha Yoga as a Global Movement." In *Gurus in America*, edited by Thomas A. Forsthoefel and Cynthia Ann Humes. Albany: State University of New York Press, 2005.

———. *Transcendent in America: Hindu-Inspired Meditation Movements as New Religion*. New York: NYU Press, 2010.

Wujastyk, Dominick. "Indian Medical Thought on the Eve of Colonialism." *International Institute for Asian Studies Newsletter* 31 (July 2003): 21.

Yadav, Kripal Chandra, and K.S. Arya. *Arya Samaj and the Freedom Movement*. New Delhi: Manohar, 1988.

Yogananda, Paramahansa. *Autobiography of a Yogi*. Los Angeles: Self-Realization Fellowship, 1998.

Zigon, Jarrett. "Moral Breakdown and the Ethical Demand: A Theoretical Framework for an Anthropology of Moralities." *Anthropological Theory* 7, no. 2 (2007): 131–50.

# Index

www.ingramcontent.com/pod-product-compliance
Lightning Source LLC
Chambersburg PA
CBHW020348270326
41926CB00007B/351
* 9 7 8 1 4 3 8 4 8 1 7 0 8 *